The Saga of Tom Horn

THE SAGA OF TOM HORN

The Story of a Cattlemen's War

With

PERSONAL NARRATIVES, NEWSPAPER ACCOUNTS AND OFFICIAL DOCUMENTS AND TESTIMONIES

By

DEAN F. KRAKEL

University of Nebraska Press
Lincoln and London

Manufactured in the United States of America

First Bison Book printing: 1988
Most recent printing indicated by the first digit below:
1 2 3 4 5 6 7 8 9 10

Library of Congress Cataloging-in-Publication Data

Krakel, Dean Fenton, 1923–

The saga of Tom Horn: the story of a cattlemen's war: with personal narratives, newspaper accounts, and official documents and testimonies / by Dean F. Krakel.

p. cm.

Reprint. Originally published: Laramie, Wyo.: Powder River Publishers, c1954.

"A Bison book."

Bibliography: p.

Includes index.

ISBN 0-8032-2719-1. ISBN 0-8032-7767-9 (pbk.)

1. Horn, Tom, 1860–1903—Trials, litigation, etc. 2. Trials (Murder)—Wyoming—Cheyenne. 3. Cattle trade—Wyoming. 4. Frontier and pioneer life—Wyoming. I. Title.

KF223.H63K73 1988
345.73'02523—dc 19
[347.3052523] 87-33019
CIP

Reprinted by arrangement with Dean F. Krakel

THE SAGA OF TOM HORN is affectionately dedicated to IRIS AND IRA DEAN

PREFACE

Today few stories are more alive, colorful and controversial than are those of Tom Horn in Wyoming. It has been approximately one-half century since the State of Wyoming took his life—yet mystery shrouds the entire affair. An atmosphere of taboo often greets the prober.

Despite numerous books, dozens of features, and hundreds of articles written about Tom Horn, some distortions, false rumors, and injustices persist. Thus this is an effort to salvage truisms from the few who knew . . . who are still living. To analyze in chronological order official records and facts of the case dating from Horn's entry into Wyoming in 1894, until the date of his execution in 1903. In his autobiography, *The Life of Tom Horn,* Horn covers his life prior to the former date. Authenticity has been the primary goal of presentation, as well as has been the preservation of the near profane atmosphere of this era.

The study has been bigger and more revealing than just that of one man. For in this minute of history was arrayed a pageant of personalities unassembled before—unequaled since. It involved the life and death of a way of living that revolved around a code of the range. The Horn trial set the stage, provided the cast, then the drama, and without warning, pulled the final curtain down—the new order had won its foothold.

But for Old Cheyenne it was a glimpse into her past—into her closet of skeletons. Into yesterday when she, like Dodge City and Tombstone, was a hell raiser. That was the heyday of homicide, the big herds, and tangled economics—with only a sprinkling of law and order to interfere. And so the Tom Horn case made her think, to remember and to pulsate—this was an anti-climax. Cheyenne was suddenly alive again—then she was suddenly sad . . . for the lifeless form of a man and a cherished way of life dangled at the end of a rope—both would be gone forever.

The personalities, the old range codes, and the atmosphere of Frontier Cheyenne are gone—but their spirit remains. This spirit has in part been kept alive by a rip snortn' show called Frontier Days—and memories of a hard bucking old outlaw by the name of Steamboat.

And so, the case marked the birth as well as the death of an era, for this was the Daddy of 'em All—this is The Saga of Tom Horn!

Dean Krakel,
Laramie, Wyoming.

ACKNOWLEDGMENT

For assistance in the collection of materials I am indebted to the Director, Mr. N. Orwin Rush, and the Staff at the University of Wyoming Library; to the Wyoming Stock Growers Association; to the late Mr. W. A. James, Clerk of Court, First Judicial District of Wyoming, for making available official documents and testimonies for both research and reprinting, and Miss Clara Ahrens of the same department; Mr. T. Joe Cahill, Cheyenne; Mr. Andrew Ross, Pierce, Colorado; Mrs. Nettie LeFors, Buffalo, for permission to use Joe LeFors' story; to the Annals of Wyoming for Edwin Smalley's account of the arresting of Tom Horn; and to the Denver Posse of the Westerners for granting permission to reprint part of the late John C. Thompson's account of the execution.

The collection of photographs for "The Pageant of Personalities" was made possible by cooperation of both individuals and institutions. I have drawn heavily from the photographic files of the L. E. Snow collection, the Wyoming Stock Growers Association, and many other collections located in the Archives and Western History department of the University of Wyoming Library. Of equal importance has been copies of prints taken from the files of the Denver Post. I am grateful to the following individuals who permitted use of photographs in their possession: Mrs. Nettie LeFors, Buffalo, Wyo.; Mr. T. Joe Cahill, Cheyenne, Wyo.; Mr. Fred Mazzula, Denver, Colo.; Mr. Andrew Ross, Pierce, Colo.; Mr. John C. Thompson, Jr., Rawlins, Wyo.; and Mrs. Leslie E. Snow, Buffalo, Wyo.

For educational and stimulating conversation of the Horn case, I am thankful to the late Mr. W. A. James, Cheyenne, Wyo.; Mr. A. S. "Bud" Gillespie, Laramie, Wyo.; Mr. Clayton Danks, Lander, Wyo.; Mr. Cleon J. Lesh, Laramie, Wyo.; Mr. Charles Farthing, Iron Mountain, Wyo.; Mr. Tom St. John, Laramie, Wyo.; former Governor of Wyoming, Mr. Fenimore Chatterton, Arvada, Colo.; and Mr. Harry Hannes, Laramie, Wyo.

In the preliminary typing and arranging of the manuscript, I was pleased to have had the assistance of Miss Dorothy Stull, Laramie. A second typing was done by Mrs. Ivan Jones, Rock Springs; and the final typing by Mrs. Lloyd Pullum, Laramie.

I feel fortunate in having been able to secure Artist Roy Hunt. He designed the book jacket and drew the illustrations for each of the three parts. Mr. Hunt resides in Denver, and is employed by the Colorado State Historical Society.

In reproduction of photographs, special thanks go to Mr. Walter B. Ludwig of the Ludwig Photo Enterprises, Laramie, for interest and professional service; to Mr. LeRoy Roman, photographer at the Ludwig Studios for interest and superb restoration work in bringing new life to many of the faded photographs; to Mr. Joe Kay of the University Studio, go thanks for excellent photographic assistance.

The dimness of many of the photographs is due to the age of the originals and should not be a reflection upon the photographers, engravers or printers who reproduced them.

I am grateful for the cooperation of Mr. Jack Costin of Laramie Printing for patience and plenty of hard work. Thanks are due Mr. Harry O. Collier, also of the same firm.

Binding was done by the Dieter Bindery of Denver.

And last but not least, to my wife Iris—for "living" Tom Horn for the past eighteen months. Her comments and suggestions have been helpful in the assembling of the manuscript.

AUTHOR.

TABLE OF CONTENTS

ILLUSTRATIONS

The Pageant of Personalities

". . . . for this minute of history was arrayed a pageant of personalities, unassembled before—unequaled since. . . ."

D.K.

THE SAGA OF TOM HORN . . .

TOM HORN

The Dr. Jekyl and Mr. Hyde of the Rangeland. "Whenever everything else fails, I have a system which never does."

(Courtesy Denver Post)

PART ONE *Another Man's Beef*

Old Paint's a good pony, he paces when he can
Goodbye Little Annie, I'm off for Cheyenne.

Goodbye Old Paint I'm a-leavin' Cheyenne
Goodbye Old Paint I'm a-leavin' Cheyenne.

—*Old Paint* (Author Unknown).

The stage that Tom Horn was to be featured on was set during the late 1880's and early 1890's—a period of tangled national economics. Silver ultimately became the hub around which the mess revolved, and politically, radical populism was born of it.

To the plight of the stockman was heaped numerous ills that, together spelled sure disaster in the industry of the open range. First was congressional action, that declared all fences and free utilization of the Public Domain unlawful. Almost overnight the big herds had to go. Then came the deadly one-two punches in the form of successive blizzards between '85 and '87. The panic of five years later capped the climax. . . .

And so, cowboys by the hundreds were without jobs. For the most part of them, punch'n cows was their only trade. Many of them had been taught how to bring in unbranded calves by their employers—a thing not considered wholly unethical in the early days of the industry. Thus, reasoning driven by short rations was comparatively simple, get a chunk of Wyoming sod, rustle a critter or two now and then, and after a few years a feller had a small spread of his own. Many learned new tricks from old nesters who, for years, had been whittling away at the fat herds. Easterners in plush Washington offices called such ingenuity individual enterprise. . . .

Peace officers did little to stop the rustlers—in many cases they were reluctant to investigate. Then too, the courts were termed by some as being "easy" on the offenders. Recorded convictions were few and far between.

Hard hit, southern Wyoming cattlemen turned to the powerful Wyoming Stock Growers Association for help. Something had to be done to stem the tide that was sweeping them down the drain of financial ruin. Two years before a "helluva" war had been fought upstate for the same reason.

The leather-booted cattlemen wasted little time in getting together in old Cheyenne. Their headquarters was in the exclusively plush and cosmopolitan Cheyenne Club. Grimly a decision was made. They decided to take matters into their own hands—rustl'n was to stop! But, not all agreed as to how far they should go in rectifying the condition. However, all approved that the first step was to collect evidence. Data on sheepmen and "nesters" was considered important.

The man they hired to collect needed evidence was Tom Horn. He had been imported as a detective by the Swan Land & Cattle Company in 1894. Their recommendation was the "cincher" for Horn.

In appearance Tom Horn was neat. His two hundred pounds was well distributed over a big boned six-foot one-inch frame. A trim mustache offset his receding hairline. While his voice was soft and clear, it contained unforgettable sharpness. Tom had a "master's degree" in the arts of assassination. He had received his baptism under fire during Geronimo's Apache war in Arizona. Horn was also well versed in Pinkerton sleuthing methods. The big man was like a bloodhound in that he loved the chase and thrilled to see his bullet cut down an unsuspecting victim. He boasted, "Killing men is my specialty; I look at it as a business proposition, and I think I have a corner on the market."

Yet, in appearance and conversation the gunman was a gentleman, a student of national affairs, an excellent roping contestant, and like a knight of old in the presence of women. In his struggle for recognition, Horn developed a dual personality: one—a perfect gentleman, the other—a homicidal maniac. Tom Horn was the Doctor Jekyl and Mr. Hyde of the rangeland.

And so, silently, the new employee began operations. During the first few months he got to know the cattlemen and the cowboys alike. In short, he became a close friend of aristocrat John C. Coble of the Iron Mountain Cattle Company. Tom spent most of his days alone in the saddle just riding, observing, and learning regional geography. Horn was said to have carried a pair of binoculars—but seldom a six-shooter. A 30-30 Winchester rifle was his favorite. Continued practice made him a deadly shot. He was furnished horses whenever he saw fit for a change. Tom affectionately called a favorite horse of his "E.W." after the former owner, Rancher E. W. Whitcomb. The horse, a splendid big chested hunter, was among several purchased by the Swan Company's Two-Bar Ranch.

A creeping paralysis swept over the region. The fear of God gripped those who had been rustling. Horse tracks, roll-your-own cigarette butts, bacon rinds, and empty food cans lying about were evidence that the "cat-like" Horn was at work.

The eager detective wanting to prove his worth, soon had his first experience with Wyoming rustlers. Single handed he arrested and escorted the Langhoff gang of thieves into Laramie and on to Cheyenne for trial when he caught them in possession of another man's beef. After a long drawn-out affair, involved action was taken by the court. One of the rustlers was sent to prison, the others given short term jail sentences and small fines. The joke was on the cattlemen. Horn's employers were stunned by the ineffectiveness of the laws. They knew they would have to contend with the thieves again. Bitterly, Tom was asked to continue his work, collecting evidence only—no more arrests were to be made.

In a matter of months the detective had prepared a lengthy report on suspects. As usual the meeting was held in Cheyenne. Suddenly Tom Horn was in his glory—he was the star in a stockman-studded show. Imported liquors, expensive cigars and fine foods suited his tastes as did unsolicited compliments. The men were quick to the point. Rustlers and Grangers were discussed in terms defined as uncomplimentary. Again, the big issue was what final action should be taken. It was inferred that the law would do nothing. Then, Horn was asked how he would remedy the situation. Strolling to the center of the floor, cigar in hand, he surveyed the group, then in a cool voice said, "Men, I have a system that never fails, when everything else has. Yours has!" Many of the cattlemen were taken back by the casualness of Horn in discussing methods of "exterminat'n." The meeting became hotter and the owners desperately divided. The Stock Growers Association officials were quick to voice a negative opinion of plans that would involve bloodshed. "Collecting evidence is one thing, assassination is another," roared the organization's president. "There ain't no more to be said, Gentlemen—Meetin's closed!"

Thus, Tom Horn was paid off and given a "well-done" pat for his work. Possibly the cattlemen would jointly hire him again, but, only as a detective. A committee was appointed to discuss less violent action against those listed in Horn's report.

The turn of events was frustrating to the unemployed Horn. He had wanted to go to "work." "Damnit all," he muttered. However, his consternation was short-lived when he was approached by radicals. They wanted the maximum penalty inflicted on the beef-stealing thieves. Thus the rift in the organization was made. And the verdict to kill was made by a few! In a matter of minutes it was settled.

A fee per rustler was set—all concerned agreed. Horn could relax. He had been retained and given enough cash so that he could stick around Cheyenne for a few weeks. Tom liked to lounge in the Inter-Ocean Hotel. It would also give him a chance to get caught up in "his bar-room life." Despite his leathery-shy exterior, he liked both women and drinks.

As the summer of '95 wore away, the thirty-seven-year-old hired assassin grew restless and tired of city life. The lower his bank roll got, the more he drank. In this state of mind he was easily offended. His backers knew it was time for action!

William Lewis, an Englishman, was the first to feel the impact of the new force. Lewis was killed with cool precision on his unplowed 160 acres in the Iron Mountain District, some forty miles northwest of Cheyenne in early August. The Lewis place was near the headquarters of Horn's friend, John C. Coble, of the Iron Mountain Cattle Company. Lewis had stolen cattle openly and defiantly boasted about it to neighbors. The rustler had been given notice to get out of the country or his life would be taken, but he ignored the notes, cussed and made accusations. On two former occasions he had been shot at.

The inquest that followed the murder of Lewis divulged practically nothing. The body was found by George Shanton. Neighboring ranchers, Shanton and Whittaker stated at the inquest: "Lewis has been very suspicious of everyone and was always accusing his neighbors of designs against his life. We know of no one who had thoughts of killing him, but believe he did not have a friend within many miles of his ranch, for he has made himself a very disagreeable neighbor."

Laramie County Coroner, Dr. Rohrbaugh, testified after examination of the body, that Lewis had been shot three times at a distance of approximately 300 yards with a weapon of about .44 calibre. The blood splattered body was buried on the spot. This evidence refutes the often repeated statements that Lewis was shot point blank with a six-shooter.

The claims against the Lewis estate exceeded the total amount received from sales. Ranchers Charles Hirsig and C. P. Organ purchased horses and cattle.

The news of Lewis' death spread like a wind-driven grass fire. The fear of God gripped all who had rustled.

More warning notes were sent out—nesters and former cowboys left the country in haste. But the sod had hardly settled on Lewis' stony grave when the crack of the assassin's rifle cut down another. Victim number two was Fred U. Powell. The Powell place, located on Horse Creek, was not more than 10 miles from Lewis'. The deceased had received a warning note telling him to leave or else... Tough and husky, despite the loss of one arm, Powell, too, was determined to make his stand.

The assassination of Fred U. Powell was a masterpiece, planned with "John Wilkes Booth-like" precision. The timing was perfect. The killer had studied the lay of the Powell ranch and Powell's working habits, and pre-determining the exact day, time and place that he would take a careful bead on Powell. There was no slip-up. The only witness* to the murder was his hired man, Andrew Ross. At the inquest Ross testified:

> "My name is Andrew Ross. I have worked for Fred U. Powell one month. We were alone on the ranch, Mr. Powell and I. We got up about 4 a.m. yesterday morning [September 10, 1895]. We got to a place about one-half mile from the ranch, down the creek. Stopped the wagon and got off. Mr. Powell told me to cut some willows so we could fix the [hay] rack. As I was cutting the second willow I heard a shot fired and I looked around. Saw Mr. Powell with his hand on his breast and I ran towards him. He exclaimed, "Oh my God, I'm shot!" Then fell. I went to him and saw he was dead. I then went to the ranch of Mr. Fay and notified him.
>
> "I examined the surroundings and from what I could ascertain the shot was fired from a ledge of rocks about 250 feet distant. I examined the body and found a gunshot wound entering the breast near the center and coming out at the right of the spine near the fourth rib. I could not see any person when I heard the shot, nor afterward."

Cowboy Ross added, "My greatest fear at the time, was that had Powell not been killed instantly, I would no doubt have tried to assist him. The assassin would have, in all probability, taken the necessary shots at me to prevent such a help." Ross described Powell's set-up for taking in company cattle as being "mighty crude."

---

*This official report, signed by Albany County Coroner Andrew Miller, is contrary to some interpretations of the assassination of Fred U. Powell. It has often been reported the only witness to the crime was Powell's six-year-old son, "Billy." And that the lad identified Horn as the killer upon seeing him in Cheyenne.

Fred Powell's funeral was held at the family home in Laramie. He was buried in the same city. A wife, Mary, and a six-year-old son, Billy, survived the deceased.

As was the case with Lewis, the killer of Powell was never caught. The two successive killings were effective in southern Wyoming. Rustling on a large scale stopped.

The killer and his supporters continued to strike. More warning letters were mailed. One was to Charles Keane. It read: "If you don't leave this country within three days, your life will be taken the same as Powell's was." Keane had been managing the Powell ranch since the death of his sister's husband—he complied with the warning.

Range talk linked the assassinations and warning letters with Tom Horn. Circumstantial evidence pointed to him, but charges were never filed. Within a few short months he had become the terror of the Wyoming range. His horse was given a free rein. . . .

During the next three years Tom Horn led a comparatively quiet life. He punched cows for the Iron Mountain Cattle Company. In his spare time he read and carved, but his favorite past time was to braid in both leather and horse hair. The hand work seemed to relax him. Horn's leather braided bridles and horse hair ropes were always in demand.

The coming of the glorious little war with Spain in the spring and summer of 1898 was invitation to excitement for the former Government scout. He read of an army pack outfit being formed in St. Louis and wasted little time in getting there to enlist. Tom hoped his knowledge of Spanish and experience as a packer would give him rank. It didn't.

Horn's role as a mule packer was one of little importance in the conflict that saw a strappling "U.S.A.," tough from decades of Indian wars, pitted against a decadent Spain. Yellow fever and dysentery were the only real victors.

In 1899 he was back on the board walks of Cheyenne, broke and weak from Yellow fever. Horn made it known around that he longed for the saddle and the nights around the camp fires, thinking and studying.

During his time in the Army, beef-stealing on a fairly large scale had been resumed. News of his return made many a rustler's spine tingle and the hair on the back of their necks crawl.

A big job was in the offing. A Cattle Baron's wild herds were being hit like clock work in the jig-saw geography puzzle of the

Brown's Park country of northwestern Colorado and southwestern Wyoming. The "Baron" needed help and Tom Horn needed a job. Necessary arrangements were made, and Horn left Cheyenne to report to the "Barron." After a few days consultation, he was outfitted and on his way to Brown's Park. A successful infiltration into the infested area was made.

He operated under the name of Tom Hicks and immediately found a job. Leads on the suspected were followed up. Cool, calm, and tight-lipped, Horn was again at work, doing a job he loved—playing man's most dangerous game. The stakes were high but the odds, like loaded dice, were always with Horn.

The basis for the trouble started with prosperity and herd expansion. The big owners' cattle and those of lesser holdings were drifting further south than established ranges; while Park cattle often moved north away from home grass. To cope with the situation, the Colorado cattlemen got together with a leading representative of Wyoming interests, "Hi" Bernard, and established a division line, to be enforced by line riders. Cattle were controlled accordingly. The Brown's Park critters were herded south and the "Baron's" north.

But the plan did not work out as hoped. The division line riders could not prevent the "tide" of Wyoming steers from moving south across the line. The big interests were further irritated by the loss of a prize range.

And so cattle were being lost by the big outfit. Some were being rustled by Brown's Park cowboys, but not all of them. Damaging evidence left by the thieves, pointedly incriminated Matt Rash and Isam Dart.

By pushing leather in the area, Horn soon spotted his "game"—victims three and four. Rash and Dart often worked together.

Matt Rash was president of the Brown's Park Cattle Association. A native of Texas, he had had a colorful and experienced past. Rash came into Wyoming in 1882 as a trail-herd boss. He then worked for the Middlesussex outfit and later for the Circle K as manager. The Texan was a top cowboy, hard worker, and had made a stake of his own.

Isam Dart was a negro, and some say, one of the best cowboys ever to mount a horse in the high mesa country. Big, husky, and smiling, he was liked by all. In 1929 George Erhard, pioneer of the Brown's Park area, reminiscing, wrote of Dart:

"I have seen all the great riders, but for all-around skill as a cowman, Isam Dart was unexcelled and I never saw his peer. He was fond of watching bucking contests and often attended at Grand Junction [Colorado]. He could outride any of them; but he never entered a contest. Isam had been a resident of the Park since the 1880's."

Suddenly Tom Horn disappeared.... Then a warning note was found tacked on to Rash's cabin door. Isam Dart, a "nigger" would not be given that much consideration. As usual, all Horn had to do was wait. Possibly he returned to "headquarters" for a final conference with his chief. Returning there would give him somewhat of a time and place alibi should he need one. The choice of victims was confirmed.

A couple of days later saw the assassin back in the Park. Matt Rash, as tough as a pine knot, was determined to make his stand. "No — — — — is goin' to scare me outta here by God!" snarled Rash to his friend Ebb Bassett as he read the warning. Leaving the country would have meant giving up all he had toiled to build. His ranch and herd were his very life blood. Besides, he had plans of marrying the prettiest girl on the mesa.

The assassin arrived at Rash's cabin under the cover of darkness, on the morning of July 10, 1900. All he had to do was wait. Matt Rash, was an early riser. Soon he had a fire going and his usual breakfast of bacon, eggs and coffee prepared. It was at this time, as he apparently began his meal, that he was killed. His saddle horse also lay dying near the cabin.

A special dispatch from Rock Springs, Wyoming, was published in the *Laramie Daily Boomerang* of July 12, 1900, and carried the story of Matt Rash's death as:

"BROWN'S PARK MURDER

"Well Known Cattleman Found Dead in Bed

"A special dispatch from Rock Springs, dated yesterday, says: Ebb Bassett, having ridden all night, arrived today from Ladore, Colo., bringing the news that Matt Rash, a stock grower and old timer in Brown's park and neighboring country, was found dead in bed with two gunshot wounds in his body at his ranch near Ladore. Everything indicated that he had been shot while sitting at the table eating. He had crawled to bed and taken off one shoe before he became too weak. His gloves and pistol were on the table. His riding horse was also found dead, having been shot.

"Rash had about 700 head of cattle and was generally respected. His brother and sister in Texas have been notified of his death. Although no explanation is given of the killing, it is conceded by some who seem to know, that it has some connection with recent happenings in Brown's Park and Ashley Valley, Utah. Developments are awaited with much anxiety."

For Tom Horn it was one down, one to go. Isam Dart was next and then Horn's deadly consecutive punches would be delivered. The plan of assassination was the same as that used on Lewis and Powell. But things were plenty hot, so he decided to not "pick off" Dart for a couple of months. However, Horn, alias Tom Hicks, continued to work in the area. He had become acquainted with Matt Rash's father during the inquest that had followed. . . .

It was a clear, crisp October morning that Isam Dart and his friends, Ebb and George Bassett stepped out of Dart's cabin and headed for the corral to saddle their horses. They were planning on a hard day's riding. All were still bereaving the death of their friend, Matt Rash. The normally grinning Dart had been silent and bitter.

A sharp report, an instantaneous thud and Dart was down. Horn's aim, as always, was unerring. The Bassetts dropped to the ground the instant Isam had been hit, and crawled to the cabin for coverage. Isam lay dead.

Isam Dart was buried in a shallow mountain grave on a hillside on Cold Springs Mountain by his friends. The service was simple, effective, and according to the code of the range. The Brown's Park people had paid their last respects to their loved friend, the "Calico Cowboy," Isam Dart.

With the killing of Dart, Horn headed his horse north, out of Brown's Park and into Wyoming. His work was done; he wanted to settle up and get back to the Laramie-Cheyenne vicinity. As always he had been effective. His employer, the "Cattle Baron," satisfied, had gone south.

Later Horn was seen at Dixon, Wyoming. Some stories have it that he became involved with some of the Posse members after the slaying of Dart, and was cut severely on the neck in a drinking brawl.

Nevertheless, with a pocket full of bills, and two new notches cut in the butt of his Winchester, Tom Horn made his way back into "home ranges." He was recognized by all and feared by many. No doubt Horn was proud of his effectiveness.

Later in a letter to Joe LeFors, he referred to his work in Brown's Park with confidence. In part the letter read:*

> "Iron Mountain Ranch Company
> "Bosler, Wyoming
> "Jan. 1st 1902
>
> "Joe LeFors Esq.
> "Cheyenne, Wyo.
>
> "Dear Joe
>
> "Rec'd yours from W. D. Smith, Miles City, Mont., by Johnny Coble today. I would like to take up that work and I feel sure I can give Mr. Smith satisfaction. I don't care how big or bad his men are or how many of them there are. *I can handle them. They can scarcely be any worse than the Brown's Hole Gang and I stopped cow stealing there in one summer.* If Mr. Smith cares to give me the work I would like to meet them as soon as commencement so as to get into the country and get located before summer...."

Tom Horn returned to the Iron Mountain district, and was possibly in the employ of his flamboyant friend, John C. Coble. Supporting evidence of this is in a letter written by Mr. M. C. Fitzmorris to Alice Smith,† secretary of the Wyoming Stock Growers Association, Cheyenne, Wyoming. The letter was dated November 20th, 1900, and written from Moore, Wyoming. In part it read:

> "Dear Miss Smith: Yours of the 14th inst. is at hand, and, as I came home from Cheyenne I stopped at the Coble Ranch, but Mr. Coble was in Cheyenne and Duncan Clark his foreman was away, but I seen Tom Horn and told him that I wanted Clark to write...."

The fall and winter of 1900 and 1901 provided the opportunity for Tom Horn and John Coble to become close friends. One was admired for his intellect and polish, while the other for his simplicity

*Letter No. 2 of the Tom Horn-Joe Lefors-W. D. Smith correspondence on file in the office of Laramie County Clerk of the Court, Cheyenne, Wyoming. Italicized portion by direction of author.

†Alice Smith was clerk for the Wyoming Stock Growers Association from 1891-95. She became Secretary in 1896 and served until 1922. Miss Smith was made an honorary life member. Her work with the Association covered the entire Horn epoch. Miss Smith, loved by all, passed away at Cheyenne, January 16, 1944.

and Western ways. Coble was born in the East of well-to-do parents. He loved to hear Tom, an excellent story teller, relate his experiences.

It was at this time that Tom Horn learned of the Iron Mountain situation, the James Miller-Kels Nickell feud, sheep, and of Nickell's violent temper. This was primarily a range, not a rustler's war. Perhaps here he heard about and met Miss Glendolene Kimmell, the dark and shapely little school teacher staying at the James Miller ranch.

As the two men became closer they confided in each other. Coble told Tom of his hatred for Kels Nickell. The basis of his seldom discussed or written of animosity had been laid a decade ago, in the same district, when Nickell stabbed and slashed Coble after the latter's foreman, George Cross and he had quarrelled over the trespassing of some cattle.*

Tom Horn was disturbed by all that he learned over the period of months in his associations at Iron Mountain.

The story of how Nickell assaulted his friend with a knife made him angry. The long scars John Coble bore were full evidence of Nickell's wrath. Horn's hatred of Nickell must have been immediate —secretly he vowed revenge and would someday take careful aim on him. . . .

Thus the friendship was consummated, Tom Horn-John Coble. It is a story almost unequaled within itself. One vowed to act—the other vowed to defend. This was the day when a man's word alone was like concrete. Perhaps one could have "talked" the other could have "fled."

Conditions around Iron Mountain did not improve as the winter of 1900-1901 wore away. Then spring saw happenings in the district like an open sore, festering with each day and irritation. However, not all was blood on the moon. Tom had been attentive to Miss Kimmell, the attractive little "school marm.". . .

---

*The article published in the *Cheyenne Daily Leader*, July 24, 1890, reads as: "J. C. Coble Cut: SLASHED WITH KNIFE BY KELS P. NICKELL: TWO QUITE SERIOUS WOUNDS ARE INFLICTED: BADLY SLASHED: J. C. Coble of Iron Mountain, was seriously stabbed at that place yesterday by Kels P. Nickell, another ranchman, and is under the treatment of Dr. Maynard at the physicians Cheyenne residence. Sheriff Martin has the assailant in the county jail.

Nickell and George Cross, Mr. Coble's foreman, quarrelled over the trespassing of some cattle. Nickell, without a word, dashed at Coble with the knife and made two effective slashes. The wounds are ugly cuts in the abdomen, and while they are serious, Mr. Coble will recover. Nickell was arrested by another ranchman and brought in on Sheriff Martin's instructions.

The proximity of the Miller and Nickell places led to an open exchange of oaths and threats between the two family heads. Even their boys were fighting whenever they met. The James Miller boys were, August and Victor; Willie and Fred were the sons of the Nickells. On one occasion Willie attempted to run Victor Miller down with his horse, when Victor's father appeared on the scene and told the Nickell boy if he did he would shoot his horse.

One thing led to another. Both Kels Nickell and James Miller started carrying rifles. It has been stated that this bitterness resulted in the accidental death of one of the smaller Miller boys, when the gun that Miller carried was accidentally discharged, snuffing out the life of his child.

When the tally sheet was totaled, according to some men, Kels P. Nickell had violated not only the code of the cattle range but also the law: (1) He had brought sheep into the heart of cow country, (2) He had attacked John Coble with a deadly weapon, seriously injuring him, (3) Defense rivalry had indirectly resulted in the death of a Miller. Thus the die was cast, whether by one, two, three or more bitter men. Kels P. Nickell was doomed from Iron Mountain. Either he would leave, or be silenced forever....

And so on October 25, 1902, the State of Wyoming convicted Tom Horn for the killing of a Nickell. Conviction was based on circumstantial evidence proved beyond a reason of doubt.

In view of this evidence perhaps the crime was committed in this way:

July 18th found Tom Horn nestled and well concealed in a wall of rocks in the proximity of a gate, about three-fourths of a mile from the home of Kels P. Nickell and Mary Nickell. Horn's horse was tethered a comfortable distance away. This could have been the dawning of the second day of waiting.

Tom was familiar with every inch of the Nickell place. He had mentally mapped out and studied the lay of the land many times. Possibly he had spent days just observing Kels Nickell and his family; he knew their work habits, the tasks performed by each.

A master strategist, the former Pinkerton Agent knew that by planting himself in the rocks near the road and by the gate, Kels would sometime during the early hours of the morning come up the road, stop his horse, and get off to open the gate. The assassin could then raise up out of his rock fortress, remain half concealed, with the sun at his back and in the eyes of the near blinded victim, and kill with ease.

But the morning of July 18th was different. Instead, the sun was not shining, it was damp, cold and cloudy. Affairs at the Nickell ranch were not going as Tom anticipated. Breakfast was a half hour earlier. John Apperson, a surveyor, was going to do some surveying for Kels. Mrs. Nickell's brother, William Mahoney, planned to assist with the surveying. Thus the boys, Fred and Willie, would possibly have to do work that their father ordinarily took care of. They had their instructions; they weren't in the habit of questioning.

Fred was to take a load of hay over the hill to the cow barn, a distance of 2 miles. Willie was to saddle-up his father's horse and ride over to Iron Mountain Station to return with a sheep herder who had left the Nickell ranch the day before. The sheep herder had wanted work, Mr. Nickell declined hiring him then, but later decided to. Because it looked like it would be a dismal day, Kels suggested that Willie wear his father's hat and slicker. It was a long ride, and it looked as if it might rain; he didn't want the boy to catch cold—Will hadn't felt too well.

Shortly after breakfast Fred had the team harnessed and was on his way up the road. The hay wagon had been loaded the day before. He would pass over the exact spot where his brother would die in almost a matter of minutes. Fred wouldn't return over this road, he would have unloaded his hay and with a lighter wagon would take the shorter but rougher route back to the ranch. Nickell, Apperson, and Mahoney prepared for the surveying. Kels had so much trouble over his boundaries he wanted to be sure of them. Willie messed around the corral talking to his horse and himself. Finally he was saddled and ready to go. He waved to his father and uncle, now some distance away. Riding past the house he bid his mother goodbye. Mrs. Nickell watched her son as he rode up the road. She was proud of William . . . but this morning she felt uneasy.

Tom Horn, hungry and cold, was cramped in the rocks. He cussed everything and everyone. He had dozed little during the night. His usual breakfast of raw bacon and bread hadn't agreed with him. And the early July morning dew added further to his misery. But the sound of snorting horses and creaking hay wagon coming up the road snapped him out of his lethargy. Instantly he was Tom Horn—wide awake, keen and cautious. As the wagon drew closer he could see a boy driving the team. No damnit, it wasn't Kels! Slowly the wagon drew up to the gate and stopped. Horn watched Fred struggle down off the load, open the barbed wire gate, drive through, close the gate, and get back on the wagon, and away. Tom cussed half aloud, jammed his binoculars back into his coat pocket, rolled a cigarette, and looked up at the sky. It wasn't clearing any. Then he looked at the ground, spit, and sat down. He gave his gun another check over . . . and began thinking about all the dirty work he had done—and what he was about to do. This was to be his final rendezvous with infamy.

In her testimony at the trial, State vs. Horn, Mary Nickell testified that Willie left the ranch sometime between 6:30 and 20 minutes of 7:00. She had been the last member of their family to see William alive.

As Willie walked his horse up the road, the same taken by his brother Fred a half hour earlier, he could see the fresh wagon tracks. It was cold and he wanted to run the horse but thought he better let him limber up first before running him. And so the time factor: Willie arrived at the gate around 7:00 o'clock—perhaps a few minutes before.

Tom Horn heard the horse and the rider long before they came into sight. He took a last drag on his cigarette, then mashed it out. Adjusting his clothes, cartridge belt, he released the trigger from its half cocked position—he was ready. Shortly Tom saw the rider slouched down in the saddle. It was Kels! He recognized the snorting horse, Nickell's hat and the old yellow slicker he had seen the sheepman wear so many times. Horn ducked down. He would wait until the rider dismounted at the gate. This was to be victim number five.

Willie rode slowly. He was always on the look-out. His father warned him to be that way. Recent experience with his neighbors made him ever alert. As the boy approached the gate his horse became nervous. The animal's ears began to turn this and that way; the horse snorted and smelled. He began to paw and dance as Willie dismounted at the fence. Willie knew horses, and respected their sensing ability—suddenly he became frightened and wanted to get through the gate. Trembling and ashen, the sickly lad began tugging at the gate post to remove it from the wire loops—he wouldn't even bother to put it back.

Tom Horn, heretofore concealed, heard the pawing of the horse and the rider dismount, then the straining of the wire fence as the boy tried to remove the gate post. He gave his gun a last glance. This was the time! He would get Kels Nickell! Like a coiling rattler, Horn slowly raised up out of the rocks with his gun elevated and finger on the trigger. The lad's sharp eye caught the movement. He turned quickly toward it. Horn and the boy stood looking at each other. The boy was paralyzed—Horn couldn't believe his eyes. A second later Willie regained his senses and whirled screaming, "Don't! Don't!" Horn was momentarily stunned. In an awful instant he had to make a death-dealing decision. He was compelled by wild desperate precaution to kill, or his identity would be revealed. Then with almost mechanical precision Tom dropped his head to the side of his cold gun barrel, clenched his teeth, caught the lad's moving form in the gunsight and squeezed the trigger in rapid succession. Fourteen-year-old Willie Nickell, reeled from the impact, ran a few feet, and dropped to the ground. Blood gushed out of his terrible wounds, taking young life with it. Over on the "fortress" Tom Horn lay momentarily prostrate on top of a large boulder. Two 30-30 shots were ringing in his ears. Gun powder smoke poured from the rifle barrel, coiling into thin air. . . . A silence that only death can cast, hung over the gate area—intermittently broken by the gurgling sound of warm human blood flowing from a lifeless body. . . .

Kels Nickell, John Apperson, and William Mahoney heard the shots just as they were ready to commence their work. They were about one mile and a half east of the house at the time. The men agreed that the shots seemed to come from the direction of the gate. At the trial Mr. Apperson testified that Mr. Nickell said something at the time to the effect that he wondered who fired the shots, and that the reports were too loud for the gun carried by Fred. He further was said to have remarked that Willie did not have a gun with him. Apparently Mrs. Nickell, busy in the house, didn't hear the shots.

Just what the assassin did after shooting the boy is a matter of speculation. Did he go to the body and inspect it? Or did he leave the scene of the crime, fearing his shots might have attracted attention?*

---

*The most accepted theory, which was also the contention of the Prosecution in State vs. Horn, was that the assassin did inspect the body. It was believed the boy had fallen on his face, and his body turned over to be inspected. Supporting evidence of this was: The body was saturated with blood, and when turned over, a large amount of gravel and dirt stuck to the face and clothing when found. The clothing directly over the wound was torn as if it had been done to make an examination. A "little rock" was said to have been placed under the boy's head.

Yet there were those who argued that the assassin never did go near the body after the shooting: The gravel and blood had clung to the boy because he had twisted and rolled in death. It was further felt that the tearing of the shirt was done by the boy as he clasped and clutched at the wounds in his dying moments. The "little rock" found under his head was cited as a mere coincidence.

(Footnote continued on page eighteen.)

As the day of the 18th wore away, work at the Nickell ranch continued as usual. Kels, Apperson and William Mahoney did the surveying. Fred returned from hauling hay, and began his usual chores around the place. Mrs. Nickell was busy taking care of the smaller children and cooking. She had prepared a bountiful meal since her brother and the surveyor were with them. Little thought was given Will; perhaps his mother mentioned at the dinner table that she wished he had returned in time for the meal.

The family was up early the next day, July 19th. They had expected their son and brother to return in time for breakfast. After the meal, Fred was told to take the cows to pasture as usual; he was cautioned to be sure and shut the gate or the cows would get out. As yet Will hadn't returned. With Fred and the other children out of the house, the elders discussed what should be done; they hadn't wanted to alarm the children. Mrs. Nickell was genuinely worried. And so, the men, undecided what to do, concluded they should wait until mid-day and start looking for Willie if he had not returned by then. In the meantime they worked on their surveying notes.

Shortly they heard a horse approaching the ranch—the men ran outside. They saw young Freddy coming back. He was riding hard and crying pitifully. Upon seeing his father he cried out, "Will has been murdered!" In reply to his father's questions, he stated that he had found his dead brother's body near the pasture gate and had started home without making further investigation.

Immediately Kels Nickell and John Apperson started for the scene of the murder. William Mahoney hastily began harnessing a wagon to take his sister to her son's body.

Minutes later Kels Nickell, with his teeth clenched and his eyes a fiery red, picked up the broken body of his son and placed it in the wagon. Mrs. Nickell, almost insane with grief, fainted upon arrival. Apperson sped over to Iron Mountain to notify the Deputy Sheriff, Peter Warlaumont by telegram.

Within a matter of hours, Sheriff Shafer and Laramie County Coroner Thomas Murray were at the Nickell home. The Coroner had been accompanied by Robert Morris, the stenographer, who recorded the testimony at the inquest.

The rock under the head story has been associated with Horn and all the cases linked with his career. It is a colorful presentation, but based on very little fact. The official inquest reports tend to refute the stories. The circumstances surrounding the Lewis and Nickell murders are the only two of the five, where the story might have been applicable. Powell and Dart were both shot from a distance and in the presence of men. Rash was killed while in his cabin and apparently died in bed.

Kels Nickell testified at the inquest that he and John Apperson found his son's body lying face down or sideways on its back in the road. A ragged hole was in his back just opposite the heart, where a bullet had torn its way into his body from behind. He further stated the boy's face, even in death, bore an expression of tense alarm. After an inspection of the scene of the shooting, it was found that stains indicated the boy ran about seventy-five feet after being shot before he fell. As he fell, it was evident that a stream of blood spurted from the wound, spattering the ground with a well-defined mark four feet from where the body lay.

The wounds on the body were described with accuracy by Dr. Amos Barber, physician, who conducted the post-mortem examination. The missiles entered the body on the left side, passing entirely through it. One wound penetrated the chest approximately on the axiliary line, striking the fifth rib, taking an inward, forward, and slightly downward course, producing a large wound of exit at the juncture of the sixth rib, with the sternum. And the point of entrance of the other wound was three inches posterior to the left axiliary line, and two inches above the ileum, taking an inward and slightly downward course, penetrating the abdominal viscera, making a wound of exit one inch above the crest of the ileum, and two inches anterior to the right axiliary line.

The mystery surrounding the murder was so complete that the peace officers investigating the case were completely stumped. Several detailed investigations and combings of the "gate" area revealed practically nothing. Only the time and place factors were conclusively established.

The most prevalent theory was that the boy had been killed by personal enemies. The fact that Freddy had passed through the gate a few minutes before his brother, discredited the belief that the assassin was out to kill the first Nickell that came along. Apparently no one at this time conceived the idea that it was a case of mistaken identity and precaution killing. It was considered incomprehensible that anyone would deliberately have shot the boy in the back. A theory of accidental death was put forward but quickly disproven by the fact that Willie was not carrying a gun at the time.

Thus the sheriff returned to Cheyenne, without clues, without arrests. And the pressure was on.

The broken body of William Nickell was taken to Cheyenne via rail. Undertaker Alex Trumbull and a Dr. Cook escorted the corpse to Cheyenne. The funeral was held in that city. A large and curious crowd attended the services.

After considerable re-questioning of the family, authorities unearthed their first clue. It was recalled by the peppery Kels that about a month before his death, Willie returned from a hunting trip almost white with fright. When asked what was the matter he said that a ranchman, whom he could not identify, had met him on the prairies and cursed him and abused him. Demanding to know where he was going, the boy had replied he was hunting. Then Will was to have said, "the ranchman drew his six shooter and waved it in my face and shouted, 'why you little ——— ——— ———, I've a great mind to kill you.' " The lad, uninjured, ran home at the first opportunity.

The information established the fact that threats were made against the boy's life. It would have been of great value had Willie known who the ranchman was. The crime still baffled authorities except for this added bit of information.

Tom Horn, once more back among friends, felt confident that his work had been effective. Perhaps he had some explaining to do. He managed to keep out of sight as much as possible doing routine work.

Despite the loss of his son Kels Nickell was defiant and determined to stay in the district. "The worst has passed," he fumed—"why leave now?" But his enemies had different ideas—they would strike again. This time at Kels for sure.

Thus on the morning of August 4th, Kels Nickell arose early. Before breakfast he went to an alfalfa patch to drive some calves in. He was unarmed. At a distance of about 600 yards from his house he was shot at several times from ambush. He ran zig-zagging and yelling for his home. He was hit in three places. One bullet shattered the bone of his left arm near the elbow, the second tore a ragged hole in his left hip and the third inflicted a slight wound under the right arm.

The wounded man was taken into Cheyenne for treatment and hospitalization by William Mahoney. Nickell made a statement implicating James Miller and his sons of the shooting.

Later that day it was learned that about 75 sheep owned by a Dr. Bennett and a Mr. Geddes, run by Nickell, were killed when four masked men attacked the herd of about 1,000 head. The sheep herder fled from the raiders and was reported to have walked all the way into Cheyenne. The herder, an Italian, told an incoherent story, and said his life had been threatened.

Feeling ran high in Cheyenne. An armed posse was formed and Deputy Sheriff Peter Warlaumont placed in charge. Sheriff Shafer had suddenly become seriously ill. As a favor, he invited Deputy United States Marshal Joe LeFors to come on the case. LeFors, a seasoned super sleuth, had heard of the "shootings" and was anxious to go to work, under cover and without fanfare.

A crowd of over 200 met the train returning with the posse that had peacefully arrested James Miller and his sons, August and Victor. The men were arrested in connection with the wounding of Kels Nickell and the killing of 75 head of sheep that he was pasturing.

> *The Laramie Boomerang* of August 8th chronicled their arrival in part as:
>
> The first man to step from the car was [Special Deputy] Sandy McKneal. He carried his Winchester and was followed by James Miller. After Miller came his son Victor carrying a Winchester rifle, then August with another rifle. Brown [another Special Deputy] brought up the rear with a short rifle. The crowd was very orderly, making no demonstration whatever aside from a jamming rush to get a look at the prisoners. Miller was apparently very unconcerned, but the boys were very nervous and evidently did not like the curiosity they were causing. The prisoners were escorted to the jail, with the crowd following on foot and on bicycles. At the court house the door of the Sheriff's office was slammed in the face of the curious, who, after waiting a short time, dispersed.

The arrest of the Millers and the investigations following brought nothing new to light. The three men furnished sufficient evidence of their whereabouts at the time of the shooting, and were released. Despite numerous inquests, rumors and jury sessions, the entire affair remained a nightmare for peace officers.

Tom Horn and his associates followed developments in the case closely—perhaps they had representatives in Cheyenne observing and reporting. They were pleased with the continued mystery and lack of evidence. Horn was confident.

September 1st saw Tom Horn back in Cheyenne participating in Frontier Days.* He won honors in the roping events and was well-

**Laramie Boomerang*, Laramie, Wyoming, September 1, 1901. ALBANY COUNTY BOYS DID GOOD WORK ON FRONTIER DAY: Tom Horn, with his famous broncho busters and fancy cattle ropers easily won first honors in the riding and roping contests Frontier Day in Cheyenne. *(See next page)*

received. It felt good to be back in the company of his old friends, particularly the Irwin brothers, Charlie and Frank.

By early October, Kels Nickell had fully recovered from the wounds he suffered. His hip had healed, and to the surprise of surgeons and friends, he regained the use of his left arm. The elbow had been shattered, at one time it was thought that the arm would have to be removed.

News that Nickell planned to sell out caused a considerable amount of "talk." At last Nickell and his sheep would go. Property was not at a premium—but Kels had made up his mind. And so, after twelve stormy years in the Iron Mountain district, Kels sold his property and sheep and took his family into Cheyenne. He found work there.

The fall of '01 was fairly open. Roundups were made in record time. Tom worked and rode, as usual for the Iron Mountain Ranch Company.† In September Horn accompanied a load of horses to Denver for stockman John Kuykendall. While in Denver the detective suffered a broken jaw after becoming involved in a drinking brawl.

Early December saw the concluding of the long and drawn out Coroner's inquest into the death of Willie Nickell. Tom Horn, fully

---

Otto Plaga did some fine work in the breaking contest. His belt caught on the pommel of the saddle, causing him to be thrown, but he quickly remounted and soon had his horse under complete control. He was given first money in this contest.

Duncan Clark did fine work in the fancy cattle roping, and is without doubt, one of the best ropers in the state; anyway he has money to put up if anyone doubts it.

Frank Stone, a well-known Albany County gentleman rode Bay Devil, a noted outlaw horse, and never was better horsemanship displayed than on this occasion. Frank rode him straight and fanned him on both sides. Bay Devil did everything to unseat his rider, but Frank was there to stay—and he stayed.

†It has been suggested many times that Tom Horn at this time was employed by the Wyoming Stock Growers Association. The following letters, now on deposit in the University of Wyoming Archives and Western History Library, Archives and Western History Department of the University of Wyoming Library, are full evidence that Horn was not working for the association and it is definitely implied that he had not been in their employ for some time. These letters were written at a time when the "pressure" was off, prior to Horn's arrest:

——————, Wyoming
Dec. 2nd, 1901

Alice Smith
Secretary Wyoming Stock Growers Association
Cheyenne, Wyoming

Dear Madam

There is a gang of thieves in this neighborhood killing cattle and stealing horses and I want a good man to help me watch and catch them. Can you send me Tom

(See Footnote on page thirty-nine.)

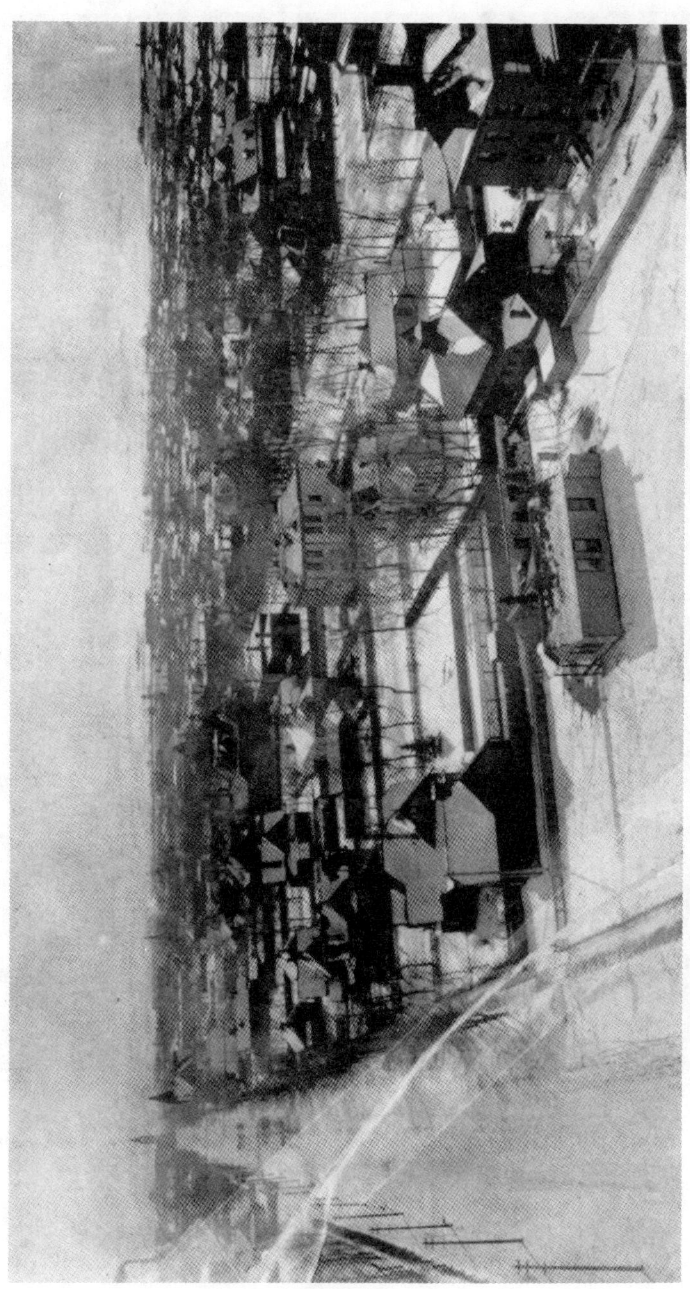

CHEYENNE OF THE TOM HORN ERA

Looking south along Capitol Avenue, taken from the Capitol Dome.

(Courtesy Archives and Western History Department, University of Wyoming Library)

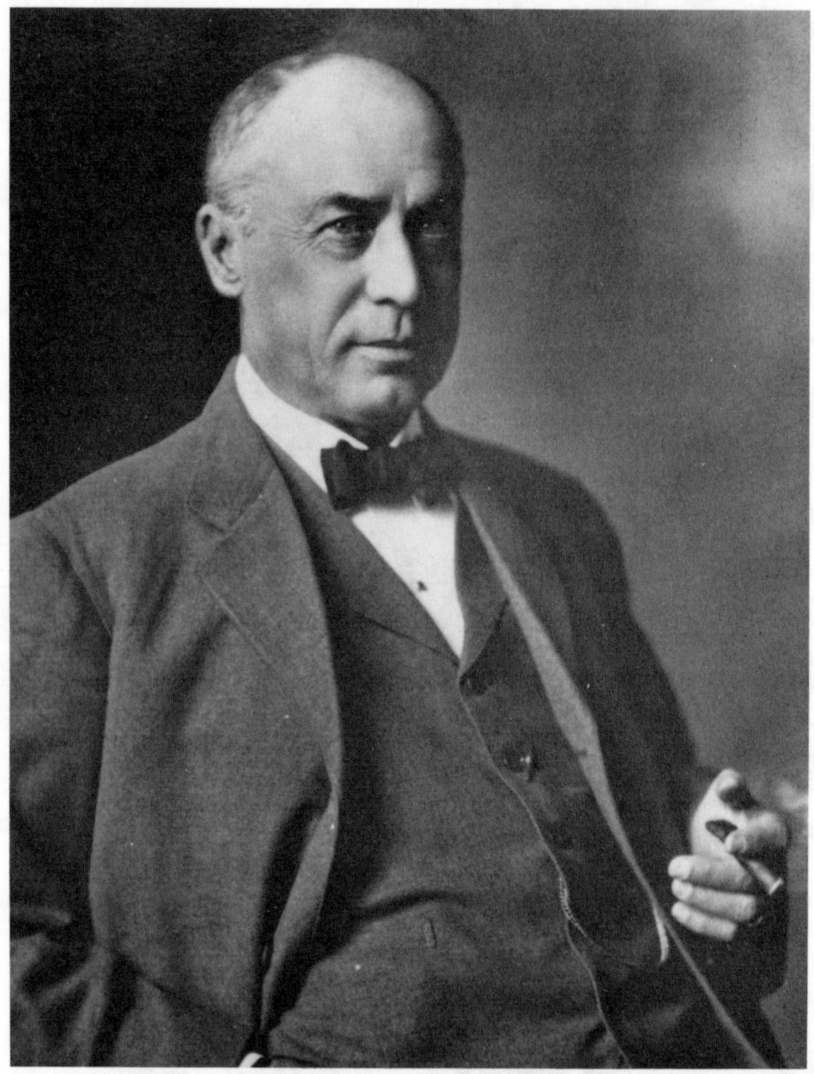

WILLIAM C. IRVINE

Mr. Irvine, a real cowman, was president of the Wyoming Stock Growers Association during the Horn episode.

(Courtesy Wyoming Stockgrowers Association Collection, Archives and Western History Department, University of Wyoming Library.)

MISS ALICE SMITH

Efficient and beloved Secretary of the Stock Growers Association from 1896 to 1922. Perhaps she knew the truth about Tom Horn. . . . Records indicate she didn't like him.

(Courtesy Wyoming Stockgrowers Association Collection, Archives and Western History Department, University of Wyoming Library.)

ORA HALEY

He was an advocate of free enterprise, but this rustlin' . . .

(Courtesy Archives and Western History Department, University of Wyoming)

THE CHEYENNE CLUB

Plush and cosmopolitan, it purchased the finest of everything. Here the "Big Operators" made important decisions.

(*Courtesy Archives and Western History Department, University of Wyoming Library*)

JOHN COBLE

Of the Iron Mountain Ranch Company. He was cultured and a good cattleman. Horn said John Coble was the best friend he ever had.

(Courtesy Archives and Western History Department, University of Wyoming Library)

The most famous of paintings that hung in the Cheyenne Club. John Coble demonstrated his marksmanship on this prize. (Arrows added.)

(Courtesy of Wyoming State Historical Department.)

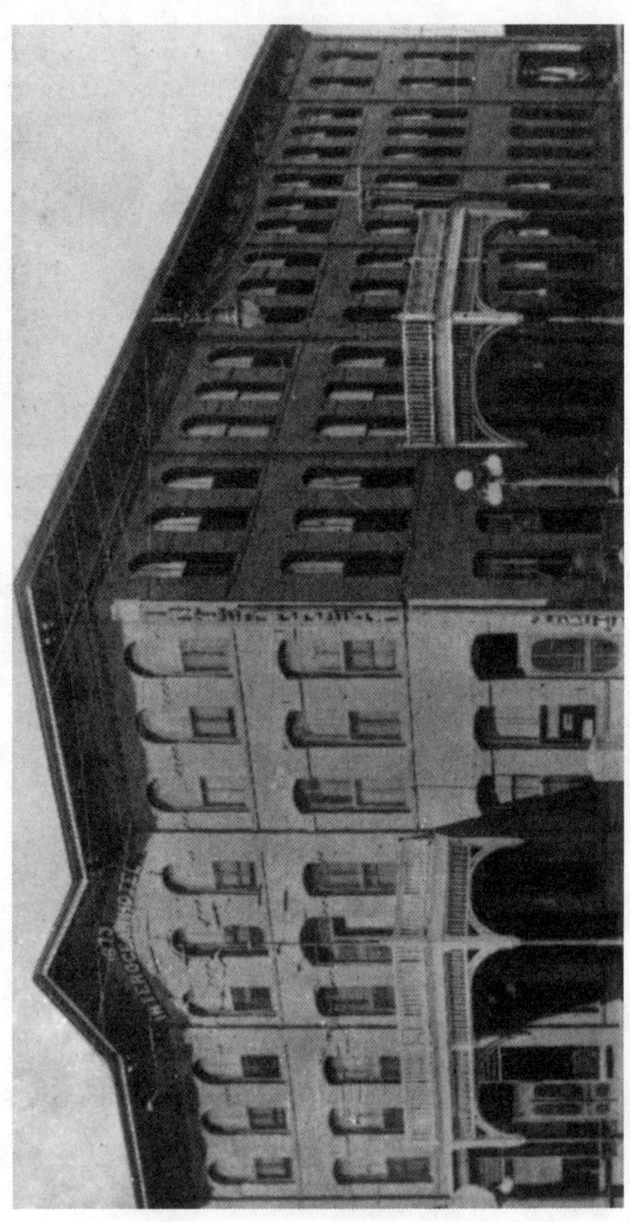

THE INTER-OCEAN HOTEL

A favorite "Hangout" of Tom Horn

(Courtesy Archives and Western History Department, University of Wyoming Library)

ANDREW ROSS

The only witness to the killing of Fred Powell. Ross testified Powell's last words were: "Oh, my God . . . I'm shot."

(Courtesy Archives and Western History Department, University of Wyoming Library)

WILLIE NICKELL

Taken shortly before July 8, 1901. His death was a case of mistaken identity, and compulsory precautionary killing.

(Courtesy Denver Post)

THE SCENE OF THE CRIME

No. 1—*The rocks the assassin hid behind.* No. 2—*The gate where Willie Nickell was shot.* No. 3—*Where the boy's body was found.*

(Courtesy Denver Post)

JOE LEFORS—WYOMING PEACE OFFICER

He alone had the daring to set the stage and trap Tom Horn.

(Courtesy Archives and Western History Department, University of Wyoming Library)

CHARLES J. OHNHAUS

As Court Stenographer he recorded the January 12th conversation between Joe LeFors and Tom Horn.

(Courtesy Archives and Western History Department, University of Wyoming Library)

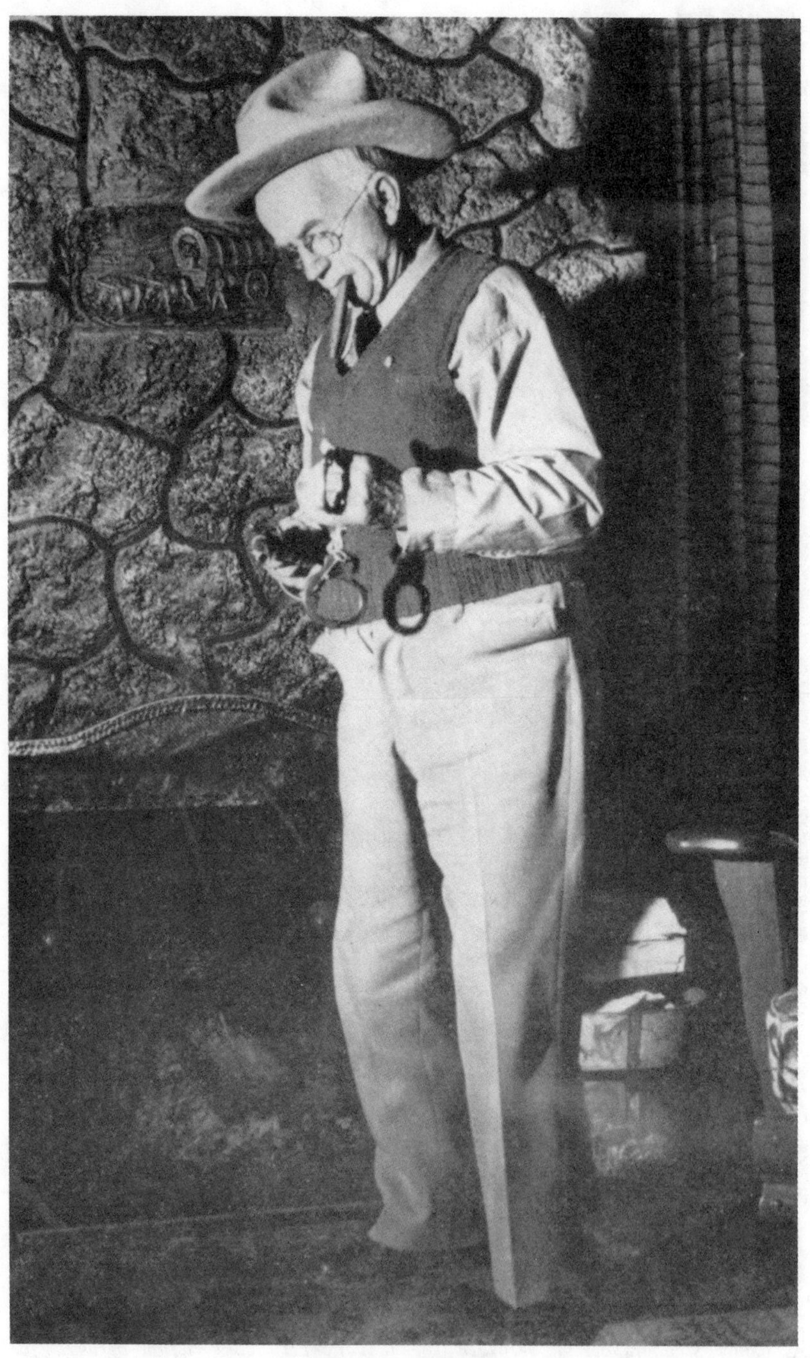

LESLIE SNOW

Deputy Sheriff of Laramie County. He testified as to the Joe LeFors-Tom Horn conversation which took place in the U. S. Marshal's Office on January 12.

SHERIFF "ED" SMALLEY (seated) and
DEPUTY SHERIFF R. A. PROCTOR

Tom was their responsibility for twenty-two months —"A mighty long time boys, a might long time."

(Courtesy Denver Post)

TOM HORN

Then a young man and pursuing his duties as a Pinkerton Detective.

(Courtesy Union Pacific Collection Archives.)

THE IRWIN BROTHERS, CHARLES AND FRANK

Put your trust alone in Jesus; never falter, never fail;
Keep your hand on the throttle; and your eye upon the rail.
—Life's Railway to Heaven.

recovered from his jaw injury, participated in the inquest and "got by" the routine with ease. Practically everyone in the district had been requested to testify.

Horn was in "wind" of work in Montana. Although the heat was off perhaps it was felt that a change of environment would be good for all concerned. The pay seemed generous to a man of his "ability." Joe LeFors was the middle man for the job. Tom was sure he could impress LeFors. . . .

THE JOE LEFORS' STORY*

. . . The Deputy Sheriff who met me at the train in Cheyenne upon my return from Aladin, Wyoming, with the counterfeiter, said that Sheriff Shafer was a very sick man and was not expected to live and that he had asked as a favor to him that I be sent to investigate the shooting of Kels P. Nickell and asked if I heard of the killing of his son, little Willie Nickell. I told the officers that the report of the shooting of little Willie Nickell came in as I was leaving Cheyenne some seven or eight days before.

They told me that Kels P. Nickell, the father, had been shot that morning and that no officer had as yet been out to Iron Mountain to investigate. Knowing from my wire when I would be back, the Deputy Sheriff said that Sheriff Shafer got permission for me to go from the U. S. Marshal's office, if I would.

I tried to get out of going as I had been up the better part of two days and nights and had had little sleep as the counterfeiter was chained to my leg.

Horn or please send me his address for reference to my standing se [see] D. R. Please answer by return mail.

Very respectively,
J. E.

E———, Wyoming
Dec. 7th, 1901

Mr. J. E.
E———, Wyoming

Dear Sir:

In reply to yours of Dec. 2nd, would say, that we think a letter directed to Tom Horn at Bosler, Wyoming, in care of the Iron Mountain Ranch Co., will reach him. You of course understand that he is not in the employ of the Association. . . .

Yours truly,
Alice Smith, Secretary

*Joe LeFors' story printed by permission of his widow, Mrs. Nettie (Joe) LeFors. Published in *Wyoming Peace Officer*, "An Autobiography by Joe LeFors," Laramie Printing Company, Laramie, Wyoming, 1953.

I finally said that I would go with Peter Warlaumont if I woke up in time to catch the early Iron Mountain train. Otto, the night policeman, said: "Fine, I'll call you." So I turned my prisoner, Becker, over to the Deputies to put in jail and I hurried home and to bed.

It seemed as if I had just gotten to sleep when Otto called me. I joined Peter Warlaumont at the train and by about 9:30 we were at Iron Mountain, our getting-off place. Warlaumont had arranged for horses and we found mounts ready and waiting when we arrived.

From Iron Mountain to the Nickell ranch was about seven miles. On arriving at the Nickell ranch and a few hundred yards from the ranch house, we met a man who at one time had been a neighbor of Warlaumont, so Peter stopped to talk to him.

I rode on, thinking Warlaumont would be more apt to get some information from his old neighbor if I left them alone. I rode up to the Nickell home, got off my horse and went to the door and knocked. A woman, in a quivering voice, asked who was there.

"An officer, Mrs. Nickell, I want to talk to you," I answered, and I further said that Mr. Warlaumont was coming a short distance back and that we had come to investigate her troubles.

She asked my name and I told her I was LeFors from the U. S. Marshal's office.

"I know Mr. Warlaumont, but I don't know you—they have killed my little boy and now my husband and I suppose it is my time next," she wailed.

I told her I had a good report of her husband's condition at the hospital in Cheyenne; that he was getting along nicely and was only painfully hurt but not dangerous. All this time I was talking through the door. At last she decided to open it.

"I suppose I might as well be killed one time as another," she said, and then I could hear her taking cord wood from the door. She had barricaded the place thinking the killer would be back.

The poor woman opened the door with tears streaming down her cheeks. She was a dear motherly middle-aged woman with three little children hanging to her skirts and all crying. A more pitiful sight I never saw.

After the door was opened she said: "We are being shot and killed off one at a time and all day yesterday not an officer came."

I then told her the Sheriff was very sick and they had been waiting for me to get back to Cheyenne as I was away on a trip.

She showed me little Willie's bloody coat that he was wearing when shot. It was hanging on the wall by the side of the door and the father's jacket was hanging by the side of it. He had been wearing it when he was shot just two days ago.

"Nothing is being done to protect us," Mrs. Nickell cried. I assured her that it was not as bad as that, saying there were lots of people that would help them.

"Who are they that will help a poor family that has nothing to pay for help with?" she wanted to know.

All this time the three little children hung onto her.

"I'll help you, Mrs. Nickell, I will get the cold-blooded murderer," I told her.

She put out her hand and I took it and promised to get the man who had been trying to kill off the family. That seemed to give her courage and the crying stopped. I told her I would need her help and said that it had been stated to me many times in the last twenty-four hours that Mr. Nickell was high tempered and talked a great deal and was accusing this one and that one of being the man that was doing the shooting.

"I want you to keep him from talking," I said. "Do not talk any more than you can help about the case and do not allow Mr. Nickell to talk. You do not know do you, who did the shooting?"

She said they did not know—that the only thing she knew was it was done on account of their sheep. That Kels had got a letter with no name signed to it saying to get out of the country with the sheep or suffer the consequences and that the morning Kels was shot the sheepherder was run off and the sheep herd was fired into. The sheep up to that time were without a herder as far as they knew.

I assured her I would investigate and get all the facts and insisted that she do no talking, or offer suggestions to anyone.

"When things quiet down," I continued, "and you think I have forgotten my promise, then I will be doing my best work."

At this point Peter Warlaumont came. I cautioned her by all means to keep my name from becoming known in the case. Of course it would be known that I went up to Iron Mountain at the time, but no one would know that I was permanently in the case.

Peter Warlaumont and I talked to all the family and found that no one saw the killer. But all the children that were up at that time in the morning and the mother had heard the shots and had seen the father running across a little meadow and heard his hollering.

Nickell had been shot as he was running, one bullet striking the arm at the elbow joint and two other slight flesh wounds. The would-be assassin fired five shots. This shooting was only a week or so after little Willie was killed at the gate, a mile to the west of the house, while he was on the way to Iron Mountain Station.

Not even Peter Warlaumont knew the extent of my talk with Mrs. Nickell regarding the catching of the assassin.

After we were satisfied we had all the information we could get from the family, we went to where the sheep had been fired into and found quite a number of sheep killed. Perhaps we could count 25 or 30 carcasses all tolled, but no doubt shooting into the crowding, jamming sheep as they ran there would be a greater number wounded. A man had been sent from Cheyenne who was gathering up and looking after the herd.

Aside from a lot of horse tracks and dead sheep there was but little information to be gathered. So Peter Warlaumont and I returned to Cheyenne that night. On arriving in Cheyenne I learned that Sheriff Shafer was very low. I never got to see him alive.

Faithful Sam Carson, the chairman of the Board of County Commissioners of Laramie County, sent me word that he would like to see me privately and for me to arrange it so that it would be a secret. I met him in the U. S. Marshal's office that evening after hours.

Mr. Carson asked what I had found from the investigation I had made. I told him that there could be only one conclusion—that the killing was the result of a sheepman's and a cattleman's war.

I told Carson: "Those killings are over the range. Kels P. Nickell had the only sheep between the Iron Mountain country and the U. P. R. R., a distance of some sixty-five to seventy miles. And there can be but one interest involved and that is the open government range. Kels Nickell is not and never has been, to my knowledge, accused of stealing."

I informed him also that there wasn't any doubt in my mind that a few of the cattlemen were interested in keeping the sheep out while they might not all sanction the methods used. So to my mind the killing was all predicated on dollars and cents. Carson told me he was perfectly satisfied that my version was absolutely right. The killing of the sheep emphasized that fact the morning Kels was shot.

I said that in order to determine who the guilty parties were, one had only to ride the range, look at the cattle brands and see for himself who was immediately interested. The finger of guilt pointed to the few cattle companies who were using that particular range.

Carson then said that if he could get my chief in the U. S. Marshal's office to consent to let me work on the case, what would I charge for running the murderer down.

I told him that I was under obligations to do all I could to land the assassin. But it would be much easier on me if I could get the consent of the higher-ups. At the same time it would be next to impossible for me to run this case down if it were known that I was working on the case. Carson said he would feel my chief out on the issue and let me know and advised me not to let my chief find out that we had had our talk, saying: "I will get him to come to you. Your chief and I have already had one talk and now I will get him to come to you with the proposition himself."

So the next day my chief came to me and asked what I thought about working on the killing and attempted-killing cases. I told him there would be no telling how long it would take to accomplish anything. Then he said that if I would undertake the case he would do as much of my work for the government as he could, so that I would have plenty of time.

He finished by saying: "If you can bring those lawbreakers to justice you can get any position the state has to offer."

At this time the feeling was running high and the demand was for justice. I could scent a lot of politics coming into the case and I knew those Cheyenne politicians were for politics first and justice next. But there was such a strong demand for the arrest of the assassin, I thought that perhaps this case would be an exception. So I told my political boss: "Once I start, I will go through with the case, and if it is in my power, I will land on everyone interested in those murders."

Hadsell then said: "Joe, go do your best."

Carson and I had another talk and I told Carson I would run the case down. I was nearly positive I could do it. At the same time I had never at any time in my life worked with a cowman or a cowpuncher in that Iron Mountain country.

My policy was, while the case was fresh, to work on the Iron Mountain bunch just when they were in Cheyenne or other towns should I meet any of them and not go out where I would create suspicion.

Cheyenne had at that time a splendid Chief of Police, a man by the name of Sandy McKneal, a real live officer. He and I were the best of friends and I knew Sandy suspected that I was working on the Nickell killing case, yet he asked me no questions, but whenever any Iron Mountainite came in I was sure to hear about it.

Information was not unravelling as fast as I wanted it to, until a couple living in the Iron Mountain country during the trouble, moved to town. These people were friends of Tom Horn.

I had now gained some knowledge of the case after I had run down one suspect, an Indian-looking painter, who had painted a barn or two in that country. I eliminated him by learning his whereabouts at the time of the killing of little Willie Nickell.

Sandy McKneal pointed Tom Horn out to me one day at the saddle shop. I asked Sandy to introduce me to him. We went into Frank Meanea's saddle shop and Sandy introduced us.

In spite of some cheap write-ups the Horn case has received, and many liars claiming Horn and I were old cronies and had done detective work together, this was the first time I had ever seen the man in my life. Neither had I any knowledge of him whatever.

Horn was buying a gun scabbard. He had his 30-30 Winchester saddle gun that he was having a scabbard made for, with him. We had quite a visit and talk about the Winchester, the sights, etc., the muzzle velocity, penetration, etc., and I found Horn very well posted on small arms and rather inclined to brag.

Horn was making his headquarters at the Bosler Cattle Company's ranch near the Bosler station on the U.P.R.R. west of Laramie City. (In a letter which John Coble wrote to Bosler on July 16, 1900, and which was later put on record in the court at Laramie, he said: "The Iron Mountain, Wall Rock and Plumbago pastures are filled with sheep and look wooly. Our she cattle are in Iron Mountain and they are doing fine, like in a meadow. When the sheep men attempt to drive or handle our cattle I will at once have them arrested. But they are scared to death, are hiring all the six shooters and bad men they can find. I want Horn back here; he will straighten them out by merely riding around).

A few days after I met Horn, I discovered the woman from Iron Mountain who had recently moved to town. She was stepping out nights with a young broncho-buster also from near Iron Mountain, while her husband was east with a bunch of polo ponies. The Missus liked her high-balls. The young man from Iron Mountain was in town only about once every two weeks and then he only stayed a couple of days. They would use a wine room in the back part of a saloon. The woman and her husband had lived near the Nickell ranch and I had picked up some information to the effect that Horn was at times stopping with them.

I was now in conference with Walter Stoll, Prosecuting Attorney, nearly every day. Mrs. Kitzmiller, Walter Stoll's stenographer, had a special book in which she compiled all the Horn data in alphabetical form. At any time I had information for Stoll in the case, I dictated it to Mrs. Kitzmiller and the Prosecuting Attorney, Walter Stoll, would read it later. In this way I was never detained in turning in evidence.

Horn let some damaging words slip in a drinking orgy in a saloon, to the effect that he sometimes got too handy with a Winchester. This talk was not made to me, but it was of public knowledge.

The young broncho-buster came to town again and had another little spree with the polo man's wife at the same wine room. I decided that next Thursday I would pump that woman and learn for sure if Horn was stopping with them during the time he was in hiding trying to get a shot at Kels Nickell.

Our court was in session and perhaps I would not be able to meet her, but I was determined to try. I took the matter up with Stoll to see if he would stand for the expense of getting a Pinkerton woman up from Denver to get those facts. A woman was put on the case and she lived out at Iron Mountain for a couple of months. But she did not accomplish much of anything. This woman lived at Hencke's place while she was investigating.

Our court adjourned and I had a man to take to the pen at Rawlins. On my way back, one of the bosses of the Bosler ranch got on my train as we passed Bosler station. I went and sat down by him and brought up the killing of little Willie Nickell.

I said, "George, what are all the Pinkertons doing around Cheyenne? I saw three there in the last three days. One time I saw them following Tom Horn around. Tom was drinking and I understood, talking about the Nickell case. Why don't you send him out of the country? Horn is going to get someone in trouble yet by his talk."

This Bosler boss said that if Horn got to talking too much they would have to bump him off themselves. This was my first real information that I could rely on—that Tom Horn was guilty of killing little Willie Nickell.

George said that he was not the man who paid for the last killing, but that he did pay Horn for the jobs committed before; that he paid Horn on the train between Cheyenne and Denver. The money, he said he paid him was in gold and paper money. I presumed the jobs before the last ones meant the killing of Powell and Lewis.

I said, "George, I've a letter here that I received from W. B. Smith, Chief Livestock Inspector of Montana. He wants me to send him a man for detective work in northwestern Montana. This might be a good place to get Horn out of sight for awhile."

George took the letter. It read:

Miles City, Montana
Dec. 28th, 1901

Joe LeFors Esq
Cheyenne

Friend Joe.

I want a good man to do some secret work. And want a man that I can trust. And he will have to be a man not known in this country. The nature of this, there is a gang over the Big Moon River that are stealing cattle and we purpose to fit the man out as a wolfer and let him go into that country (and wolf).

And if he is the right kind of a man he can soon get in with the gang. He will have to be a man that can take care of himself in any kind of country.

The pay will be $125.00 per month and I believe a man can make good wages besides.

Joe if you know of any one who you think will fill the place let me know. There will be several month's work.

Yours truly,
W. D. Smith

P. S. Man will have to report in Helena.

George thought it just the thing to get Horn out of the country; that he would see John Coble and talk the matter over with him. If Horn did not want the job they would make him take it whether he wanted it or not.

In a few days Coble came to Cheyenne from Bosler and came up to my office and wanted to see a letter that I had mentioned before to George and asked if the Montana people still wanted a man. I told John Coble they did. I said that I had not sent anyone as yet but that I had two or three people in mind.

Coble then asked if he could take the letter back to Bosler with him and that he would have Horn answer it in a couple of days. I gave the letter to him and said to tell Tom to make up his mind pretty quick, that I would have to do something soon.

Coble asked if I would be in town for two or three days and when I said yes, said that Tom would answer by Friday or Saturday. That would give him time to get back to the ranch at Bosler and for Tom's letter to reach me.

Horn's letter:

Iron Mountain Ranch Company
Bosler, Wyoming
Jan 1st 1902

Joe LeFors Esq.
Cheyenne Wyo.

Dear Joe

Recd yours from W. D. Smith Miles City Mont. by John Coble today. I would like to take up that work and I feel sure I can give Mr. Smith satisfaction. I don't care how big or bad his men are or how many of them there are. I can handle them. They can scarcely be any worse than the Browns Hole Gang and I stopped cow stealing there in one summer. If Mr. Smith cares to give me the work I would like to meet them as soon as commencement as to get into the country and get located before summer.

The wages $125.00 per month will be satisfactory to me. Put me in communication with Mr. Smith whom I know well by reputation and I can guarantee him the recommendation of every cow man in the State of Wyoming in this line of work.

You may write Mr. Smith for me that I can handle his work and do it with less expense in the shape of lawyer & witness fees than any man in the business.

Joe, you yourself know what my reputation is although we have never been out together.

Yours truly
Tom Horn

P. S. Enclosed find enclosure of Mr. Smith
Tom

A few days later I received another letter from Tom. It was the letter I wanted.

Iron Mountain Ranch Company
Bosler Wyoming Jan 7 1902

Joe LeFors Esq
Cheyenne Wyo.

Friend Joe

Recd your Jan 6th to day and contents noted. Joe I am much obliged to you for the trouble you have taken for me in this matter and I will do my best to give satisfaction. I will get the men sure, for I have never yet let a cow thief get away from me unless he just got up a [and] jumped clean out of the country.

I will come to Cheyenne to get my pass as I can get one to Helena or any other point from Cheyenne. I can go at any time after ten days. I will see you in Cheyenne when I come in. Again thanking you for your trouble.

I am yours truly
Tom Horn

Enclosed find letter of W.D.S.

With Horn coming into Cheyenne I put everything in readiness and planned to have the U. S. Court reporter and the deputy sheriff hide behind the door in the Clerk's office and take down a conversation between Tom Horn and me.

I had Peter Burgesson, a key maker, fix the door between the Clerk's and Marshal's office so that it could be locked and had him give it plenty of clearance so it would not drag. We had about two inches of clearance under the partition door between the two offices.

I told the County Prosecuting Attorney Stoll all my plans. Walter said, "Fine." And then he suggested that the U. S. Court Reporter come to his office just as quickly as he could after he took down the conversation.

Just before I received Tom's letter, I got sight of the polo man's wife on the street. The detective woman from Iron Mountain was in town so I hunted her up and told her of a little scheme I had to get a good story of Horn's whereabouts for a few days prior to the killing of little Willie Nickell. She was right in for it. I also got sight of the broncho-busting friend, too, so I went to Sandy McKneal and asked him to see to it that this cowboy broncho-buster was entertained until at least twelve o'clock that night. Sandy promised he would see that he was kept entertained until that time.

After we had a late dinner the woman detective and I went to the wine room, got some glasses and all kinds of drinks and waited. We left the wine room door ajar so the woman from Iron Mountain would be sure to look in. Sure enough about 9:00 p.m., she came, pushed open the door and looked in. She got such a pleasant and appealing invitation to join us that she came right in, apologizing as she came, saying she had her own party coming in a few minutes, but she would not mind one drink with us.

As no one came, it was another and another drink until she had about enough. We told her we were going to Salt Lake City from Denver. She soon got to talking, giving us the history of her adventures and related the story of the shooting of Kels P. Nickell and told us she had carried sandwiches to Horn while he was lying in hiding to get a shot at Nickell, the father of little Willie Nickell. We then sent her home and we wrote up what she had told us. And the next morning we took the story to Attorney Stoll.

I saw this woman on the street a time or two the next day, but tried to keep out of her sight, but she saw me and asked me who I was and learned my name. She went upstairs across the street and sent a man to ask me to come to see her in the Senate Building. I went to her living room with quite a bit of suspicion.

When I met her she asked if I had all the information from her that I wanted. I told her she volunteered all the information I had. She asked if Horn was now suspicioned. I told her she must have some suspicion that he was in hiding for some purpose.

She said, "I did not know it at the time but I do suspect him now."

I said, "Well, forget our talk," and I told her that I thought everything would come out all right and for her just to forget it.

She laughed and said, "When I sent for you I fully intended to kill you but I believe you are all right now." While she was talking she shook a keen edged dagger out of her sleeve.

"I didn't know what you wanted," I told her, "or who I was going to meet with you when I was coming upstairs," and I shook an automatic out of my sleeve. She laughed and we shook hands and declared we would be friends.

The woman was just about as dangerous as Horn himself. I think she was about one-half Spanish or something, not entirely all American.

The information she gave us was of the shooting of the father and we intended to prosecute Tom for killing the boy. So this information could not be used only in case of a prosecution for the shooting of Kels P. Nickell himself. Walter Stoll often stated we must be careful in the trial of this case in order not to allow grounds for a reversal in case of a conviction and a new trial. For that reason much evidence was left out at Tom Horn's trial.

Horn reached Cheyenne on the Sunday appointed. I met him myself at the train and I know that he was not drunk, as has been so often claimed. Snow and Ohnhaus were hidden close to the door in the next room. Charlie Ohnhaus took down the conversation between us in shorthand. Most of this is given in 73 Pacific Reporter as follows:

After LeFors and Horn entered the marshal's office, the former handed the latter a letter, remarking, "Here is your letter of introduction to Mr. W. G. Pruitt, which reads as follows," and he proceeded to read it aloud.

Then Horn said: "I want to go on the U.P. I know the route, and I don't know the others."

LeFors: "It is about as near one way as the other, and you will get there about the same time."

After one or two remarks on this line, Horn said, "Well, Joe, do you know anything about the nature of the work I will have to do up there?"

LeFors: "Tom, they are good people. I have worked for them five or six years. You will have to get right in among them, and gain their confidence, and show them you are all right."

Horn: "I don't want to be making reports to anybody at any time. I will simply have one report to make, and that will be my final report. If a man has to make reports all the time, they will catch the wisest S.O.B. on earth. These people are not afraid of shooting, are they?"

LeFors: "No, they are not afraid of shooting."

Horn: "I shoot too much I know. You know me when it comes to shooting. I will protect the people I am working for, but I have never got my employers into any trouble yet over anything I have done. A man can't be too careful because you don't want any——— ——— officers to know what you are doing."

LeFors: "Tom, I know you are a good man for the place. You are the best man to cover up your trail I ever saw. In the Willie Nickell killing I could never find your trail and I pride myself on being a trailer."

Horn: "No, ——— ———; I left no trail. The only way to cover up your trail is to go barefooted."

LeFors: "Where was your horse?"

Horn: "He was a ——— ——— long ways off."

LeFors: "I would be afraid to leave my horse so far away; you might get cut off from him."

Horn: "You don't take much chances. These people are unorganized, and anyway I depend on this gun of mine. The only thing I was ever afraid of was that I would be compelled to kill an officer, or a man I didn't want to; but I would do everything to keep from being seen, but if he kept after me, I would certainly kill him."

The conversation then continued as follows:

LeFors: "I never knew why Willie Nickell was killed. Was it because he was one of the victims named, or was it compulsory?"

Horn: "I think it was this way. Suppose a man was in the big draw to the right of the gate—you know where it is—the draw that comes into the main creek below Nickell's house where Nickell was shot. Well, I suppose a man was in that, and the kid came riding up on him from this way, and suppose the kid started to run for the house, and the fellow headed him off at the gate and killed him to keep him from going to the house and raising a hell of a commotion. That is the way I think it occurred."

LeFors: "Tom, you had your boots on when you ran across there to cut the kid off, didn't you?"

Horn: "No, I was barefooted."

LeFors: "You didn't run across there barefooted."

Horn: "Yes, I did."

LeFors: "How did you get your boots on after cutting your feet?"

Horn: "I generally have ten days to rest after a job of that kind. Joe, do you remember the little girl?"

LeFors: "Who do you mean?"

Horn: "The school marm. She was sure smooth people. She wrote me a letter as long as the Governor's message, telling me in detail everything asked by Stoll, the Prosecuting Attorney. Stoll thought I was going to prove an alibi, but I fooled him. I had a man on the outside keeping me in touch before I showed up with everything that was going on. I got this letter from the girl the same day I got my summons to appear before the Coroner's inquest."

LeFors: "Did the school marm tell everything she knew?"

Horn: "Yes, she did. I would not tell an individual like her anything; not me. She told me to look out for you. She said, 'Look out for Joe LeFors; he is not all right. Look out for him; he is trying to find out something.' I said, 'What is there in this LeFors matter?' She said Miller didn't like him, and said he would kill the S.O.B. if God would spare him long enough. There is nothing to those Millers. They are ignorant old jays. They can't even appreciate a good joke. The first time I met the girl was just before the killing of the kid. Everything you know dates from the killing of the kid."

LeFors: "How many days was it before the killing of the kid?"

Horn: "Three or four days maybe. Damned if I want to remember the dates. She was there, and of course, we soon paired ourselves off."

LeFors: "What nationality was she?"

Horn: "She was one-quarter Jap, one-half Korean, and the other German. She talks almost every language on the earth."

LeFors: "Tom, didn't Jim Dixon carry you grub?"

Horn: "No one carried me grub."

LeFors: "Tom, how can a man that weighs 204 pounds go without eating anything so long?"

Horn: "Well, I do. For sometimes I go for days without a mouthful. Sometimes I have a little bacon along."

LeFors: "You must get terribly hungry, Tom."

Horn: "Yes, sometimes I get so hungry that I could kill my mother for some grub, but I never quit a job until I get my man."

LeFors: "What kind of a gun have you got?"

Horn: "I used a 30-30 Winchester."

LeFors: "Tom, do you think that will hold up as well as a 30-40?"

Horn: "No, but I like to get close to my man. The closer the better."

LeFors: "How far was Willie Nickell killed?"

Horn: "About 300 yards. It was the best shot I ever made, and the dirtiest trick I ever done. I thought at one time he would get away."

LeFors: "How about the shells? Did you carry them away?"

Horn: "You bet your ——— ——— life I did."

LeFors: "Tom, do you need any more money for this trip?"

Horn: "No. If I get a pass, I will not need any more money. If I have to buy a ticket, I must have a little more money; but today is Sunday, and I will have to wait until tomorrow."

LeFors: "Well, it is afternoon, and I will go home, and see you again this afternoon or this evening, when we can talk this matter over."

Horn: "All right, I will be back. I want to know all about these people before I go up there."

LeFors: "Tom, let us go downstairs and get a drink. I could always see your work clear, but I want you to tell me why you killed the kid. Was it a mistake?"

Horn: "Well, I will tell you all about it when I come back from Montana. It is too new yet."

Horn and Lefors then left the office, but they returned in the afternoon, when the conversation was continued as follows:

Horn: "Joe, we have only been together about fifteen minutes, and I will bet there is some people saying, 'What are those S.O.B.'s planning now, and who are they going to kill next?' We have come up here because there is no other place to go. If you go to the Inter Ocean [hotel] to sit down and talk for a few minutes, some one comes in and says, 'Let us have a drink,' and before you know it you are standing up and talking, and my feet get so ——— ——— tired it almost kills me. I am 44 years, 3 months, and 27 days old, and if I get killed now I have the satisfaction of knowing I have lived about fifteen ordinary lives. I would like to have had somebody who saw my past and could picture it to the public. It would be the most ——— ——— interesting reading in the country; and if we could describe to the author our feelings at different times it would be better still. The experience of my life, or the first man I killed, was when I was only 26 years old. He was a coarse S.O.B."

LeFors: "How much did you get for killing these fellows? In the Powell and Lewis case you got $600 apiece. You killed Lewis in the corral with a six-shooter. I would like to have seen the expression on his face when you shot him."

Horn: "He was the scardest S.O.B. you ever saw. How did you come to know that, Joe?"

LeFors: "I have known everything you have done, Tom, for a great many years. I know where you were paid the money on the train between Cheyenne and Denver. Why did you put the rock under the kid's head after you killed him? That is one of your marks, isn't it?"

Horn: "Yes, that is the way I hang out my sign to collect money for a job of this kind."

LeFors: "Have you got your money yet for the killing of Nickell?"

Horn: "I got that before I did the job."

LeFors: "You got $500 for that. Why did you cut the price?"

Horn: "I got $2,100."

LeFors: "How much is that a man?"

Horn: "That is for three dead men and one man shot at five times. Killing is my specialty. I look at it as a business proposition, and I think I have a corner on the market."

Horn and I exchanged some stories and then left the Marshal's office, with the understanding that he was to leave for Montana the next day.

Ohnhaus, the Court Stenographer, hurried and got everything typed Sunday night. Warrants were all prepared for Horn's arrest the next morning, and the arrest was made Monday morning by Edward J. Smalley, Sheriff; Dick Proctor, Under-sheriff; and Sandy McKneal, Chief of Police, in the lobby of the Inter-Ocean hotel. I was looking on only a few feet away. Horn did not offer the slightest resistance. . . .

"ED" SMALLEY'S NERVE*

"After Horn's confessions were recorded, I was given the warrant for his arrest. I learned that Tom was in the lobby of the Inter-Ocean Hotel, where he was stopping, so I with my deputy, R. A. Proctor, went on down there. We found him sitting on one of the leather settees in the lobby and talking to a Union Pacific special agent by the name of Wheeler. Tom usually wore his coat and his vest unbuttoned and carried his gun thrust into his trousers, fastened, of course, to the trouser belt. The butt of his gun, rested right at the pit of his stomach which made it easy for him to draw in quick time. I called 'Hello Tom,' and he got to his feet and put his hand out to greet me and said 'Hello Eddie.' He called me Eddie. I shook hands with him with my right hand and at the same time grabbed his gun with my left. He was mildly surprised at my taking his gun, but showed no inclination to fight. I said, 'Tom, I have a warrant for your arrest.' 'The h-- you have! What for?' he demanded. I then

*Annals of Wyoming, Vol. 13, No. 1, pp. 69-72.

read the warrant to him and said, 'You'll have to come along to the jail with me, Tom.' 'All right,' he said, 'but say Eddie, leave my gun at the desk and ask them to take care of it for me, will you?' 'No, I'll put it in the safe at the jail, Tom, for safe keeping,' I told him.

"He came along with me without any protest whatever. I didn't even put the cuffs on him. As we were walking along I asked, 'How much do you weigh, Tom?' 'I weigh about two-hundred one pounds.' he said. 'How old are you Tom and what is your height?' I asked. 'I'm forty-four years, forty-four months, forty-four days, forty-four hours, and forty-four seconds, and I'm six foot one inch tall,' he answered with his usual joking manner. After I locked his cell he asked to see LeFors. He smelled a rat, all right, (it was Joe LeFors, Deputy United States Marshal who had secured Tom Horn's confession through a ruse). I telephoned LeFors who was down at Walter Stoll's office. (Walter Stoll was the County Prosecuting Attorney.) LeFors said he didn't want to see Tom, but I suggested he might come and talk to him for a little. He did, but only a few minutes. Horn said to him, 'They got me in here for killing the kid.' Joe said, 'the h - - - they have.' There was not much said between them . . ."

Sketch of Attorney Stoll questioning Kels P. Nickell.

(Courtesy Denver Post)

PART TWO *The State of Wyoming vs. Tom Horn*

Oh, hitch up your horses and feed 'em some hay,
And seat yourself by me so long as you stay.

Goodbye Old Paint, I'm a-leavin' Cheyenne
Goodbye Old Paint, I'm a-leavin' Cheyenne.

—*Old Paint* (Author Unknown).

Horn was arrested on January 13th. The preliminary hearing was held January 24th. Judge Becker was to preside.

The intervening two weeks were busy ones. Horn's backers had time enough to line up his Defense. Five attorneys were hired, representing the best "legal brains" in the State of Wyoming. They were Judge J. W. Lacey; T. E. Burke, the District Attorney for the U. S. for the District of Wyoming; Burke's partners, Clark, Matson, and T. Blake Kennedy, late of Syracuse, New York.

Almost unheard of Walter R. Stoll, Laramie County Attorney, Clyde Watts and H. Waldo Moore represented the prosecution. Few conceded to the idea that Horn would not be released by the time the grass was green again.

Ten o'clock January 24th saw the stage set and the play ready to start. The Court Room was packed. However, this was to be only a dress rehearsal. Bigger things were to come.

Judge Becker started the precedings by asking the attorneys if they were ready to proceed. W. R. Stoll asked the record show what Horn was arraigned for. The request was granted and the trial proceeded.

The first witness called by the Prosecution was the father of the murdered boy, Kels P. Nickell. He described in detail events at the ranch preceding the dastardly crime, and then of finding the body.

John Apperson testified that he was at the Nickell ranch. His story of events on the day of the killing corroborated the testimony of Mr. Nickell.

Doctors A. W. Barber, J. H. Conway, and G. P. Johnston were sworn in and testified that they held the post-mortem on the body of the deceased. Jointly they testified, "The body was in an advanced state of decomposition when examined, being swollen and discolored. Death was produced by two gun shots, either of which the examiners felt could have been fatal."

Laramie County Coroner T. C. Murray, testified that at the inquest he found the imprint of a gun butt behind the pile of rocks from where it was ascertained the shots were fired.

The next to be called to testify were Mr. and Mrs. John Ryan, who were employed at the Coble ranch. Both stated that Tom Horn was not on the ranch the day of July 18th and did not return until the 20th of the same month.

John Clay, a ranchman, testified Horn had made his headquarters with him for many years.

The Court was recessed for dinner, upon the completion of Mr. Clay's testimony.

First to be called to the stand at the afternoon session was Victor Miller, son of Nickell's neighbor, James Miller. The lad stated that Horn was at the Miller ranch on Tuesday, July 16, two days preceding the shooting. The boy further testified that Tom Horn did some practice shooting at that time.

The sensation of the day was the testimony of Deputy United States Marshal Joe LeFors. LeFors related in detail his conversation with Horn which had been recorded by Clerk of the Court Charles Ohnhaus and heard by Deputy Sheriff Leslie Snow. The conversation was held at the Sheriff's office on January 12, 1902.

The "confession" had been successfully kept a secret by the Prosecution. The Counsel for the Defense was somewhat surprised by Prosecutor Stoll's sharp move.

And thus, the "confession" supported by "pointing" circumstantial evidence warranted the Court's requesting Tom Horn to be held for trial in the district Court for the death of Willie Nickell.

It was determined that Horn would be held in the District Court without bail. Judge Lacey made a strong and lengthy argument against the decision; he based his claim upon his interpretation of a Constitutional provision, which he cited:

> *"All persons shall be bailable by sufficient sureties, except for capital offenses when the proof is evident and the presumption great."*

The Court held that the proof was evident and the presumption was great, and the prisoner was committed without bail.

The Defense was again stunned by their rebuttal. They began to view the case with considerable more concern. Confidence had been somewhat shaken.

As the winter of 1902 wore away, it was well into spring before any further legal action was taken. The date of the trial as yet had not been selected.

Tom Horn was in almost daily conference with his attorneys. They worked hard. Cases were reviewed, precedences established and the approach planned and then discussed in detail. The "what ifs" and alternatives were prepared.

As Tom conferred with his attorneys he became more confident. He cheerfully exchanged greetings and joshed with his friends on the outside through the jail bars. He had a steady stream of visitors, and did not want for anything except his freedom.

It has been estimated by some old-timers that the aggregate wealth pledged to Horn's cause probably exceeded half a million dollars. Other cowboys have stated that a large portion of the money poured into the Defense was done so by certain stockmen bankers from an adjoining state. . .

On Friday, May 23rd, Prosecuting Attorney Walter Stoll filed his information on the case with the court.

THE PROSECUTION OPENS THE TRIAL

Further action was not taken until September. The Prosecution asked that the trial be postponed until November. However, the Defense successfully fought the action and the tentative trial opening date was set for October 7th.

A jury was finally selected after considerable complaints from both sides. The first had been selected in January. Upon examination of the list by the Jury Commissioners by the recommendation of the Court, it was found that one-third of those selected were not qualified.

The names of new Jurymen* were then drawn from a list of 1,000 names placed in the Jury box. Jury Commissioners, County Clerk Cowhick, County Treasurer Schunemand, and County Com-

*The names, residences, and occupations of the Jurors were: O. V. Seeburn, ranchman in Goshen Hole country; Homer Payne, cowboy employed by the Two Bar outfit; F. F. Sinon, foreman of White ranch on Little Horse Creek; H. W. Thomas, ranchman residing near LaGrange; T. R. Babbit, ranchman near LaGrange; Amos Sarbaugh, foreman of Two Bar ranch; J. E. Barnes, butcher, Cheyenne; G. W. Whiteman, ranchman residing near Uva; Charles Stamm, ranchman on Wheatland flats; C. H. Tolson, porter, Cheyenne; H. W. Yoder, Goshen Hole ranchman; E. C. Metcalf, blacksmith, Wheatland.

—*Cheyenne Daily Leader*, Saturday, October 25, 1902.

missioner Carson, drew the names in the presence of Judge Scott and attorneys for both sides.

Twelve men were finally selected from the thirty-six final names drawn. It was thought that the trial, scheduled to start on the morning of October 10th would have to be postponed, however, it was only delayed until the afternoon of the same day.

All of the witnesses were on hand for the trial. There were over one hundred of them. It was stated that many of the witnesses were subpoenaed and would testify with reluctance. Silent fear was still a common denominator. Before the Court was to be arrayed a pageant of personalities, a group unassembled before—unequaled since.

Prosecuting Attorney Walter Stoll made the opening address to the jury. The presentation was considered a master-piece and was the keynote of the brilliance and intense excitement that was to unfold. This was the case that was to capture the interest and imagination of the entire west.

The second day of the trial, October 11th, was a drizzly and gloomy morning. However, the court room was packed—an air of anticipated excitement hung over the room. Judge Scott did not arrive until after the time set for the convening of the court.

The morning was taken in the introduction of witnesses. Testimonies described the country in the immediate vicinity of the gate.

Mr. William S. Ingham, City Surveyor of Laramie, was the first called to the stand. He presented a map showing the country from the gate to Laramie City. Mr. Ingham testified he had ridden over the Iron Mountain country and was familiar with all roads and trails in the area. He further stated that the distance from Laramie to the gate was thirty-two miles, and it would take hard riding to make it in three hours time.

Mr. Zorn, City Engineer of Cheyenne, was the second witness introduced. His testimony was substantially the same as Mr. Ingham. He introduced a map that gave the elevations of the key points in the "gate vicinity." The map also contained all the roads and trails near the Miller and Nickell ranches.

The third person to take the "chair" was Photographer W. S. Walker. He had been hired to take pictures of the Iron Mountain district. The photographer presented eleven different views of the "gate area" and explained each with the aid of maps to the court and jury. The court was then adjourned until two o'clock in the afternoon.

The first witness of the afternoon session was Mr. Edward Titus, a rancher of the Laramie Plains district. The rancher testified that he had lived in the State of Wyoming for fourteen years and had been acquainted with Tom Horn for the greater part of the time. He further stated that on July 19th he had taken a drink with Tom Horn at the Kuster House Bar in Laramie. The witness stated he hadn't noticed anything peculiar about Horn's clothes at that time.

The second to testify during the afternoon session was Mr. William Mahoney, brother-in-law of Kels P. Nickell. He stated that he was at the Nickell home on the morning of July 18th. Mr. Mahoney reviewed the events of that morning. He said that they arose at 5:30, ate breakfast, and of Willie leaving for Iron Mountain Station. The purpose of young Nickell's mission, he stated, was to return with a sheep herder who had left the day before. The brother-in-law then related the events of the entire morning. He testified that he, Kels Nickell, and John Apperson had begun surveying east of the ranch at the time shots were fired. The three men concluded someone was hunting in the "gate direction." He further added that when they returned home nothing was thought of Willie's absence as his errand might have taken longer than anticipated.

The next witness was Mrs. Mary Nickell,* wife of Kels P. Nickell, and mother of the deceased. A silence hung over the court room. The grief and anxiety of the preceding months were evident in her face. Her testimony is given as follows:

DIRECT EXAMINATION BY MR. STOLL

Q. Please state your name and residence?
A. Mary Nickell, Cheyenne.
Q. You are the wife of Kels P. Nickell?
A. Yes sir.
Q. You lived on the ranch at Iron Mountain, known as the Nickell ranch, in July, 1901?
A. Yes sir.
Q. State to the Jury what time it was you ate breakfast on July 19th, 1901?
A. About 6 o'clock.
Q. Tell the jury what you recollect at the time?

*Testimony taken from the State of Wyoming records, State of Wyoming vs. Tom Horn, on file with Clerk of the Court, Laramie County, Cheyenne, Wyoming. Testimony of Mrs. Mary Nickell, pp. 46-51.

A. We had breakfast early that morning to send the boy after the sheep herder.
Q. What was your usual time for breakfast?
A. We always had it at 6.
Q. On this occasion you had it at 6?
A. Yes sir.
Q. How old was Willie?
A. He was 14.
Q. How large a boy was he?
A. Not quite as tall as I am.
Q. How much did he weigh?
A. I don't know.
Q. Was he heavy or medium?
A. He was quite heavy set for a boy of his age.
Q. What time did you get through breakfast that morning?
A. We were all eating breakfast that morning.
Q. About how long?
A. I could not say.
Q. Was Mr. Apperson there?
A. Yes sir.
Q. How long after breakfast was it that Willie left for Iron Mountain?
A. About half past 6 or 20 minutes of 7.
Q. Why do you fix this as the time he left?
A. We were in a hurry to get him off to start him off as quick as we could.
Q. The family ate breakfast and he went off to get his horse?
A. Yes sir.
Q. Did he leave for Iron Mountain before Mr. Apperson, Mr. Nickell and Mr. Mahoney went to work?
A. It was after.
Q. When was the last time you saw him alive?
A. When he was going around the house up the road.
Q. He was on his way to Iron Mountain?
A. Yes sir.
Q. How was he dressed?
A. In overalls, white shirt, vest and white hat.
Q. State to the jury whether he had anything whatever in the nature of firearms or weapons of any kind?
A. No sir, he did not.
Q. When did you next see him?
A. When he was on the road dead.

Q. What time was that about and what day?
A. The next day after he left for Iron Mountain.
Q. About what time of day?
A. It must have been about 8 o'clock in the morning.
Q. How did you come to find him dead?
A. Freddie went to take the cows out and came back and told us Willie was killed.
Q. Then you and Mr. Apperson and the rest of the family went out to the gate?
A. Yes sir.
Q. Tell the jury what condition you saw him at the gate?
A. He was lying down with his face up toward the sun and a rock under his head and his shirt open exposing the wounds.
Q. How was his shirt open?
A. Just pushed open like somebody had pushed it open and looked at it to see where he was shot.
Q. And the shirt kind of stiffened up in that position?
A. Yes sir.
Q. Were his clothes bloody in parts; if so describe how the blood was?
A. His shirt was bloody and his clothes were bloody in parts.
Q. State whether or not his face and his clothes any part of them contained small gravel and dust?
A. Yes sir, his face contained small gravel and dirt.
Q. How was this gravel; did it seem to be imbedded in the face?
A. Yes sir, it was imbedded on his face.
Q. How was his hands?
A. Laying down by his side.
Q. When you saw him?
A. Yes sir.
Q. Were you the first one there?
A. No, my husband was the first one there.
Q. Did you hear any shots?
A. No, I didn't hear any shots.
Q. State whether or not you saw anyone whatever excepting Willie, Mr. Apperson, Mr. Mahoney and the members of your family that whole day?
A. No sir, I didn't see anybody but the members of my family that day.
Q. When you found his body near the gate, state whether there was any weapons, firearms or anything of that kind about the body?
A. No sir, there was not.
Q. Did you notice how the gate was situated?
A. It was laying down.

CROSS EXAMINATION BY JUDGE LACEY

Q. You had your breakfast that morning you think about 6 o'clock?
A. Yes sir.
Q. You don't hardly know how long it took, but you think about a quarter or twenty minutes after 6 breakfast was over?
A. Yes, we had breakfast in a hurry that morning.
Q. The first thing after breakfast, Mr. Nickell, Mr. Mahoney and Mr. Apperson went on surveying business?
A. Yes sir.
Q. And then the next thing Willie went after the sheep herder?
A. Yes sir.
Q. His route would be up from the house to the gate?
A. Yes sir.
Q. You did not see him again until the next morning?
A. No sir, I did not see him until the following day.
Q. I understand that Freddie came down and told you?
A. Yes sir.
Q. Something about the cattle caused Fred to go there, what was there about that?
A. We put all our milk cows out there every morning. Fred went out to put the cows out and came back and told us that Willie was dead.
Q. How was the gate when Freddie got there, you don't know?
A. No sir.
Q. He turned the cows through the gate?
A. No, he found Willie dead and left the cows scatter.
Q. The cows were put out there the morning before?
A. Yes, Freddie put them out.
Q. When?
A. It was just a little before Willie started.
Q. Then how did they come back?
A. We didn't go after the cows that night, they came back themselves.
Q. Evidently they came back down through the gate?
A. Yes sir, through the gate, the gate was left open and we didn't go there that night.
Q. Freddie came back and told you about Willie?
A. Yes sir.
Q. You all went up to the gate?
A. Yes sir.
Q. Mr. Nickell got there ahead of you?
A. Yes sir.

Q. When you got there you say that Willie's hands were down by his side?
A. Yes sir.
Q. And the clothes were stiffened and standing out from the wound?
A. Yes sir.
Q. And there was some gravel on the clothes?
A. Yes sir.
Q. Where the blood stains were?
A. Yes sir.
Q. Also on his face?
A. Yes sir, on his face.

Mr. Nickell was the next witness called before the Court.* Nickell corroborated the testimony of his wife.

DIRECT EXAMINATION BY MR. STOLL

Q. State your name, occupation and residence?
A. Kels P. Nickell, 47 years old, Cheyenne.
Q. You are the father of the boy Willie Nickell concerning whose death we are now inquiring into?
A. Yes sir.
Q. Can you tell the jury how large a boy he was at the time of his death?
A. He was just about an average size boy for a boy of 14 years old. I could not say just what the boy would weigh, or how tall he was; he was what you would call an average size boy for that age.
Q. State to the jury when you last saw him alive?
A. It was on the morning of the 18th of July.
Q. Where was he then?
A. The last I saw of him, he started off from the corral toward the house. I would not be just positive whether he had started for the house or whether he was just cinching up his saddle when we saw him from the wagon going toward the creek to survey.
Q. Where was Willie going, and what was the object of his visit?
A. He was going to Iron Mountain for a man to go to work for me.
Q. Had that man been previously at your house?
A. He had been there the night before, that was the 16th; he had been there and stayed all the night of the 16th and went away the morning of the 17th.
Q. What was he seeking when he came there?
A. A job at herding sheep.

*Ibid, pp. 51-62.

Q. You did not give him a job?
A. No sir.
Q. Afterwards you concluded you wanted him?
A. Yes.
Q. How did you know he was in the direction of Iron Mountain?
A. When he went to Iron Mountain the day before, Willie went for Apperson's surveying tools; when Willie came back he told me he saw this man at Iron Mountain when he left there at 2 o'clock. That he was going to see Mr. George Mathews. Mr. Mathews carried the mail to Sybille Post Office and back; when Willie came home it was late in the afternoon and I knew Mathews did not get home until very near night; that if he did not get home his usual time this man would be apt to stay until next morning, and that would bring him there in the morning; I started the boy over to get him.
Q. What hour did you get breakfast?
A. It was not far from 6 o'clock.
Q. What time was it you started for your work? That is when you saw Willie going toward the house or cinching up his horse?
A. As near as I can remember it was close around 6 o'clock that he left the house. He hitched the team up at the corral and as soon as he got the team hitched we got ready to go down the creek and do some surveying.
Q. What time did you say that was?
A. That was a little bit after 6 o'clock, I could not say just how much. As well as I remember about that time we left the house I noticed the clock, it was just about 6, right close around 6 o'clock; I couldn't say just to the minute.
Q. At what time did you hear shots fired that morning?
A. It was right around 7 o'clock.
Q. How do you fix that as the time?
A. From the time we started to go from the house down to work it would take us, I should judge about that time to go down there and unhitch the team, tie the team and get the instruments and things out to go surveying; when we got the instruments out of the wagon and were getting ready to go off and start the survey from the corner stone to tie a ditch to the creek. It would have taken that length of time to get down there and got around. We heard the shots just as we were getting ready to do the surveying.
Q. What direction did the sound come from?
A. Right direct from this gate as near as I can fix it.
Q. Did you give any heeding or pay any attention to the shots?
A. Yes sir, the remark was made they came from right about that gate. It must be somebody shooting or hunting deer up there.

Q. What kind of a horse was Willie on and what kind of a horse was he?

A. It was a bay horse. My horse.

Q. The one you usually rode around?

A. Yes sir.

Q. Was the absence of the boy from home that night a matter of alarm to you?

A. A little bit.

Q. Yet you made no effort to locate him that night?

A. No sir, because I expected this man, as I told him when he started; if this man had left Iron Mountain that he would go down the Chug; he was going from Iron Mountain to Casper he told us. If he rode the horse he had at the ranch it was a very poor horse for a man to get over the country; if he rode that horse and had not traded with Mathews as he calculated to, I thought he would overtake him about the time he got to Diamond station; I supposed he followed him by not coming home to the ranch.

Q. State whether or not you saw any other person beside your immediate family and Mr. Apperson and Mr. Mahoney anywhere in that section of the country that day?

A. I did not.

Q. Now state the circumstances of finding the body the next morning and the condition that you found the body in and all the surrounding circumstances?

A. Mr. Apperson and I were sitting at the table fixing up some notes of the surveying he had done the day before and Freddie, a younger brother, who usually took the cows in the morning—some mornings he started out with the cows at half past 6 and some mornings not until half past 8. He started to take the cows out and come back riding, crying and told us Willie was killed at the gate. Mr. Apperson and myself started right away for the gate where the boy was; my wife's brother was there and I told him to go down and get a team and for my wife to get in the wagon and come right on up there. Mr. Apperson and myself went up to the gate ahead of the rest; just before we got to the gate we found the boy lying in the road with his head toward the house lying on his back. It looked where he was lying there as though he had been turned over, because all the clothing was saturated with blood; there was blood splashed on his clothing and his face, and his right hand was lying about like that and this hand was lying right straight out like that; right here by the side of him was a little pool of congealed blood; he must have been turned over. His shirt and vest were open and pulled up in that kind of shape; it stayed there and the blood had been almost dried and the shirt was open and exposed the wound. It remained standing up in that position. We looked to see if we could find any tracks of anyone around there and we could find no tracks of anyone. The stake was taken loose from the gate and throwed down near the post. We will say this is the fence and the gate was here; right west of this here the gate was in that way about; take this post for instance, about that distance and there was a little congealed blood there. It was just as though he was going in this direction and the blood splashed. We hunted around and could find no trail or sign of anyone except his own horse; his own horse's tracks were west of the fence; he had grazed around there quite awhile probably all day before he left. We took him then to the house in the wagon.

Q. Did you see how many wounds he had received?
A. Yes, just 2.
Q. Did you see anything under his head?
A. Yes sir, there was a little rock under his head.
Q. Under the back of it?
A. It seemed to be under this part of the head.
Q. Slightly behind the ear?
A. Yes sir. He was lying on his back and there was a little rock under the head; the head was kind of propped up; I took it for granted it was put there to keep it from falling over.
Q. It did not look like a rock that layed there naturally?
A. No sir, it was not; at that time there was very few rocks in the road.
Q. Were his feet toward the gate?
A. Yes sir, they were.
Q. Did you see whether the boy was armed when he left the house in any way?
A. I did not; he went from the corral to the house after I saw him.
Q. Were there any fire arms of any character whatever about his body when you found him?
A. No sir, not at all.
Q. State whether or not you marked the place where the body lay?
A. I did.
Q. How did you indicate that place?
A. I put some rocks there.
Q. I will ask you to point on this exhibit No. 2 the photograph, the rocks that you placed where the body lay.
A. This is the gate here; the stay of the gate is there; this is east where the boy lay; this pool was right here. It is 60 or 30 feet from the gate, I don't remember just which.

CROSS EXAMINATION BY JUDGE LACEY

Q. Did the boy ever have trouble in that vicinity?
A. Yes sir.
Q. Much trouble?
A. He had quite a little trouble with the Miller family.
Q. Which members of the Miller family?
A. Miller himself, principally the boys.
Q. Which boys?
A. Gussie and Victor.
Q. Do you know how serious the trouble had been?
A. I do not, because I never saw any of the trouble myself.
Q. Do you know anything about their having had serious trouble, fights and rows?
A. Just what was reported, I never saw it.
Q. Did you notice anybody was carrying any guns in relation to the matter?
A. What do you mean carrying guns? In fact I did, and most every ranchman does more or less carry a gun when he goes out.
Q. Did you know of it more than that?
A. No, not necessarily, I did not.
Q. You were not present at any of the rows between any of the boys or any of the Millers?
A. No sir.
Q. He had reported them to you and that was all?
A. Yes sir.
Q. Had they been frequent?
A. No, not frequent, they had trouble, that is little rows.
Q. There had been trouble between you and Miller likewise?
A. Yes sir.

OBJECTED TO AS NOT PROPER MATTER AT CROSS EXAMINATION. BY THE COURT—I think the objection is well taken and will be sustained, to which the defendant, by counsel takes exception.

Q. Now when you went up there to the gate that was after the cows had come down the night before?
A. The cows came down the night before down the creek.
Q. They did not go through the gate?
A. No sir.
Q. They came down the creek?
A. Yes sir.
Q. Were there any tracks at the gate at all?

A. When we went there that morning? Yes sir.
Q. What kind of tracks?
A. Tracks of my horse.
Q. Any other tracks?
A. There were tracks of a pony. There is a little pony.
Q. What other tracks?
A. There was tracks of cattle between the gate and where the boy was.
Q. Cattle tracks between the gate and where the boy lay?
A. Yes.
Q. Were the cattle tracks as far as the gate?
A. I think they were.
Q. They reached up to the gate?
A. Yes sir, there might have been cattle tracks through the gate.
Q. It looked as if some of the cattle went that way?
A. I don't think the cattle went through that morning.
Q. The tracks went between the boy and the gate and maybe some of them outside?
A. They might possibly I can't say positively.
Q. Did you notice how many cattle tracks there was in that vicinity?
A. It is hard to count the tracks of six or eight cows.
Q. It seemed like a good many tracks?
A. Yes sir.
Q. You say that the boy's shirt was stiff when you saw it?
A. Yes sir.
Q. And his hands, one of them near his side, his right hand?
A. Yes sir.
Q. Not straight down, but doubled up in this fashion?
A. Yes sir.
Q. And the other thrown out in this way?
A. Yes sir.
Q. That hand was clear on out?
A. Yes.
Q. The shots you heard, how were they all together, or how?
A. At the time of the inquest my mind was clear on that I think, whatever statement I made at that time, I would rather have go. I think that the way the shots was; it was two shots and then a little bit of a lull and then a third shot; it might have been that it was one shot then a little bit of a lull and then two shots. We made the remark at the time that it must be someone hunting up there.

Q. Your recollection would be that it was first two shots in fairly quick succession and then one shot later?
A. Yes, about as quick as ordinary shooting. Not like two guns understand; it was not two persons.
Q. They were in quick succession, one person might have fired them as quick as they were together?
A. Yes sir.
Q. Did you not say in your testimony before that the two first shots were fired as quickly as one could fire a Winchester and then there was a little lull and then the next shot fired?
A. As I said a few minutes ago I am not positive whether that was the way it was; if that is the way the testimony was taken I am perfectly satisfied to submit that as right.
Q. You were asked this question—"How were those three shots fired with relation to their succession, one after another?" Your answer was, "Two was fired as fast as a man could fire a Winchester rifle, then a little pause and the other one was fired." Does that recall it to your recollection?
A. No, it does not, that must be right.
Q. You don't remember whether that was the way you testified or not?
A. I could not remember now at this time; whatever way I said at that time, I am satisfied it was.
Q. How far outside of the gate to the west of the gate was the blood you found farthest west?
A. The farthest blood we saw west of the gate when the gate was stretched across; I don't think it exceeded four feet; I didn't measure it.
Q. From there the blood trailed back to where the body was found east of the gate?
A. Yes sir.
Q. You don't recall whether it was 20 or 60 feet from the gate where the body was?
A. No, I do not, I don't recall the exact feet now.
Q. Did Willie generally carry a gun?
A. No sir, once in awhile he carried a .22 rifle.
Q. You generally carried a gun, but he did not?
A. Yes sir.
Q. Do you know whether the Miller boys generally carried a gun?

OBJECTED TO AS NOT BEING PROPER CROSS EXAMINATION. Objection sustained to which defendant, by his counsel, takes exception.

RE-DIRECT EXAMINATION BY MR. STOLL

Q. State if you know whether or not Freddie had driven the cattle through the gate when he had taken them up to the pasture the morning the body was found.
A. I was a little confused about those tracks, I am not positive right now whether he did or not.
Q. You spoke of looking for tracks, I presume you mean a man's tracks?
A. Yes sir.
Q. And you found none?
A. I did not.
Q. State over what vicinity your examination extended?
A. Mr. Apperson and I went together over quite a little circuit around there, maybe part of it 100 yards and some other parts 150 yards; I don't think we did at that time—we came back afterwards with Mr. Reed and Mr. Davidson and quite a number of us and went out at different times and searched for two or three hundred yards and further around to find tracks.

RE-CROSS EXAMINATION BY JUDGE LACEY

Q. The truth is that the country is very rocky and a man's tracks would not show at all?
A. Around there there is a good deal of it that way.
Q. That comes right up to the road, so that they would not show except in the road?
A. Not necessarily, there had been a sprinkling of rain the day before.
Q. I mean outside of the road?
A. It is hard granite substance and granite formation and the soil is granite.
Q. It would not show tracks?
A. It would not show tracks.
Q. Most places it would not?
A. Where there was rocks it would not.
Q. There is rocks over most of the country?
A. There is lots of rocks.

The third member of the Nickell family to testify was young Freddie. The lad told of finding his brother's lifeless body in a precise but pathetic way. Tears came to his eyes when he described the scene.

The next witness called to the stand was J. A. B. Apperson. He testified as to the circumstances related by other witnesses, and of finding drops of blood all the way from the gate to where the body lay. Apperson stated that the character of the soil near the gate was such as to leave no tracks. He felt it was almost impossible to determine whether the body had been moved by the nature of the soil.

Laramie County Coroner T. C. Murray then took the "chair." He testified that he arrived at Iron Mountain on the morning of July 20th. He said he had arranged for the shipping of the boy's body to Cheyenne. Coroner Murray described the "gate area" as had been done in previous testimonies. He added that a pile of rocks was to be found at a distance approximately 300 yards from the gate. The Doctor said that he had found a print of a rifle butt in the soil near the rocks.

Dr. Amos Barber testified that on the 21st of July he and Doctors Conway and Johnson of Cheyenne, held the post-mortem. And that they found two gun shot wounds in the body of the deceased. The first wound had made an incision three-eighths of an inch in diameter and shattered the fifth rib coming out just left of the breast bone; the exit was one-inch in width. The doctor described their report as stating the second wound was the same size as the first at the entrance and one-half inch at exit. Both took the same direction and from the proximity to each other concluded they were evidently fired in rapid succession. He stated that both wounds might have been received while running, and either would have been fatal.

Dr. Barber's testimony was the last of the day. Court was adjourned, Judge Scott granted the Jurors permission to attend services on Sunday at the Methodist church.

MONDAY, OCTOBER 13

The convening of court on Monday saw the court room filled again, many were standing. The Prosecution spent the morning in trying to establish the calibre of the gun that fired the shot that killed Willie Nickell.

The first witness called was H. Waldo Moore who testified that on the Monday following the assassination, July 22nd, he went to the "gate area" and examined the surroundings carefully looking for shells and other evidence. He said he was unable to find anything.

Surveyor J. A. B. Apperson took the stand for the second time during the trial. He testified as to the identity of the clothes worn by the deceased at the time of his death.

The next witness was Alfred Cook, the Sheriff of Albany County, of which Laramie is the County Seat. The Sheriff testified that he examined the horse left at the Elkhorn Barn in Laramie by Tom Horn. He told the court that the animal was a dark bay. He said he made a drawing of the brand and sent it to Deputy Sheriff Peter Warlaumont in Cheyenne. The drawing of the brand was made in the presence of Mr. Marsh and Mr. Wallis, also of Laramie, ten days after the death of Willie Nickell. It was further brought out in the examination that this horse weighed between 1,050 and 1,100 pounds.

Judge Lacey in his cross-examination of Sheriff Cook* asked him when was the first time he had seen Tom Horn after the murder. The witness testified that it was on the 21st day of July; and that Horn was wearing a dark suit of clothes and straw hat at that time.

E. T. Cook was the next witness. He stated that on July 19th he received a message requesting him to come to Iron Mountain at once. Cook testified that he found a perfect imprint of a horse's hoof and had tracked the animal a distance of 250 yards from the rocks. He said he had made a drawing of the hoof print, however, it was not submitted as evidence.

The next witness was Mrs. Nickell.† Her testimony is as follows:

DIRECT EXAMINATION BY MR. STOLL

Q. Mrs. Nickell, you may look at these clothes under the table, and state if they were the clothes that were on Willie?
A. Yes sir.
Q. When did you take them off?
A. When he came to town I took them off at the coroner's inquest; I think we didn't take them off at home.
Q. Before the body was submitted to the doctors you took the clothes off before the inquest?
A. They did not take them off at home; I think they brought them on him in town; I didn't go out in the room.
Q. You do not know when the clothes were taken off?
A. No, I do not; Mr. Turnbull came out and attended the boy.
Q. Mr. Turnbull was the undertaker?
A. Yes sir.

---

*It was reported that during the examination of Cook, Horn displayed his first real concern during the proceedings and was in frequent whispered consultation with his attorneys.

†*op. cit.* p. 95.

Q. Do you know as a matter of fact whether they were taken off at the house or in town?
A. I do not.
Q. Who does know?
A. My husband ought to know.
Q. These are the clothes, however?
A. Yes, those are the clothes.

Peter Ferguson, a gunsmith for thirty-five years, was then requested to appear. Mr. Ferguson, by virtue of his trade, was considered an expert on ballistics and the calibre of guns. Prosecutor Stoll asked him to state to the best of his judgment on the size of the bullets that struck Willie Nickell down. The expert replied that he believed it was either a 30-30 or 32 calibre. The Prosecution then asked Mr. Ferguson how it would affect the point of the bullet to carry it in the magazine of a rifle for some time, jarring it against 'the butt of another. The witness stated that it would make a larger hole. A discussion of powder types in relation to the size of holes concluded the balance of testimony.

The next witness was Dr. Maynard who described the size of the wounds. The doctor stated that any resistance offered by clothing would cause the expansion of a bullet and thus make a larger wound. Dr. Desmond then was called. His testimony supported that of Dr. Maynard. Dr. Barber was next. He said the distance in range would make a difference in the size of the wound.

At 12:20 the court was recessed until 2 o'clock.

With the convening of court, the Prosecution introduced two more witnesses. The first of these was James Mathison, manager of the *Laramie Republican* which had published an account of the killing of Willie Nickell. The Prosecution desired to establish a date in view of the succeeding witness—a Will Eagen, manager of the Union Pacific Hotel of Laramie. Eagen's testimony consisted in part of identifying the entrance of a key witness at the Union Pacific Hotel.

Sheriff Peter Warlaumont was then called before the Court. He exhibited the drawing of the brand sent him by Sheriff Alfred Cook of Laramie.

Duncan Clark, ranch foreman for the Iron Mountain Cattle Company, then took the stand. He said that Tom Horn had been at the Iron Mountain Ranch before the killing of Willie Nickell and had also departed before this time. The leathery cowboy stated that after leaving the ranch he did not see Horn until July 20th when he met him in Laramie. Duncan established the time of their meeting in Laramie as being about 4 o'clock in the afternoon.

Mr. and Mrs. John D. Ryan, who were both working for the Iron Mountain Cattle Company at the time of the shooting, were asked to appear.

Mr. Ryan testified that Horn left the ranch almost a week before July 18th, and that he didn't see him again until the 20th when he came in for dinner. He said Horn changed his clothes at that time, and gave him twenty-five cents to pay for a message Horn had already sent to Laramie. The witness said the Defendant left the ranch about 3 o'clock, riding away on a bay horse. Mrs. Ryan corroborated the story of her husband. Testifying that Horn came to the ranch between 10 and 11 o'clock on the morning of the 20th. She said she had agreed to do some washing for Horn—adding that he would send her money for the work from Laramie.

The last witness of the day was Hiram Davidson. He was the mail man at Iron Mountain Station. Davidson testified that he had not seen Tom Horn from the 15th to the 23rd of July, 1901.

The trial was gaining momentum as it progressed. Business was almost a stand still as all western-clad and boot-shod Cheyenne took time out to follow the drama. So many were implicated, and it was feared many more would be—especially if Horn told all.

TUESDAY, OCTOBER 14

The events of the day's session proved to be the most startling to date, as the brilliant Prosecutor, Walter Stoll, wove the web of evidence around the Defendant, despite the capable stand taken by the Defense.

First to testify was Freddie Nickell, son of Kels and Mary Nickell and brother of the deceased. The lad related how he found a 30-30 calibre shell near the scene of the crime on the 28th—just ten days after his brother had been killed. He told the Court that he did not find the horse his brother had been riding until a week later. When found, the animal was still carrying the saddle.

Victor Miller* was then called to the stand. The boy testified as follows:

**op. cit.* pp. 183-190

DIRECT EXAMINATION BY MR. STOLL

Q. State your name, occupation and residence?
A. Victor Miller, Iron Mountain, Wyoming; ranchman.

Q. How old are you?
A. I will be 19 in December.

Q. You are the son of James A. Miller?
A. Yes sir.

Q. Do you know the defendant Tom Horn?
A. Yes sir, I have saw him and met him.

Q. State when you saw him in July 1901?
A. I think it was on the night of the 15th.

Q. What night of the week was that?
A. It was Monday night, I think.

Q. You can look at the calendar in front of you, and state where he was and the circumstances of your seeing him?
A. It was about ten o'clock at night, right in front of my father's house.

Q. Turn to the map behind you and point out his house.
A. That is the place marked Miller's ranch on this map.

Q. It was there you saw him that night?
A. Yes sir.

Q. What did you see him do that night?
A. I saw him turn his horse loose; then he went into the house and had some supper, and then went out and went to bed.

Q. Did he or not stay there at your house all night?
A. Yes sir, he stayed there.

Q. Where did he go to bed?
A. He went out to the tent.

Q. Explain that to the jury?
A. The tent was about sixty feet in front of the house; we had a tent out there and us boys slept there during the summer; he went out there and went to bed with us.

Q. Did he or not sleep there in the tent all night?
A. Yes sir.

Q. Who was in the tent besides the defendant?
A. My brother and I.

Q. What was your brother's name?
A. Gus Miller.

Q. State what Horn did the next day if you know?
A. We were doing different things like shooting and fishing.

Q. As a matter of fact state whether he stayed there at your house during the next day, Tuesday?

A. Yes, he stayed there until about 3 o'clock, and then he saddled up his horse and rode away; he rode south of our place.
Q. Referring to this map, Exhibit 4, and tell the Jury in which direction he rode?
A. He rode south.
Q. Point it out on the map?
A. This would be south from the road in this direction. I didn't watch him only for about two hundred yards; I didn't notice where he did go then.
Q. Did he tell you when he returned where he had been?
A. I was not there when he returned; I was fishing when he returned. After I had been there my mother told me...

OBJECTED TO.

Q. Did he himself tell you or was it in your presence where he had been?
A. No, I don't think he did.
Q. I will ask you to point out on that map the Colcord pasture.
A. It is on the North Chug down this creek. I don't know exactly how far it would be.
Q. It would be somewhat to the east or northeast of the ranch of Kels Nickell?
A. It would be toward the east.
Q. What time did he return?
A. I don't know exactly what time he did return, I was out fishing; when I returned about six o'clock he was there.
Q. State whether or not he was there at your house at that time?
A. Yes, he was.
Q. How long did he remain there then?
A. He stayed all that night.
Q. All Tuesday night?
A. Yes sir.
Q. What did he do the next morning?
A. I got up and ate breakfast with him, he went in the front room and was talking there when I left.
Q. What time did you leave?
A. I don't remember what time it was, it was probably about 8 o'clock.
Q. You left the ranch house to go about some business of your own?
A. I was going down to the lower ranch to look after some things.
Q. Did you see Horn again anywhere in that vicinity?
A. No sir, I don't think I did.

Q. When did you see Horn again the next time?
A. The next time I saw him was here in Cheyenne.
Q. About when was that?
A. It was along in the afternoon some time.
Q. Of what day and month?
A. I don't remember what day it was.
Q. Was it a considerable time after this?
A. I think it was when they were holding the coroner's inquest.
Q. You did not see him in the vicinity of Iron Mountain a week after of this time you saw him on Wednesday?
A. No sir.
Q. What kind of a horse did he have?
A. I call it a black horse, some might call it a dark brown.
Q. Describe the horse a little more fully to the jury.
A. I think the horse had a roached mane.
Q. Was it a large heavy horse or rather a short chunky horse?
A. If I remember right it was kind of a long bodied horse and slim. It was a horse that would weigh maybe ten to eleven hundred.
Q. How was it branded?
A. I don't remember the brand.
Q. Did you see whether Horn had any firearms with him or not?
A. Yes sir. All that I saw was a 30-30 Winchester rifle.
Q. Do you know whether he had anything tied on his saddle?
A. I don't remember whether he did or not.
Q. Have you any recollection as to how he was dressed?
A. Yes sir, some.
Q. Tell how it was.
A. He had on a pair of light striped pants and a light striped shirt and a light hat with a high crown.
Q. When you say light striped pants do you mean a whitish or grayish color?
A. I think they were of a grayish color.
Q. What did the man say, if anything, as to what he was doing in that section of the country or what was the object of his visit?
A. I don't remember what he did say now exactly.
Q. Did he say anything about the object of his visit there?
A. If I remember right about he was watching the sheep of Nickell to see whether or not they got on deeded land.

CROSS EXAMINATION BY JUDGE LACEY

Q. You say that the Colcord place is east of Nickell's, do you know about how far?
A. Yes sir, it is from three quarters of a mile to a mile.
Q. Right out east of Nickell's?
A. Yes sir.
Q. Do you know of any other deeded land that the Iron Mountain Ranch Company had in that vicinity.
A. No sir, I don't believe I do.
Q. That Colcord place was part of the deeded land of the Iron Mountain Ranch Company?
A. That don't belong to the Iron Mountain Ranch Company, it belongs to the Swan Land and Cattle Company.
Q. Did the Swan Land and Cattle Company have any other ranches in that immediate vicinity?
A. Not right close around there, they have the AL Ranch six or eight miles southeast of there or almost east.
Q. But rather off to the south?
A. Yes sir.
Q. Which would be the way to go to the place from your house?
A. We would go from our house almost east.
Q. You might strike off south over in this direction?
A. You go a little south and then east.
Q. Now you spoke of the way Tom was dressed when he was there at your place, did he have a coat on or was he in his shirt sleeves?
A. He was in his shirt sleeves.
Q. Had a vest on?
A. I think he did.
Q. Didn't have any sweater on?
A. Not that I saw.
Q. Had none with him that you saw?
A. Not that I saw.
Q. You saw him there for two days?
A. Yes sir, just for one whole day.
Q. That was Tuesday?
A. That was Tuesday.
Q. You saw him a little while on Wednesday?
A. Yes sir.
Q. As I understand you, all the firearms you saw with him was a 30-30?
A. Yes sir.

Q. You think you would have noticed it if he had any there?
A. I think so.
Q. That is all you saw?
A. Yes sir.
Q. So far as you remember you saw nothing on his saddle?
A. No sir.
Q. Nothing in the way of firearms?
A. No sir.
Q. No other garments on his saddle?
A. Not that I remember.
Q. Not even a slicker?
A. No sir.
Q. Now when did you first see Tom Horn?
A. I saw him on Monday night July 16th about 10 o'clock.
Q. That was the first time you ever saw him?
A. Yes sir.
Q. He had not been at your house before this so far as you know?
A. No.
Q. You were asked something about what he talked about. What did he talk about when you saw him there?
A. I don't remember what he did talk about now.
Q. Do you remember what he talked about in the tent as you were going to bed?
A. I don't believe I do.
Q. Did he talk about the robbers?
A. Oh yes, I remember about that.
Q. What was it he told you?

Objected to as not cross examination.

Q. In a general way without going into the details of what he was talking about, did he say that he had killed the train robbers that robbed the Union Pacific, killed five of them at once off down in Colorado—was not that what he was talking about?
A. Yes sir.
Q. At that time he told you he killed the last one of them when he was nearly dead from lack of blood by putting his pistol over his shoulder and shooting him in the mouth?
A. Yes sir.
Q. Five of them all at once, the train robbers from Wilcox?
A. Yes sir.
Q. Did he tell any other stories of that kind?

Objected to because not proper examination. Objection sustained, to which defendant's counsel takes exception.

Q. As a matter of fact there is a good deal of trouble in that neighborhood between Nickell and his neighbors?

Objected to as not proper examination, as immaterial. Objection sustained and exception taken by defendant's counsel.

Q. Personally you had trouble with Willie Nickell yourself?

Objected to as improper cross examination and immaterial. Objection sustained and exception taken by defendant's counsel.

Q. You had once in your father's presence a difficulty with him when you offered to fight him, and your father told you to fight him. And Willie run you down with a horse and your father pulled a pistol and told him if he did that he would shoot the horse—that is a fact is it not?

Objected to for the same reason. Objection sustained and exception taken by defendant's counsel.

Q. That occasion you had such trouble with Willie in June? Whether such a trouble did not occur in June immediately prior to the killing of Willie Nickell?

Objected to for the same reason. Objection sustained and exception taken by defendant's counsel.

Q. While Tom was there, nothing in the world was said about killing Willie Nickell?
A. No sir.

Q. No arrangement of that kind that you know anything about?
A. No sir.

Q. No talk of any such thing as that?
A. No sir, none at all.

Q. He left some time on Wednesday forenoon?
A. Yes sir.

Q. And you did not see him any more in that vicinity?
A. No sir.

RE-DIRECT EXAMINATION BY MR. STOLL

Q. With reference to knowing whether anything was carried on his saddle or not, state whether or not you made any observation to determine what he had on his saddle, or whether you passed it by without making any observation?
A. I passed it by without making any observation.

Q. You spoke of his shooting, how was his shooting?

[Possible Omission in Court Records]

A. Mr. Horn, my father, my brother and myself.

Q. In that way you determined the kind of a gun that he had?
A. Yes sir.

RE-CROSS EXAMINATION BY JUDGE LACEY

Q. Your father and your brother and yourself had guns, 30-30 and Tom Horn had a 30-30?
A. Mine was a 30-30 and my brother's was a 30-40.
Q. Did your father have a new gun at that time?
A. I think he did.
Q. Didn't he get a new gun after that?
A. It was afterwards he got it, I remember now.
Q. He was shooting with his old gun or your 30-30?
A. He was shooting with my 30-30.
Q. In addition to his gun what was it Tom had on his saddle, was it not a field glass?
A. Yes, I believe he did.
Q. You were looking through that field glass that day?
A. I think not.
Q. That glass, to the best of your recollection he had fastened to his saddle?
A. Yes sir.
Q. You saw the saddle with it on and was looking at it?
A. Yes sir.
Q. That was the time you noticed he hadn't any slicker?
A. If I remember right he had a field glass hung over his saddle horn, I think he didn't have anything more on his saddle.

Gus Miller, brother of Victor, was next to be called before the Court. His testimony corroborated that of Victor except he added that the horse ridden by Horn was branded C A P. While in the vicinity, he said Horn was generally watching Nickell's sheep.

Mrs. James Miller and her daughter, Eva, mother and sister to Victor and Gus, were the next two to testify. Their testimonies were substantially the same as that of the two boys.

Kels P. Nickell was then asked to appear. He testified as to the location of John Coble's east fence in which there was a gate. This fact had not been brought out in previous testimony.

John Bray, a neighboring ranchman to the Nickells, stated that he had seen Tom Horn near his place on Wednesday evening, July 17, at about 6 o'clock.

Mr. Robert Morris, the Court stenographer, was called on to read from the transcript of evidence. He related that Horn had been seen at William Clay's place on July 14th and 15th; at Innis' ranch also the 15th, then 16th and 17th; near Chugwater on the 18th and at the Fitzmorris place on the 19th.

The most startling testimony of the day was that of Frank Irwin,* resident of Laramie. Irwin told the Court that on the morning of the assassination he was riding after some of his cows that had strayed away. While continuing his search east of Laramie on the road to Iron Mountain, he met Tom Horn, who he said, was riding in the direction of Laramie. He stated Horn's horse was covered with a lather and apparently near exhaustion. Horn carried a gun and had a bundle back of his saddle. The witness followed Horn to Laramie and said he saw him ride into the Elkhorn Barn at 11 o'clock.

Following Frank Irwin's testimony, Court was adjourned until 2 o'clock.

An air of anticipation hung over the Court Room as it was called to order by Judge Scott. Many spectators had not left their seats during the recess—fearing they would not be able to get back in if they left.

Frank Irwin continued his testimony. He testified that he saw Tom Horn in the evening of that same day in "Ed" Allen's saloon. Horn was described as wearing a dark and wide brimmed hat at this time. The witness related how he and the Defendant had words, when the latter threatened to come to his place and examine some hides there, which the detective had intimated were taken from Iron Mountain Company's herd. Irwin concluded his testimony by stating that he had no particular love for Tom Horn but he had not let that fact affect his testimony.

Charles H. Miller of Cortez, Colorado, then took the stand. He had been one of the operators of the Elkhorn Barn in July of 1901. Miller said that he recalled keeping a black horse brought there by Tom Horn. The horse was branded C A P. Miller said the horse had been taken away early in July. On the 21st of the same month the witness recalled that Horn rode in on a large bay horse sweating and showing evidence of having been ridden hard.

Judge Lacey offered to prove that the horse was brought into the barn on the 20th and not the 18th. The books of the Elkhorn were brought in and examined by the Court. The Defense Attorney pointed out the entry indicating that Horn was charged with the board of a horse from July 20th to the 30th. The former liveryman

*This Frank Irwin is not to be confused as the brother of Charles Irwin, of Cheyenne.

explained the entry was made by his partner and their custom was to make the entry on the day the horse left and not when it came in, thus indicating there might have been a mistake.

Deputy Sheriff Peter Warlaumont was the next witness. He produced the shell found by Freddie Nickell. The cartridge had been picked up by the young Nickell boy ten days after the death of his brother.

Alfred Reed, a former employee of the Elkhorn Barn, testified that he remembered Horn bringing in a bay horse. He said he remembered it because the animal was covered with sweat indicating he had been ridden hard.

Mr. George Matlock, proprietor of a shoe store in Laramie told that on a day shortly after the assassination of Willie Nickell, a large dark man with slightly stooped shoulders came into his store and asked permission to leave a package there for a few minutes. The witness related to the Court how he had obliged the man—giving the matter little thought, if any. When the man did not return for the package, he said he became curious and took the liberty of opening it. In it he testified was found a dark blue sweater covered with dirt and blood. Mr. Matlock stated that he gave the sweater to his partner who sent it to the laundry to have it washed and that he had worn it since. He testified that he could not swear that Tom Horn was the person who left the sweater, but to the best of his recollection, Horn resembled this man.

The next witness was George T. Powell, Matlock's partner. Powell told a similar story, only he was positive that the original owner of the sweater was Tom Horn. Powell described the sweater as being covered with grass and gravel. He said that he noted the man as he walked out the door and walked on down the street. Attorney Stoll, in his questioning of the witness, asked him if he could identify the man if he could see him walk. Attorney Stoll then asked the witness just how he could tell. Powell replied, "The man who came in the store had a peculiar kind of swing and I would know it again anywhere if I saw it."

The Defense protested, and said they refused to let their client submit to such examination. Judge Lacey then asked the witness what he had done with the sweater. The witness replied, "I sent it to Tom Horn at Cheyenne in care of Sheriff Smalley."

Mr. Roy Campbell was the next witness to be called before the Court. Campbell was from Denver, Colorado.

Attorney Stoll requested the witness to state to the Jury if he had ever seen Tom Horn before and when.

Campbell said he had seen Horn in a saloon in Denver when Horn had done some boasting to the effect he was the "main guy" in the killing of Willie Nickell. The witness further related how Horn had tried to cash a check in another Denver saloon to pay for drinks, but it was too large, and the bartender could not cash it. He testified that Horn had bragged about the Nickell shot being the best he ever made.

Mr. D. R. Cowhich was the last witness in the long session. He produced a certified brand book of the county and pointed out the brand discussed in the case and identified its owner.

Court was then adjourned.

As the large crowd filed out of the small Court Room many lingered and talked. Some were pleased, others displeased. Some indicated a concern for Horn in their conversation. Among those who bore a look of anxiety was John C. Coble, former employer of the Defendant. He had talked with Horn on one occasion during the day.

Many noted that Tom Horn was beginning to lose his confident air although he was calm and composed as usual.

An incident that apparently caused considerable amount of interest and "talk" in Cheyenne involved Kels P. Nickell. Nickell's name was familiar to all because of the case—otherwise perhaps it would not have received much attention.

The following was printed in the *Laramie Boomerang*, Tuesday, October 16, 1902 as:

NICKELL A FIGHTER
Attacks a Man Last Night
At Cheyenne

Special to the Boomerang:

Cheyenne, Wyo., Oct. 15—Kels P. Nickell who has figured so conspicuously in the Tom Horn case is employed by the U.P.R.R. as a night watchman. Last night a man named Whitman attempted to enter the shops when he was halted by Nickell who demanded that Whitman show his pass which he refused to do. Thereupon Nickell attempted to arrest him and a fight ensued in which Whitman was badly beaten up by Nickell.

WEDNESDAY, OCTOBER 15

The first witness of the day was Frank A. Mullock, of Denver, who had previously testified that he had met Horn in Denver during the month of October, 1901. The witness stated he and the accused had drunk together. Horn, Mullock testified, said he was the best rifle shot in the United States and the killing of Willie Nickell was the dirtiest piece of work he had ever done. He said the Defendant had told him that lots of Cheyenne people were mixed up in the affair. Horn he said, was drunk at the time, and came to him the following day and asked him if he had been talking. When Mullock told him that he had talked, Tom asked him not to say anything of the matter to anyone.

Robert C. Cousley, also of the Colorado capitol city, appeared following Mullock. He corroborated the evidence presented by Mullock's testimony. The witness stated to the Court that he had met Tom Horn in the Scandinavian Saloon in Denver, and at the time Horn told him that he was a stock detective in Wyoming. Cousley said he asked Horn why he did not go after the reward money offered for evidence leading to the arrest of the killer of Willie Nickell, he said Horn replied, "Why that's all right, I'm the main guy in the case." Then Cousley added, that the accused bragged and said, "That Nickell was the ——— best shot I ever made."

The next "called up" was one Lyman Murdock who gave his address as Havana, Illinois. He testified that during the summer of 1901 he worked on the Coble ranch. He recalled meeting Horn on July 16th and that Horn was wearing a dark blue sweater, similar to the one exhibited by the Prosecution. He said this meeting took place north of Laramie.

Sheriff "Ed" Smalley's name was called. Smalley testified as to the sweater sent to him by Powell of Laramie. The Sheriff said he took it to Horn and the latter said, "I guess that's my sweater all right." Deputy Proctor supported Smalley's testimony regarding the sweater.

Deputy Marshal Joe LeFors was next to appear before the Court. The perspiring Peace Officer started his testimony by stating that on January 12, 1902, he had a talk with Tom Horn in the office used by the United States Marshal. LeFors said he told Horn that W. G. Pruitt of Miles City, Montana, wanted a man for a job in Montana. Horn asked him the nature of the work offered.

Then he (LeFors) let Tom read a letter from Pruitt. In the conversation that followed, LeFors said he associated Horn with the Nickell murder, and added he (Tom Horn) was a "slick" man to follow, as he had not been able to find any tracks. To this Horn had replied that he left no tracks as he went barefooted, adding that was the only way to keep officers off the trail. Horn said he left his horse a long way off. Tom then told him, LeFors continued, how it was possible for a man to be killed in the draw at the Nickell place. When LeFors asked if the murder had been compulsory, Horn replied, it was obliged to be as the lad had started to run to the house and it was necessary to kill him to keep him from raising a disturbance at the ranch. As the detective continued, he said Horn estimated the distance at 300 yards. Then Horn said, "It was the best shot and the dirtiest trick I ever done." They then discussed the type of gun used, Horn stating that he preferred a 30-30 to a 30-40 as the former would carry better, and the closer he was to his man the better he liked it.

LeFors testified he asked Horn if he wasn't provided food by Jim Dixon. To this he said Horn replied that when he went on a job of that kind he always carried a little bacon and bread. Then LeFors added that Horn had remarked that sometimes he got very hungry—so hungry that he could eat his mother.

LeFors said, personally that he could not have run across the ground barefooted. Horn replied that he did, but that he always had ten days rest after such a job.

In reply to LeFors' question about what he did with empty shells, Horn told him he took them with him to keep officers from finding them.

The witness concluded his testimony by stating that the Defendant said he got $600 for the Powell job and $500 for the boy. And he had received $2,100 for three men and one he had shot at five times. The accused said he placed a rock under the boy's head, this way he hung out his sign, so he could collect his money. Killing people was his specialty. It was his business and he had a corner on the market.

Judge Scott rapped his gavel and called for order in the Court as LeFors stepped down from the stand—the court was again quiet.

Attorney Stoll then exhibited three letters of the LeFors-Horn-W. D. Smith correspondence. The letters were circulated among the Jurymen.

Cheyenne Policeman D. A. "Sandy" McNeal, was next. He told the Court that he had seen Tom Horn on the Sunday, the day of his alleged conversation with LeFors. He met him in the stairway leading to the Marshal's office in the Idleman block. McNeal stated Horn seemed perfectly sober, though he seemed noisy and talkative.

Others to testify in regard to Horn's condition on this same Sunday (January 12th) were bartenders Vincent McGuire and E. O. Robertson. Both testified that Tom Horn appeared sober. The latter added that he thought it strange LeFors and Horn were together, he added he thought the two a "funny pair."

Louis Hall, bartender in Idleman's parlor, then recalled for the Court that he had seen Tom drunk at times and that he did not appear to be on this particular day.

A Paul Bailey was the next witness to be examined. He testified that he had been in the room with LeFors and Tom Horn a few minutes before their conversation.

Under-sheriff Leslie Snow related that he was in the private office of the U. S. Marshal the Sunday before the arrest of Tom Horn, and that he heard the conversation between the men. He stated that the conversation was practically the same as Joe LeFors had given in his testimony.

Charles Ohnhaus was the next witness. He was the United States Court Stenographer and testified that he was in the adjoining room when LeFors and Horn had their conversation and that he had taken it down in shorthand. The Court then asked Ohnhaus to read his report of the conversation, which he did.

During cross examination by Stoll, Ohnhaus testified that he could both see and hear Horn and LeFors, as there was a crack in the door, and that the door had been altered to permit sound to come through. The Court Stenographer added he could see Horn very plainly, and added that once Horn arose and walked to the window. LeFors, he stated, sat behind a desk and toyed with a revolver. He said that he had seen Horn both sober and drunk, and this time he was sober.

Following the testimony of Ohnhaus, the Court was recessed for ten minutes, after which Attorney Stoll announced that the Prosecution would rest the case at this point.

Judge Scott then adjourned the Court until 9 o'clock the following morning.

THURSDAY, OCTOBER 16

A large and eager crowd gathered early at the Courthouse—anticipating the opening of the Defense. However, developments were disappointing to many. Most of the morning was spent in an attempt to prove whether Tom Horn had been drunk at the time of his conversation. The afternoon was taken up in the discussion of the size of the wounds and the calibre of the gun. The untiring Stoll spent two and one-half hours cross examining one witness.

The first called to testfiy was Grover Reise, a bell boy at the Inter-Ocean Hotel. He testified that he had known Tom Horn for three years and had seen him intoxicated several times. He said that on January 12th he saw Tom between 12:30 and 1:30 at the hotel and he appeared to have been drinking; he judged he was "half-shot" at this time. The witness added that when the accused was sober he was very quiet, but while drinking he was inclined to be talkative.

Al Leslie, bartender for Harry Hynds, stated he saw Tom Horn on January 12th and he and Horn had drunk a considerable amount of whiskey and beer—too many to recount.

An Andrew Nelson was the next witness. He said that he saw Tom Horn on the morning in question and that he (Horn) was drunk and spinning yarns about the Mexican Army.

Frank Kerrigan testified. His story corroborated that of Nelson.

The proprietor of the Inter-Ocean Hotel, John Fullerton, told the Court that he saw Tom Horn at one o'clock on Sunday, January 12th. He described Horn's condition as being "loaded."

Dr. George P. Johnston was the next witness to be called. He told the Court that he had made a study of the gunshot wounds. In his opening statement he testified that the wounds that took the life of Willie Nickell were larger than a 30-30. However, upon being cross examined by Mr. Stoll, he said the wounds might have been by a 30-30 altered or deformed bullet. The doctor stated in his testimony that if the body had been turned over 3 or 4 hours after death, the blood might have flowed for at least 20 hours in the hot sun.

The next witness was Dr. Lewis, an Army surgeon from Fort D. A. Russell (present-day Fort F. E. Warren). The surgeon stated he entered the Army in 1893, and since that time he had treated an estimated 250 wounds. Three-fourths of these were made by 30-30 calibre rifles and 37 calibre pistols. The doctor said that he thought that the body must have been turned over 3 to 6 hours after death.

When the Court convened after the mid-day recess, the attendance was the largest since the trial began. The entire affair was beginning to assume monstrous proportions.

Army Surgeon Lewis was recalled to the stand. Prosecutor Stoll subjected the witness to vigorous questioning. He asked Dr. Lewis if the examinations of wounds he had made were on living or dead bodies. The witness replied, "mostly on living bodies." The fact was also brought out that in general, wounds on living would be small and on dead bodies they would be somewhat larger. Attorney Stoll then read an article written by authorities on the subject, in an effort to prove his point. Dr. Lewis acknowledged the authority, but said it was impossible to tell anything about the size of the bullet. In concluding, the witness somewhat upset by the vigorous cross examination he had been given, "fired" back at the Prosecutor that the wound might have been caused by a 30-30 soft nosed bullet.

Dr. Conway was the last witness of the day. He had testified at both the preliminary examination and at the Coroner's inquest. His testimony was much the same as his colleagues. However, during the two and one-half hour cross examination he became confused with the attorney's rapid and clever cross examination.

FRIDAY, OCTOBER 17

This was one of the most dramatic days of the long trial—Tom Horn was called to take the stand as the last witness of the day.

The first to be requested to appear was Dr. W. A. Burges, who gave an opinion on the size of the bullets that took Willie's life.

Dr. W. L. Davis, surgeon on the Denver Police Force, testified of Tom Horn's being in Denver on September 30, 1901, and that the Defendant had a fractured jaw and could not talk because of this condition. Dr. Davis on cross examination testified that the Carnival in Denver opened on September 30th instead of October 1st as he formerly testified.

John Wallis of Laramie, co-owner of the Elkhorn Barn, further testified regarding the date that Tom Horn rode into their barn. The cross examination brought out that the books were in an unorganized state, and it was difficult to learn much from them.

W. S. Carpenter was then called to the stand. He told of being at the Bosler ranch on July 20th when Tom Horn got the horse "Pacer" to ride to Laramie.

Duncan Clark, ranch foreman for the Bosler Company, said he knew Tom Horn rode to Laramie City on Saturday, July 20th. He stated that Tom had never worn a black or blue sweater, but had seen him wear a dun-colored one at various times. Later he admitted, to the Court, that he never paid much attention to Horn or his clothing.

Albany County Sheriff Alfred C. Cook took the chair and testified concerning the sketch of the brand that he sent to Sheriff Peter Warlaumont. It was the TY brand. He conceded on cross examination that his information had been obtained from John Coble and employees at his ranch. The Court was then recessed.

The first witness after the mid-day recess was Attorney T. F. Burke of Cheyenne. He stated that Mr. Kennedy, Judge Lacey and he had visited the "gate area." He described the site as being covered with sharp gravel, briars and cactus. The attorney said that he believed it impossible for a man to walk barefooted across the ground. Gravel was exhibited by the witness. He added it would be impossible for a man to be seen in the draw.

Defense Attorney, T. Blake Kennedy, corroborated Mr. Burke's testimony.

Frank Stone of Laramie was the next witness called before the Court. He stated that he saw Tom in Laramie on July 21st. "We bummed around town all day," he added. In describing the evening of the same day, Stone said he was with Horn and put him to bed when he became drunk, and that he saw no blood on Tom's clothing. He also removed the intoxicated man's socks and said he did not notice any bruises on Horn's feet. The witness then recalled that he took the horse and Horn's six-shooter to the ranch on the 29th of July. Frank Stone concluded his testimony by reiterating that he knew Tom had a yellow sweater.

Light-hearted cowboy Otto Plaga was the next witness to take the stand. His testimony to become controversial, is as follows:*

DIRECT EXAMINATION BY JUDGE LACEY

Q. You may state your name, age, place of residence and occupation.
A. Otto Plaga, age 24, Sybille, ranchman.
Q. How long have you resided in Wyoming?
A. Eighteen years.
Q. How long in the country where you now reside, or in that vicinity?

**Op. cit.*, pp. 568-581.

A. The greater part of the time.
Q. Are you acquainted with the defendant?
A. Yes sir.
Q. How long have you known him?
A. Since 1894.
Q. Are you acquainted with the horse that Tom Horn used to ride?
A. Yes sir.
Q. You may describe it?
A. A black brown horse.
Q. What size?
A. He is about 900 pounds or over.
Q. Do you remember the brand that was on him?
A. Yes, C A P.
Q. Do you know what the horse was called?
A. Yes sir, Cap.
Q. The same as the brand?
A. Yes sir.
Q. How was his mane?
A. It was roached.
Q. Do you remember where you were on the 18th of July, 1901?
A. Yes sir.
Q. Where were you?
A. I was up in the hills.
Q. Up in what hills?
A. In the Fitzmorris country.
Q. How far is that from your ranch where you were living?
A. About eight miles.
Q. Where is the ranch where you were living, how far north of here? What direction from Iron Mountain?
A. It is in a north westerly direction I should judge.
Q. Do you know where the Nickell ranch is?
A. Yes sir.
Q. How far and in what direction was your place from the Nickell ranch?
A. In a westerly direction, I should judge about twenty-five miles.
Q. It is about twenty-five miles from your place to the Nickell ranch?
A. From the place where I seen Horn.
Q. I am asking how far from your place to the Nickell ranch.
A. About eighteen miles or seventeen.

Q. Now, as I understand you were still west of your place on the 18th of July 1901?
A. Yes sir.
Q. What were you doing up there?
A. I was gathering cattle and prospecting.
Q. Now, what time in the morning did you get up there, or was it in the morning or afternoon?
A. In the morning.
Q. About what time?
A. About eight o'clock.
Q. What time did you have breakfast?
A. About six.
Q. You went up there eight miles after the cattle?
A. Yes sir.
Q. How soon did you start after breakfast?
A. Right away.
Q. Now, did you go on horseback or how?
A. I went horseback, yes sir.
Q. Now, if you saw anybody up there who was it?
A. Tom Horn.
Q. Where did you see him?
A. I seen him up in that place in a south westerly direction from the Fitzmorris ranch.
Q. Do you remember with reference to the branches of the Sybille, the Berner creek as it is called or the Middle Sybille and main Sybille?
A. It was in between Middle and Main Sybille.
Q. That Middle Sybille is sometimes called by what name?
A. Berner Creek.
Q. A man by the name of Berner lives on the creek?
A. Yes sir.
Q. What was Mr. Horn doing there?
A. He was riding.
Q. Riding in which direction?
A. In a southwesterly direction.
Q. What kind of a horse did he have?
A. A blackish brown.
Q. Do you know whether this horse he has ever ridden before?
A. Yes sir.
Q. What horse was it?
A. It was that Cap horse he used to ride.

Q. What way was he riding as to whether rapidly, slowly or medium?
A. Just riding along on an easy trot.
Q. How did the horse seem as to whether he was fresh or tired?
A. He appeared very fresh; he didn't show wet or lather.
Q. Now, how close were you to Tom Horn?
A. About one hundred and fifty yards I should think.
Q. In which direction did you say he went?
A. In a southwesterly direction.
Q. How long did you watch him?
A. I should judge two or three minutes.
Q. How far did he go in the time you watched?
A. About two hundred yards.
Q. Did you get anything up there that day?
A. Yes, cattle and calves.
Q. How many cows and calves did you get?
A. Two cows and two calves.
Q. What did you do with them?
A. Took them home and branded them.
Q. If you mentioned to anybody that day anything in reference to Mr. Horn state to whom you mentioned it?
A. I mentioned it to Raymond Hencke.
Q. Who is Raymond Hencke?
A. He is my stepfather.
Q. Now, this point at which you saw Tom Horn how far was that from Nickell's ranch in your judgment?
A. About twenty-five miles I should judge.
Q. State whether Horn saw you?
A. No sir.
Q. Did you speak to one another or anything?
A. No sir.
Q. What were you doing at the time you saw him?
A. I was cracking quartz rock.
Q. Were you higher or lower than Tom?
A. I was higher.
Q. Where was he in a ravine or hill?
A. Just coming down beneath me in a little draw.
Q. Neither of you spoke to the other?
A. No sir.
Q. What kind of a horse did you ride that morning?
A. A dark iron gray.

Q. You say that you got two cows and two calves, what did you do with them?
A. Took them home.
Q. Do you know what was done with them the next day?
A. Yes, branded them.
Q. Branded the cows and calves?
A. Branded the calves.
Q. A couple of cows bearing Mr. Hencke's brand?
A. Yes sir.

CROSS EXAMINATION BY MR. STOLL

Q. Did you have some mining claims, Mr. Plaga, in that locality?
A. I did at one time, some prospects.
Q. Your claims filed?
A. No sir.
Q. So that if you were prospecting you were prospecting on claims that had not been recorded?
A. Yes, I was prospecting from a distance where I had seen some claims, and I intended taking up one.
Q. At the time you were prospecting did you have on record in Albany County or elsewhere the claims that you were prospecting?
A. No sir.
Q. Have you filed on that claim since?
A. No sir.
Q. So that you were not prospecting in the sense of locating a claim?
A. Yes, I intended to.
Q. But did you do it?
A. No sir.
Q. And you have not done it yet?
A. No sir.
Q. What was the object of your going out there that morning, the prospecting or the getting the cattle?
A. I was going for both.
Q. Now, do you remember of making a statement in my office on February 7th, relating to seeing Horn?
A. Yes sir.
Q. On this occasion do you remember of saying at that time you were prospecting?
A. Yes sir.
Q. And you did not say anything about hunting any calves?
A. I can't answer that question.

Q. But you were asked what you were doing there, and you said you had located some claims and you were prospecting?
A. I believe if I remember right I said I was going after cattle.
Q. You think you stated at that time you were after cattle; that is your recollection on the subject?
A. My recollection on the subject is that I was going after cattle and in the meantime I was prospecting.
Q. Now in regard to the time of day, what time of day did you say it was you saw Horn?
A. About eight o'clock.
Q. What enables you to fix the day?
A. I left home right after breakfast and went straight up in the hills, and I should judge I could ride eight miles in two hours.
Q. So you think it would not be much later than eight o'clock?
A. Not much I do not think.
Q. If the distance were only eight miles it would scarcely take you as long as that?
A. In a smooth country, no sir.
Q. Will you point out to the jury where it was? Look at that map behind you and put the point on the map if you can locate approximately the point where you saw Horn?
A. I do not understand the map; I can't point out the place; there is none of the tributaries on there at all.
Q. Will you point out generally the direction it was in?
A. It was in this direction up in the country.
Q. Somewhere in that locality?
A. Yes sir, there is little tributaries.
Q. And the place you have pointed is a place on the map an inch and a half a little southwest of the name Fitzmorris—is that the place?
A. I am not sure from the map. There is none of these little tributaries; this is very rough country.
Q. You spoke of seeing him about a mile and a half southwest of the Fitzmorris place?
A. Yes sir, a mile and a half.
Q. Do you mean a mile and a half southwest of the Fitzmorris house?
A. Yes sir.
Q. So that you would locate the point in that way without being able to point it out definitely on the map?
A. Yes sir; that is the best I can see it on that map.
Q. Was Horn going on any road or was there a trail?
A. There was an old trail.

Q. Was that off from a road or was it a trail that led into any of those roads?
A. It is a tributary that leads down into the main Sybille.
Q. Here is the road indicated along the main Sybille; now where does this trail come from and where does it go?
A. If you follow the trail down there is two branches, one turns down the main Sybille, another turns over into the Long Canyon country.
Q. Take that pointer so that the Jury can get some idea.
A. I cannot see the Long Canyon country at all. It is up here somewhere I should judge. There is Dick Latham's place and the Swan Land & Cattle Company are somewhere in that locality.
Q. Was the trail north or south of the road of the one marked the main road on the Sybille?
A. It was on the south side.
Q. It was going southwest, the trail?
A. As far as I could see; then it turned down towards the main Sybille where Fitzmorris lived, and the other trail turned off to Long Canyon country.
Q. Where does that trail that goes southwest go to?
A. It goes into the country road at Sybille Springs.
Q. About where is the Sybille Springs?
A. I can't see them on this map.
Q. In what direction from Fitzmorris' house?
A. I should judge in a southwesterly direction.
Q. About how far from his house?
A. I think they call it twelve or fifteen miles.
Q. You were well acquainted with Horn?
A. Yes sir.
Q. You have been for a long time very friendly with him?
A. Yes sir.
Q. You consider yourself one of his particular friends?
A. I can't say a particular friend of him.
Q. You were quite intimate with him and have ridden together with him a great deal?
A. Yes sir.
Q. Was there anybody around with you at that time?
A. No sir.
Q. You were all alone?
A. Yes sir.
Q. Why didn't you call to him, or say something to him as he was passing by?

A. I was cracking this quartz and didn't pay no attention to him as I wanted to keep that to myself.
Q. Do you know whether he had any rifle, Winchester rifle with him?
A. I didn't see any.
Q. What is your best impression, did he have one or didn't he?
A. He might have had one on the other side.
Q. Which side were you on, his right or left side?
A. I was viewing him from his right side.
Q. The side those guns are usually carried on?
A. Some carry them on the left and some carry them on the right side.
Q. Did you notice anything as to his dress?
A. He had a light striped shirt on and a vest.
Q. Anything tied on his saddle in any way?
A. No sir.
Q. Did you notice the kind of hat?
A. He had a light gray felt hat.
Q. It might have been as late as 8:30?
A. I don't hardly think so.
Q. You had a time piece or something to indicate the time?
A. No sir.
Q. Now, can you fix the hour in any closer limits; can you say it was close to eight or eight thirty?
A. I judge it was close to eight.
Q. In your statement made, to which I have referred, on February 7th, I will ask you to state whether or not you did not say it must have been eight or half past when you saw him?
A. Perhaps I did; it was either close to eight or a little after; I didn't exactly state the particular time.
Q. So that if you stated it was eight or half past eight you wish now to be understood as saying close to eight o'clock?
A. It was eight or a little after; I can't exactly tell the time.
Q. You say that this was the 18th of July?
A. Yes sir.
Q. How do you know that it was the 18th of July?
A. It was two days afterwards I heard of the boy being killed.
Q. So that it was the fact that Willie Nickell was killed that fixed this matter in your mind?
A. Yes sir.
Q. How do you know that it was two days afterwards?
A. It was on mail day.

Q. Because it was mail day is that the reason you fix it the 18th of July?
A. Yes sir, it is; it was on Saturday the 20th, mail day, we heard the news the boy was killed; it was the 18th; I remember the time.
Q. So far as anything occuring at the time when you heard of the killing of Willie Nickell, you have no reason for fixing this date except the mere fact that it was two days before mail day; why couldn't it have been three days, or one day before mail day?
A. Because we do not receive our mail there.
Q. How often do you receive your mail?
A. We receive the mail twice a week.
Q. It gets back to the mere matter of memory after all?
A. Yes sir, I recall the incident.
Q. Could it have been the day after, that is the 19th?
A. No sir.
Q. Why could it not have been one day before mail day if it is a mere matter of memory, two days before mail day that you seen Horn?
A. Because I recall the time of the incident; because I heard the boy was killed and it was only two days before that I seen Horn. I never gave it any particular attention at the time in regard to Horn.
Q. So the mere fact that you seen Horn at the time you were out there in these hills did not make any impression on your mind?
A. It did to a certain extent.
Q. You were in the habit of seeing him quite frequently?
A. Used to.
Q. He rode around in that section and you met him quite often?
A. I have met him before, yes sir.
Q. You saw him and whatever the impression may have been on your mind it was not sufficient to cause you to address him and say, Hello, Tom?
A. At that time I never paid no particular attention; he rode by and I attended to my work.
Q. He merely passed by, and his passing by was not a matter of much moment to make an impression?
A. He made a kind of an impression. I was thinking of there being some rustling in that country.
Q. And yet there was nothing said on the subject of rustling, or nothing about the time of day, or where he come from or where he was going to?
A. No sir.

Q. Whatever the impression was, it was not sufficient to cause you to address him in any way at that time?
A. No sir.
Q. Now you went home and pursued your usual vocation at home, I believe you worked in haying?
A. I worked the day before in the hay field.
Q. You worked the next day in the hay field?
A. Yes sir.
Q. You didn't mention the matter to Mr. Coldick who was working with you of seeing Horn?
A. No sir.
Q. So that it did not make any impression on your mind, so much so at least that you spoke of it to the man that was working with you?
A. I didn't think it was necessary for him to know; he was working there and a green hand in the country.
Q. There was not anything further to fix in your mind except what you have stated?
A. Yes sir, Saturday when we received the mail I heard the boy was killed. I recalled the incident when Mr. Hencke said that if I seen Horn, he didn't see why they should be looking for him over there.
Q. Who told you Willie Nickell was killed?
A. Raymond Hencke told me.
Q. When he told you, you immediately thought of Horn?
A. No sir.
Q. There was nothing in the fact that the mail carrier told you Willie Nickell was killed that caused you to think of Horn?
A. There was some talk suggesting who might have done it, Coldick said they might accuse me being I was gone that day. We were talking that evening about the Nickell and Miller feud, and we thought it was something like that.
Q. When did you have a conversation with Mr. Coldick?
A. On Saturday evening.
Q. What did Mr. Coldick say in that conversation as to where you were?

Objected to as not cross examination. By the Court: It is testing his memory. To which defendant by counsel takes exception.

A. He said it would be a joke if they blamed it on to me being as I was out riding the range.
Q. When the matter was brought to your attention did you think of Horn then?

A. Not just then.
Q. So that when Raymond Hencke told you that Willie Nickell had been killed you did not think of Horn?
A. No sir.
Q. When Coldick told you about being accused of it yourself, you did not think of Horn?
A. No sir.
Q. When did you think of seeing Horn up there?
A. A short time afterwards.
Q. About how long?
A. About two weeks.
Q. How did it come then you thought of Horn?
A. Because I was asked if Horn was seen in the country.
Q. Until you were asked if Horn was seen in the country the matter did not occur to you?
A. Not in regard to Horn.
Q. Or in regard to seeing him in that locality?
A. I thought of seeing him.
Q. You said there was something you wanted to keep to yourself up there, what was that?
A. In regard to rustling.
Q. In regard to cracking the stone?
A. I thought I had a lead there that looked very good. It was iron and I wanted to keep it myself.
Q. The next day after you saw Horn, what was it you said you did?
A. Branded calves and worked in the hay field.
Q. It was the next day after that, it was mail day?
A. Yes sir.
Q. You said if that was a smooth country, a man could ride 8 miles in less than two hours, what kind of a country is it?
A. It is very rough rocky country.
Q. You cannot make very rapid progress even on horse back?
A. No sir.

Dr. Conway was then called to testify as to the kind of ruler he used in making measurements.

Mr. Raymond Hencke corroborated Otto Plaga's testimony. He said he recalled Plaga telling him that he had seen Horn on the 18th. He testified that he remembered the day because they had branded calves at the time.

Al Leslie was next to take the sand. The Prosecution asked him if he had been with Tom Horn all day on July 19th in Laramie. He replied with an emphatic "no."

Then a silence fell over the Court Room as the composed Horn took the "chair." All had awaited his appearance. Tom Horn was sworn-in on his own behalf, his testimony is as follows:*

DIRECT EXAMINATION BY JUDGE LACEY

Q. State your name?
A. Tom Horn.
Q. Your place of residence just at present?
A. In the county jail.
Q. Are you the defendant in this case?
A. I am.
Q. Where did you reside prior to July 1901?
A. I made my home for a long time at Coble's ranch at the Iron Mountain Ranch Company.
Q. You mean by that the ranch, just north of Laramie?
A. It is at the present time; formerly it was in the Iron Mountain country.
Q. What is your business?
A. My business has been to ride on the range alone and look after the interests of the company.
Q. What do they generally call that?
A. I am recommended—I don't know as I am by Mr. Coble—by the people in general as a stock detective.
Q. What was the purpose of that riding?
A. To keep track of the cattle in the country in a general way and as closely as I possibly can to shove all the cows and calves that I found—you understand this country is all fenced—wherever I found cows and calves belonging to the company in anyone else's pasture, I drove them home to brand them—that is the nature of the work. I also keep as good track of the people in the country as I can that are killing and marketing beef; everything of that nature that will have a tendency to protect the interests of the company.
Q. How long had you been engaged in that business prior to July 1901?
A. Perhaps 8 or 10 years.
Q. Now without going over all of the movements from the very first of July, suppose we begin with the time you stopped at Billy Clay's after the middle of July, or about that time, do you remember that circumstance?
A. I remember very distinctly having stopped there.

**op. cit.*, pp. 595-608.

Q. When was it you stopped at Billy Clay's?
A. It was on Sunday evening.
Q. Do you remember the day of the month, if not, you may look at the calendar.
A. I can tell what day of the month by looking at the calendar; at that particular time I didn't pay any attention to the day of the month. I remember it was Sunday. Sunday on a ranch is a kind of rest day.
Q. Is that the calendar for 1901?
A. Yes, I should say from looking at it, it must have been the 14th of July.
Q. When we speak of Billy Clay, is that the witness that was on the stand here?
A. Yes sir.
Q. How long did you stay at Mr. Clay's.
A. I stayed all night.
Q. Then what did you do the next morning?
A. The next morning I went out in his pasture.
Q. To look over his pasture?
A. Yes sir.
Q. When you got through doing that what did you do?
A. I came again to his house.
Q. About what time of day was that?
A. I presume it was afternoon, they had had their dinners and had gone back to the hay field.
Q. You did not notice just the time of day, only they had had their dinners?
A. Mrs. Clay told me that the men had eaten their dinners and gone out.
Q. Where did you go from there?
A. From there I went across up through Clay's pasture again and out through what I think is Mr. Nickell's pasture, and on over into Mr. Coble's pasture.
Q. The large pasture of Mr. Coble's you went to this time?
A. We designated it on the ranch as the north pasture.
Q. Where is it with reference to Mr. Nickell's premises?
A. It runs up within a couple of miles of Nickell's house.
Q. In which direction?
A. I think Mr. Nickell's pasture joins Mr. Coble's pasture 2 or 3 miles from his house, I think the dividing fence between Nickell's and Coble's comes right up to Coble's.

Q. From there where did you go? This would be Monday about what time that you were down at Coble's pasture?
A. After I got lunch at Mr. Clay's I went back over in that country and stayed over there as long as I could see.
Q. Where did you go that night?
A. I went to Jim Miller's ranch.
Q. What acquaintance did you have with Miller before this time?
A. None at all scarcely.
Q. Had you ever met him prior to this time?
A. I think once, I don't believe oftener.
Q. You had met him you think once?
A. Yes sir.
Q. What if any invitation had he given to you if you should ever get in his neighborhood?
A. He told me if I ever come in his neighborhood to be sure and call.
Q. You went to his house Monday night, that would be?
A. Yes sir.
Q. How long did you stay there?
A. I stayed all night. It was quite late, they had all gone to bed when I got there; when I left up in the hills it was dark.
Q. It was late when you got to Miller's house?
A. Yes.
Q. You stayed all night there?
A. The balance of the night.
Q. What did you do the next day?
A. I didn't do anything in particular the next day. I laid around Miller's ranch and went fishing in the front part of the day; laid around and went up the creek to see where Mr. Nickell's sheep were located.
Q. About what time of day was that that you went out to see about the sheep?
A. I should say about the middle of the afternoon.
Q. What time did you get back?
A. They hadn't had supper when I got back, I don't think it was sun down, it was only a short distance up there. They were up there in a pasture that I think belonged to Miller.
Q. Were they in any of Coble's pastures?
A. No, I went up to see if they were in Coble's pasture, and they were not.
Q. When you found they were not, what did you do?
A. I went back to Miller's.

Q. Had they been trespassing so far as you ascertained upon any of Mr. Coble's ranches?
A. The only way I had to tell, was by looking for tracks and signs of sheep; I saw they were not in the pasture, the sheep themselves and I didn't see any indications whatever of them in the pasture.
Q. You didn't see they had been there at all?
A. I settled it definitely in my own mind, they had not been there.
Q. You went back to Miller's ranch, where did you stay that night?
A. I stayed at Miller's again that night.
Q. With whom did you talk mostly while you were there?
A. I think the principal part of my conversation was with a young lady by the name of Miss Kimmel.
Q. When did you leave the ranch?
A. I left the next morning, which I suppose would be Wednesday morning as it is figured out here.
Q. Look at the calendar and keep these dates as nearly correct as you can, as a matter of fact in riding about that way, do you keep track clearly of dates?
A. I do not keep track of the dates or days. And I never would have kept track of these if I had not been arrested in connection with this murder; I would not have given it a thought.
Q. Wednesday, you would say was the day you left there?
A. Yes sir, Wednesday, the 17th.
Q. Do you remember about what time?
A. I remember it was after Miss Kimmel had left to teach school.
Q. That is as near as you can fix the time, do you remember how shortly after she went to school?
A. I should say very shortly, I saddled up my horse, I was not in a particular hurry, I hadn't any particular place to go.
Q. You have spoken of your horse, state what horse you had?
A. I was riding a horse they call Cap.
Q. What color?
A. Very dark brown, or black; he is black in the winter time when he is not sun burned. In the summer time he is smoky color, most people would call him black in the summer time too.
Q. How was he branded?
A. C A P on the shoulder.
Q. Anything peculiar about his mane?
A. Nothing peculiar only it was roached.
Q. What fire irons did you have?
A. A rifle.
Q. What else?
A. Nothing else.

Q. What kind of a rifle?
A. A 30-30 Winchester.
Q. Did you have anything else on your saddle?
A. Field glasses.
Q. What else?
A. Nothing else.
Q. How were you dressed, or do you pay much attention to your dress, can you recall how you were dressed?
A. No, I could not recall.
Q. State what you had if anything in the way of a sweater with you?
A. I never had a sweater; sweaters are worn in the winter time; this was in the middle of the summer.
Q. You didn't wear a sweater in the summer time?
A. No sir, I didn't even have a coat with me.
Q. Now, when you left the Miller ranch on the morning of Wednesday the 17th of July, where did you go, which direction did you leave the Miller ranch?
A. I left the Miller ranch and turned right up the creek.
Q. Which direction would that be, north, south, east or west?
A. I could not say as to that.
Q. Was it towards Nickell's ranch or from it?
A. Directly away from it; that was only two or three hundred yards you might say.
Q. Then where did you go?
A. Then I swung around and crossed the South Chug in below Nickell's ranch.
Q. What was there over there if anything that you were looking after?
A. There was a piece of land there, just a small piece of meadow, belonging to the Swan Land and Cattle Co. that we called the Colcord Place.
Q. Did you look to see the situation of the land?
A. I looked to see if Mr. Nickell's had any sheep in there.
Q. What did you find about that?
A. There was not a sign of sheep there.
Q. There being no further about that what direction did you go?
A. I headed back home towards the Laramie Plains, in fact I started back towards the Laramie Plains when I left Miller's. I left Miller's with the intention of going through the Colcord Place. After I left the Colcord Place I went along up through Mr. Nickell's pasture.
Q. Which pasture was that of Mr. Nickell's?
A. I know the pasture very well, I don't know what he called it.

Q. Which direction from his house?
A. It is a pasture that lays directly between his house and Mr. Clay's house.
Q. It would be up to the north or northeast direction?
A. Northeast I should say.
Q. Which direction with reference to the gate at which Willie Nickell was killed, same direction or opposite direction?
A. I was not going out at any time toward the gate Willie Nickell was killed.
Q. When you left and went on up through Mr. Nickell's pasture where did you go from there?
A. I went over Billy Clay's pasture.
Q. Now, at that place where you crossed Billy Clay's pasture, about how far were you from Mr. Nickell's house?
A. I can't say; it was east; it was below across towards Mule Creek; where I crossed the creek was below his house, perhaps from a mile and a quarter to one and one-half, I can't say as to miles, just making a guess; I crossed the south Chug a mile and a half below Mr. Nickell's house. I know the gate very well where the boy was killed; it is estimated about a mile above Mr. Nickell's house.
Q. Pretty near opposite direction from where you were from the Nickell's house?
A. Yes sir.
Q. Where did you go from the place across the Nickell pasture?
A. I went in Mr. Nickell's pasture.
Q. Where did you go then?
A. I worked through Mr. Clay's pasture.
Q. Who did you see in that vicinity?
A. I did that night; Johnny Bray.
Q. You seen Johnny Bray?
A. Monday morning when I was leaving Clay's I saw him coming up there when I was getting ready to leave. I have known him a long time and I spoke to him. I heard Mr. Clay say John Bray is coming back to help me hay. This particular Monday morning before I left John Bray came along and evidently went to work. I went along about my business. On this Wednesday evening I was down in the lower part of Clay's pasture and I saw Johnny Bray going home.
Q. On what creek was that?
A. Mule Creek we call it.
Q. In what direction from Billy Clay's?

A. He lives on Mule Creek, this was right down the creek from Billy Clay's.
Q. As to north, south, east, or west, do you know the direction that way?
A. I am more certain by saying directly down the creek from Billy Clay's.
Q. Where did you go from there—you were going down Mule Creek, which way was John Bray going?
A. He was going home, I suppose—I don't know that he was. I heard Billy Clay say he was going to help him hay, and he would have to go home as his wife was alone.
Q. You took it he was going home?
A. Yes sir.
Q. Did you watch him until he got home?
A. I don't suppose I watched him a minute.
Q. You went on from there in which direction after you saw John Bray?
A. I crossed on to the Sybille.
Q. Did you go as far on Mule Creek as to where John Bray lived?
A. I went on past there but not directly by his house.
Q. Which direction did you turn then?
A. I swung off to the left like, heading across into the Sybille country. Judge, let me explain. It was after I left Bray's and had ridden a mile or two and it began to get dark—you understand I saw Johnny Bray, I didn't meet him. I saw him; I should judge now to the best of my recollection about sundown.
Q. Do you know whether he saw you or not at the time?
A. It didn't look to me as if he did; he rode right along; he did not check up his horse.
Q. You do not know that he seen you?
A. I was there in plain sight, but it occurred to me that he didn't see me.
Q. After passing his place it began to get dark?
A. Yes sir. I wanted to go out on the other side of the branch of the Sybille that was right there close to me. There was a continuous line of settlements on the Sybille and I wanted to cross that line of settlements that night because there were pastures there in very close to those ranches, and I have to work these pastures. Of course, it is just the least bit embarrasing when a man riding through the country in that way, to ride into a man's pasture and look over his pasture and have the man come along. Too, also if there is anybody in the country that are disposed to shove cattle out of the road before you come along—it gives them an

opportunity to get in cows and calves. For instance, if anyone knew I would be through their pastures and they had one of my calves, they could shove them over to some other pasture they thought I would not go into. The consequence was as regarded that country I had no particular desire to be seen by any of the ranchmen.

Q. Where did you get that night?

A. I slept out on a little branch that puts into the Sybille there—known as Berner Creek. No, it is not Berner Creek, it is a branch you crossed before you get to Berner Creek.

Q. Had you crossed that branch that night?

A. I crossed it that night.

Q. And slept where?

A. I slept on one of the short tributaries.

Q. This was the night of the day you left Miller's?

A. It was.

Q. Where did you go the next morning?

A. I left Miller's in the morning and saw Johnny Bray in the evening at sundown, and that evening I slept on the branch.

Q. You left Miller's on Wednesday, what day was that?

A. Naturally Thursday would be the 18th, I would infer from the calendar.

Q. Where did you go that morning?

A. I went on up towards the head of the Sybille country. I was headed there mainly from the time I left Miller's; I was virtually headed towards home.

Q. This was taking you off in the general direction of home?

A. Yes sir.

Q. In going home you were intending to make these pastures, make these investigations?

A. Yes sir. I don't have any particular place to go, or any particular time. I don't work under any particular instructions at any time. I am supposed to go when I please and where I please, and how I please. The boss or foreman of the ranch, the manager of the ranch leaves that entirely to myself.

Q. Now, Thursday morning the 18th, you were working on back towards the Coble ranch, and you were working through these pastures?

A. Yes sir.

Q. Do you remember when it was, what time of day you got in the vicinity of Marble Top Mountain, or up between that somewhere and the Sybille?

A. Thursday morning I crossed through there.

Q. Do you remember now what time it was you got up there?
A. That is quite a hill.
Q. Well, now where did you spend the time on Thursday?
A. On Thursday I was all day all around there on some of the forks of the Sybille, and even up as far as the Divide, at some of the heads of Chug, I was in that country all day.
Q. On Thursday night where were you, where did you sleep Thursday night?
A. I know the exact springs.
Q. Maybe you can describe it so that we can know what springs it is?
A. I can't no more describe it more than to say it is a little spring that is really one of the very headwaters of the Sybille.
Q. What kind of a country is it in?
A. All of the country is rough country.
Q. All of the country you were riding through was a rough and rocky country?
A. Yes sir.
Q. Through such a country you can't ride rapidly?
A. If a man wants to ride rapidly, he can ride rapidly. People in that country naturally ride faster in the mountains than a man out in the flat country. You can ride as fast as a cow can run. I don't use a fast gait, I go along on a jog trot. If I start anywhere, I ride fast.
Q. Do you take notes of the distances you travel each day, anything like that?
A. No sir—how do you mean?
Q. How many miles it was, or anything like that?
A. No.
Q. You took notice of when it was that you were there?
A. I know where I was. I was not taking any particular notice.
Q. Which side of the Sybille was it that you slept on Thursday night?
A. It was really on the head of the Sybille. On Thursday I had made up my mind in going home. When I started home from Miller's, I says to myself, I will go across the Colcord Place and over on the Sybille and take a look down on the Fitzmorris place —there had been some complaint made to me about Fitzmorris dogging cattle that drifted down on him. I thought I would go down there and look around that day and see if I could see anything of his dogging cattle, look around so that I would know the condition of the country.
Q. Did you go down there?

A. I started down there on Thursday; then there was a portion of the country up on the Divide between the Chug and the heads of the Sybille that I hadn't been through, and didn't want to leave the country because I was virtually satisfying myself that everything was right in that country before I would leave that district and go to work somewhere else. So Thursday I started as though I had intended to go down to Fitzmorris' as I got in the neighborhood of that country. I says I will ride up and ride out the rest of this country between the Sybille and the Chugwater and then go to Fitzmorris and go home; then I would satisfy myself as to the condition of the entire country.

Q. You rode some back and forwards so as to cover that country?

A. Yes sir. I naturally go all over the country, or else I would not know what was going on.

Q. When was it that you saw the Fitzmorris place?

A. On Friday morning I went down close to the Fitzmorris place.

Q. Did you see Fitzmorris?

A. I didn't see Fitzmorris myself. I don't remember having seen him.

Q. Did you see anybody there?

A. Yes sir.

Q. Who was it you saw there?

A. I didn't know the man; he was off perhaps a half mile from me; I could see him as plain as if I had him sitting on my knee with my field glasses.

Q. What time of day was it that you saw these people at Fitzmorris'?

A. I saw a man working around there. I should say the time (to make a rough guess) was from 9 to 10 o'clock. I saw this man there all that day off and on.

Q. You were looking around so as to satisfy yourself if they did any dogging of cattle?

A. That is what I was doing.

Q. Friday night that would be the night of the 19th, where did you stay?

A. On Friday I camped still on the Sybille that is all the Sybille country, I call that all the Sybille country. On Friday night I was still on the Sybille on the tributary of another fork.

Q. Off more towards the home ranch?

A. Not directly towards the home ranch.

Q. How far from the home ranch did you camp Friday night?

A. I should say ten or twelve miles.

Q. What did you do Saturday?

A. Saturday I went to the home ranch.

Q. This distance of ten or twelve miles, what means of knowing what it is?

A. Anytime that I mention any distance, I am simply guessing at it. I guess ten or twelve miles. Just after dark that night I watered my horse, and took a drink from what I call Blue Grass Spring.

Q. Is that a well-known spring?

A. It is very well known to me.

Q. It is well known in that region, you think that is a well-known place?

A. That place is called Blue Grass country; further across the Sybille is called the Sybille country.

Q. You took a drink that night at the Blue Grass Spring—how close to that did you camp?

A. I camped a mile or so from there. I went rather in the direction of the ranch, more in the direction of the ranch than away from the ranch.

Q. The next morning was Saturday morning the 20th. What did you do that morning?

A. Saturday morning the 20th, I went home to the ranch.

Q. Do you remember what time it was you got there?

A. I should say somewhere along in the middle of the forenoon.

Q. Did you make any particular note of the time when you got there?

A. No sir, I had no occasion to.

Q. Who was it that was there at the ranch when you got there?

A. Jack Ryan and his wife were in the house. Carpenter was at the stable.

Q. Do you know what Carpenter was doing?

A. He was tending to the putting up of the hay. He told me what he was there for, that was the first time I had ever seen him on the ranch there, on the place.

Q. All of this time from the time you left Miller's ranch until you got to the home ranch, and saw Carpenter, what horse did you ride, or if you changed horses, what horse did you ride?

A. I did not change horses from the time I left the ranch on the trip; I started to ride the C A P horse and came home riding him.

Q. You came home riding C A P your black horse?

A. I did.

Q. Did you have any talk with Carpenter there at the corrals or barn about the horse when you got in?

A. When I got in I went to the house and got my mail; after reading my mail, I wanted to go to Laramie City, I had an appointment to go to Laramie. I calculated originally to go to Laramie on this Saturday evening. After getting my mail in the house I wanted to go right away, so I telephoned; there is a telephone running from the ranch to the railroad station; I telephoned a message over to the telegraph operator at the station to send to Laramie. I went out and Carpenter was in the stable and I asked him what horses were there, I wanted to go to Laramie right away. The horses that were there right in that pasture close to the house were little old sticks of ranch horses like I didn't care to ride. Mr. Coble's private horse was there—previously in the house Mr. Ryan had told me that Mr. Coble had gone east and I knew he was not there and the horse was a big fat snorty horse and Carpenter told me it was the only horse there that was any good, so I got him in a little pasture close to the house; I went out and drove him into the corral.

Q. Describe that private horse of Mr. Coble's that you got.

A. He is a very dark bay or brown horse, handsome appearing horse, has a kind of racking, shuffling gait until he strikes a run; he has a very high life and he always acts as though he had a little touch of the weed we call it, a little kind of crazy, snorty, flighty.

Q. Do you know what his name is?

A. We call him Pacer.

Q. You got Pacer then, you know he was branded?

A. He is branded lazy TY.

Q. Do you know whose brand that is?

A. The cows now belong to Duncan Clark.

Q. Whose brand was it originally?

A. John Coble's.

Q. When you got that horse up and started you went where?

A. To Laramie.

Q. Do you know how long it took you to go to Laramie?

A. No sir, I don't know how long. He wanted to go and I didn't care to disappoint him and I let him go.

Q. Do you remember whether you had anything to eat before you left the ranch?

A. I had something to eat.

Q. What time of day, if you know, was it when you got into Laramie, or did you notice particularly?

A. I didn't notice particularly. I didn't have any particular occasion to notice.

Q. What day of the week was it that you got to Laramie?
A. It was on Saturday; the same day I got into the ranch.
Q. What day of the month was this?
A. I see now it was the 20th.
Q. Saturday, July 20th?
A. Yes sir.
Q. Where did you take the horse?
A. To the Elkhorn barn.
Q. Now when you put that horse in the Elkhorn barn, you may state whether or not you took it out again for the next week?
A. I have not taken him out yet. [Laughter]
Q. Who took him out?
A. Frank Stone.
Q. You rode then when you left Laramie in what way?
A. I went up on the Little Laramie with Frank Stone.
Q. How did you ride?
A. I rode in a 2-wheeled cart. He had a couple of broncs hitched to a cart. He had a boy who was to fetch him and I rode in the cart.
Q. From the time you reached Laramie on the 20th, until you left there with Frank Stone on the 30th, state whether you left town at all?
A. No sir.
Q. Now, Mr. LeFors has said some things that you said to him, you may just explain to the jury what it was that you and LeFors were doing, when you had that talk with Joe LeFors that was overheard by Les Snow and Charlie Ohnhaus.
A. We were just joshing one another, throwing boquets at one another you might call it.
Q. What intention, if any, did you have in any way in the world to seriously admit that you had killed Willie Nickell?
A. I never had anything to do with the killing of Willie Nickell; I never had any cause to kill him. And I never killed him. He was joshing me about it and I did not object.
Q. You did not object to the joshing?
A. No sir.
Q. State whether in that conversation you intended to admit that you really did kill him as a serious proposition or in any other way than mere joshing?

A. There was nothing serious about the talk at all, it was all a josh all the way through. There was no concealment. If they were there at the table I would probably have gone on all the same, I don't think that would have made any difference.

Q. You heard these men testify as to some talk you had during the first week in October as they put it, the festival week in Denver? What have you to say about that? Was that a true statement of anything you said to them or was it not?

A. There could not have been any truth about it at all, not one word of truth could there have been about it.

Q. Where were you the first week of October, 1901?

A. I was in the hospital in Denver, St Luke's Hospital.

Q. Do you remember what it was that caused you to be there?

A. I lost the fight.

Q. Lost it in such a way you were injured, in what way?

A. I had my jaw broken to the extent that I had to go to the hospital.

Q. How long were you in the hospital?

A. 20 or 21 days.

Q. Now do you remember what night it was you got your jaw broken in that fight?

A. It was Sunday night.

Q. Was there any opportunity in the world for you to, the next day, go up town and tell Mr. Mullock as he states that you had been talking too freely the night before?

A. The next day it was impossible for me to communicate with anyone except by writing. I could not speak a word. He also said on the witness stand that I was making some arrangements trying to buy a ticket. I had no occasion to buy a ticket as I took a carload of horses and had a pass with the horses.

Q. Was Sunday night the only night you were drinking in Denver on that trip there?

A. It was.

Q. And the result was that you didn't talk with anybody for three weeks?

A. I think 20 or 21 days I was in the hospital.

Q. Something has been said here about a sweater, here, a navy blue sweater, was that sweater yours?

A. No sir.

Q. When it was brought to you, did you have any knowledge beforehand that it going to be expressed to you?

A. The jailer brought me a letter written to Mr. Smalley, that letter, says Mr. Smalley, Tom Horn left a sweater here with me which I send to him by express. Mr. Smalley has perhaps got the letter; I had the letter in the cell for two days. The jailer then come and asked if I had the letter; I said it is perhaps there in the rack; I had a little rack fixed in the cell. I gave it to him and haven't seen it since.

Q. When was it that the letter arrived with relation to the sweater?

A. Sometime after, I don't know exactly.

Q. What did you say about the sweater at the time you got the letter?

A. There was nothing to say.

Q. Did you tell the jailer you had left no sweater there?

A. I asked the jailer who this man was that was sending this sweater; I didn't know anything about the sweater; he told me he was some shoemaker in Laramie the sheriff told him. The shoemaker I know was Pete Rauner. I asked if this fellow worked for Rauner; there was some conversation about the sweater; it occurred to me they were jobbing me about the sweater.

Q. When the sweater actually came, what did you say?

A. When it actually came the sheriff and jailer brought the sweater in; the sheriff said here is an express package for you, I don't know whether it is yours; I says, I suppose it is that sweater they wrote me about; I was sitting on the floor cutting rawhide. I cut the strings and got it out; it was an old dirty sweater; I said all sweaters look alike to me. I think they took up the sweater and took it out. I said to the jailer if that is mine, you had better have it washed; I never saw it before or I never seen it since. Judge, in connection with the sweater, I would like to say further that the only sweater I had for four or five years is a kind of yellow tan colored sweater, and Dunc Clark has been wearing that all the while.

Q. It might be called a dirty white, dung colored, but not a navy blue?

A. Yes sir, I have not worn that much, Dunc Clark has worn it most of the time.

Q. You heard the testimony of Frank Irwin that he saw you there in Laramie on the 18th, what is the truth about that?

A. I was not there.

Q. You heard the testimony of Ed Titus that he drank with you on the night of the 19th? What have you to say to that?

A. He did not drink with me on the night of the 19th—I did not go into Laramie until the 20th.

SATURDAY, OCTOBER 18

Sunrise on this day saw many about Cheyenne trudging toward the heart of the Old Frontier town to the County Courthouse. It was a typical Wyoming morning—slightly chilly, if anything. Few mentioned the weather; the Horn case was foremost in their minds. Today would be another big day. Arriving early insured them of a seat in the court room, that would perhaps be described during the day by one onlooker to another as ". . . damned crowded ain't it?"

At 9 o'clock the "cast" was assembled in the Court. The longevity and tenseness of the situation had taken its toll, all appeared tired.

Judge Scott started the events of the day with the vigorous rapping of his gavel on the bench. In an instant the conglomeration of voices stopped. Court was in session.

On this day Walter Stoll would cross examine Horn.

Stoll had a break, he could warm up on Frank Stockton, Peace Officer from Arapahoe County, Colorado. The sheriff was called to testify as to the character of Mullock who told of Tom Horn's "confession" in Denver. The sheriff testified as to Mullock's long criminal record.

Attorney Stoll asked the sheriff if he had a copy of this record. The witness said yes. The Prosecutor objected to the document stating it was a copy and not an original.

The crowded Court room had become somewhat out of hand during Stockton's testimony. They were anticipating Horn taking the stand, and were paying little attention to the first testimony. Judge Scott frequently pounded for order. A silence filled the room as the bailiff called, "Next witness, Tom Horn."

This was it! Walter Stoll had turned his plan of interrogation over in his mind many times—perhaps a hundred or more. He had taxed his legal knowledge to the maximum in preparation of the hours he would face Tom Horn.

Horn's "brain trust" gave him a nod of approval as he left their table. Straight and quick-like, Tom walked past the Jury box, up to the chair where he lithely sat down. He winked at a friend, then became as composed as any man in the Court room and perhaps more confident than most. Other than his skin being bleached from his extended confinement, he was as usual. And so with nervous confidence, Prosecutor Stoll began the duel that was to last the entire day. If a death struggle can be waged with words, this was it.*

*Ibid, pp. 612-701

THE "PLACE"

The Laramie County Courthouse, Cheyenne. It was here that the drama unfolded. Cross on the left was location of Tom Horn's cell. The cross on the right indicates the location of the Court Room.

(Courtesy Denver Post)

JUDGE RICHARD H. SCOTT
He heard the dramatic case in its entirety.
(Courtesy Denver Post)

"JUDGE" J. W. LACEY

Chief Counsel for the Defense, a brilliant legal mind.

(Courtesy Wyoming State Tribune)

T. F. BURKE

Keen Defense Attorney for Tom Horn.

(Courtesy Wyoming State Tribune)

EDWARD T. CLARK

He argued for the life of Tom Horn.

(Courtesy Leslie Snow Collection)

T. BLAKE KENNEDY (left), R. N. MATSON (right)
They completed the five-man "brain trust" for the defense of Tom Horn.
(Courtesy Wyoming State Tribune)

WALTER R. STOLL

The brilliant and unrelenting Prosecuting Attorney.

(Courtesy Wyoming State Tribune)

CLYDE M. WATTS
Assisted the Prosecution.
(Courtesy Wyoming State Tribune)

H. WALDO MOORE

He helped prepare the State's case against Tom Horn.

(Courtesy Wyoming State Tribune)

THE JURY

They decided the fate of Tom Horn.

Upper line, reading left to right—John Rees, bailiff; O. V. Lebern, E. C. Metcalf, H. W. Yoder, Amos Sarbaugh, F. S. Simon, Homer Payne, George Proctor, bailiff. Lower line, reading left to right—J. E. Barnes, Charles Tolson, T. R. Babbitt, Charles Stamm, H. W. Thomas, George A. Wrightman.

(Courtesy Denver Post)

MARY NICKELL

The tragedy of it all . . .

(Courtesy Denver Post)

FREDDY NICKELL AND HIS SISTER, MRS. COOK

Fred found his brother's body—on July 19, 1901

(Courtesy Denver Post)

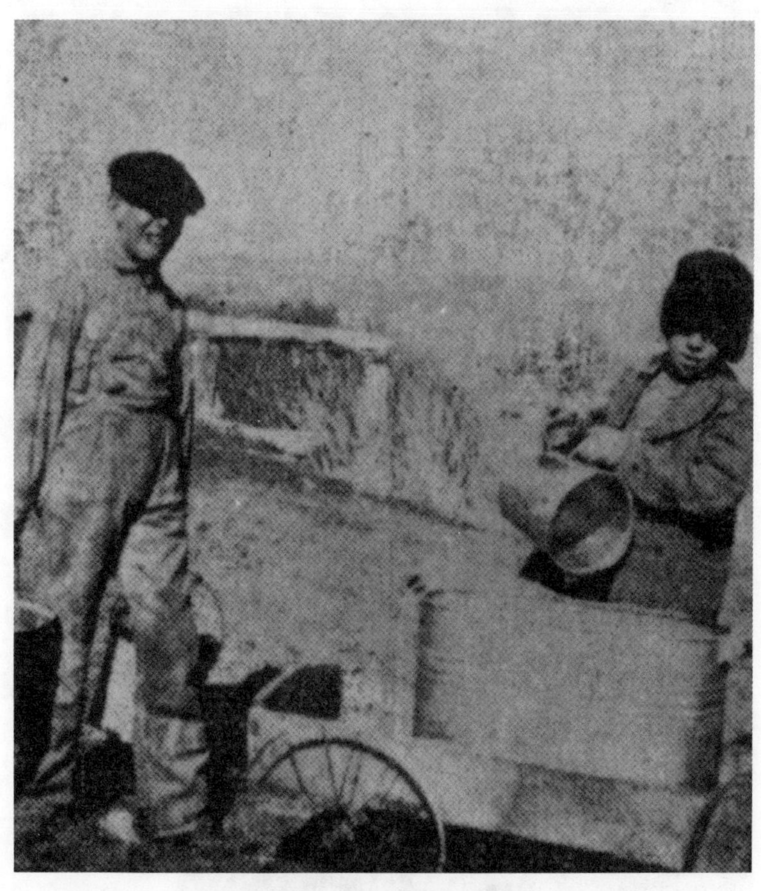

THE MILLER BOYS

Victor (right), Gus (left). They were caught in the whirlpool of circumstances.

(Courtesy Denver Times)

COURT ROOM SCENE
Taken during the trial of Horn.

(Courtesy Leslie Snow Collection)

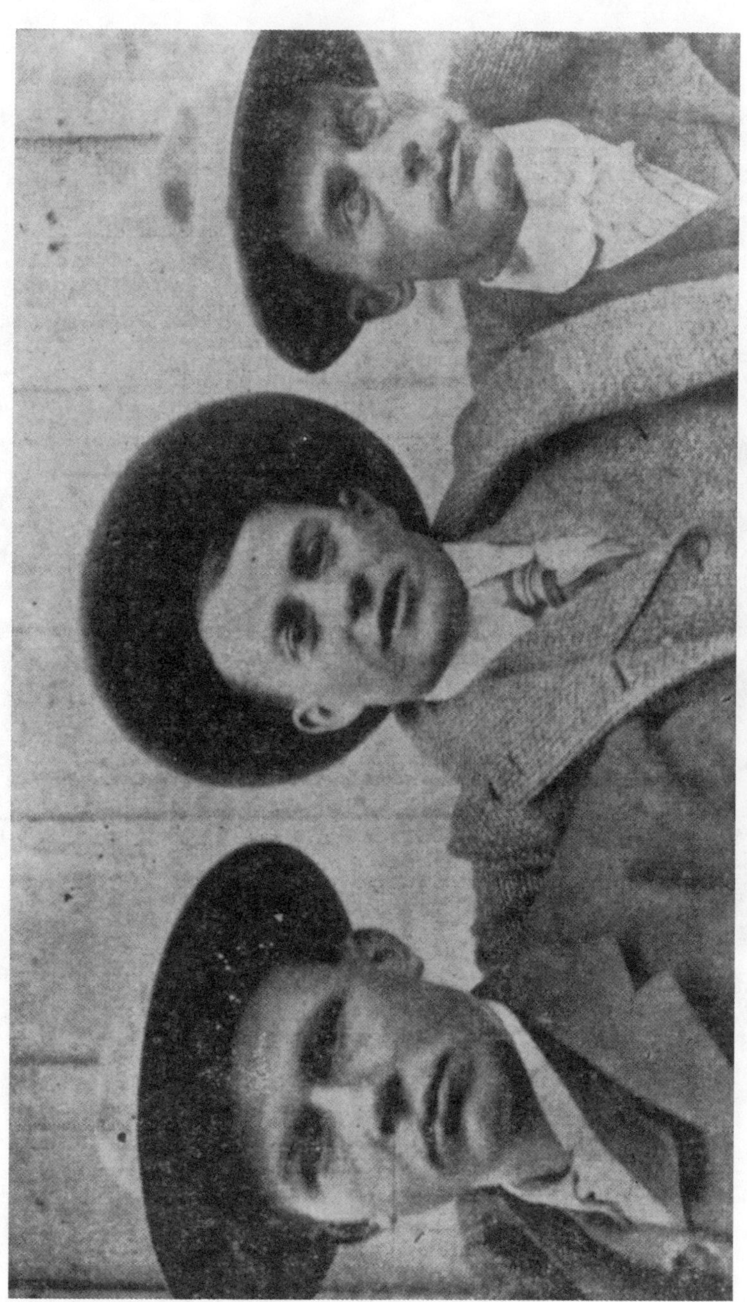

COWBOY WITNESSES FOR TOM HORN

Left to right: H. Waechter, Otto Plaga and O. Colchrist.

(Courtesy Rocky Mountain News)

WITNESSES

Left to rights Dr. G. F. Conway, Dr. George P. Johnston, Captain W. S. Lewis.

(Courtesy Leslie Snow Collection)

CROSS EXAMINATION BY MR. STOLL

Q. You said your business was that of a stock detective. I will ask you to state whether or not, your business as a stock detective as you use that term did not include more than we understand by that term, merely a stock detective?

A. It does. My understanding of the word stock detective, my position includes more.

Q. It included so much did it not that your method detecting the stealing of stock resulted in no necessity for the trials by a jury, witnesses in court, attorney's fees or anything of that kind?

A. Ordinarily not.

Q. In your letter of January 1st, 1902, to Joe LeFors, in which you say "I do not care how big or how bad his men are, I can handle them, they can scarcely be any worse than the Brown's gang, and I stopped the cow stealing there in one summer," does that refer to legitimate work of detecting thieves, or does it refer to the well-known fact that there were two men killed down in Brown's hole while you were there and in this way cow stealing was stopped?

Objection is made to so much of the interrogation as it makes assumption to men being killed.

By the Court—I think that is right Mr. Stoll, I don't think you ought to put that in your question.

Q. What is referred to in this statement that I have just read to you, "They can scarcely be any worse than the Brown Hole gang and I stopped the cow stealing there in one summer"?

A. It would apply the same to any position, but would necessarily need somewhat of an explanation to the first question that you asked me.

Q. But it meant simply legitimate work?
Judge Lacey—Go on.

Q. Finish your answer.

A. You asked me in the first place, if my work was more than that of the ordinary stock detective's work, I said it was the reason I said it was, was this—ordinarily a man out handling stock in all manner of shape and form in connection with their detective work, the ordinary detective as I understand them are men who go around and put up jobs on this man and that man and some other man, and that is something I have never done. I have got out where the stealing was going on and remained continuously in the country where it is a matter of stealing calves, I associate myself so directly with the neighborhood that stealing cannot go on without my being present; if they steal I will catch them in the act of stealing on account of being there consequently if a man is caught stealing he gets out of it the best way he can.

Q. That is what you refer to in this letter to LeFors? "I don't care how big or bad his men are or how many, I can handle them, they can scarcely be worse than the Brown's Hole gang. And I stopped cow stealing there in one summer."

A. It never cut any figure with me wherever my work called me I went.

Q. The work was always of the character you have described, and that is the meaning you endeavored to convey?

A. I think Mr. LeFors understood it that way.

Q. Always finish your answer.

A. Some of those questions in the answering yes or no would reflect considerably on me, where an explanation would give a better understanding.

Q. I am asking you for your explanations of these expressions.

A. I will give it.

Q. You say you associate yourself so closely with the people that no stealing can take place unless you are present at the time?

A. With the people in the country.

Q. When you associate yourself so closely with them that you are present at the time of the stealing, then what is the character of your business—that of filing complaints, reporting the commission of crime, to officials, and having the people tried, or as you say in your letter, avoiding the matter of witness fees—

Objected to because it does not correctly read the letter, does not state the letter, but assumes a thing contrary to what the letter says; The letter says less expense for lawyer fees.

Q. The expression is "You may write Mr. Smith for me that I can handle the work and do it with less expense in the shape of lawyer and witness fees than of any man in the business."

A. I can give you an illustration of what I have done in this country of which you are familiar, that of catching one of the most notorious cow gangs in the country, the Langhoff outfit; there were five of them if I remember distinctly engaged in the killing of cattle, calves, and I caught them directly in the act at 9 o'clock at night and just gathered them in myself and took them off to jail; that was all there was to them; there was no expense to the county or the people that hired me.

Q. That was 10 or 12 years ago in which the Langhoffs were arrested?

A. It was not 12 years or 14 years ago, I was not in the country then.

Q. It was 12 years ago at least was it not, it was in the year 1890 was it not?
A. It scarcely could have been as I was not in the country at that time.
Q. When were you first in the country?
A. I think I came in 1894, if I remember correctly.
Q. You must be mistaken, a few years in the dates, I don't want to get you confused in the matter of dates.
A. I am not going to get confused, but I simply said that you knew of the affair; my supposing you did know of it as every other person in this entire county knows that had knowledge of the Langhoffs; I think everybody knew about them. I did not say you were officially connected with them on this occasion.
Q. In your letter of January the 7th, you say "I will get the men sure, for I have never yet let a cow thief get away from me unless he just jumped up and got clear out of the country." You mean by that that you arrested a man and your business was that of arresting the man who committed a theft?
A. I did not. I meant that no one can remain in the country without my being present on some occasion if I am present I use them as I did the Langhoff outfit, that is all there is to it.
Q. What cow outfits have you arrested since you arrested the Langhoffs if you did arrest the Langhoffs?
A. That broke up the stealing so far as I know of any stealing in the hills.
Q. That Langhoff outfit was in this section of the country? That was considerable time ago?
A. The Sybille country is not the Iron Mountain country.
Q. That is the Sybille country that you referred to in your testimony in chief?
A. Yes sir.
Q. The Langhoff ranch now is occupied by what person, whose name appears on the map?
A. I think Martin lives there.
Q. The name of Martin occupies the place where Langhoff lived at that time?
A. I think he probably does.
Q. Since that time, you have not arrested anyone in that section of the country and brought them to Cheyenne for trial, or preferred any complaints against them?
A. No sir, I have not.
Q. You claim your presence and your business as a detective have broken up or has a tendency to prevent cattle stealing?

A. As it will any gang, anybody that gets in and pays attention to their business. The stock detective that goes out and stays around this stealing, it scarcely occurs. If they know a man is watching them it certainly has a tendency to keep them from stealing. The cow man hires a detective for when a thief steals cattle he never recovers the cow, if he prevents stealing but preserves his cattle.

Q. That is your statement when you say I will get the men I don't care how big they are or how many there are? It is not a question of getting them and arresting them and putting them in the pen; it according to your interpretation the fact of stopping stealing by your presence that is what you mean?

A. Yes sir. In a new country it would be necessary to arrest some of them, don't you understand as soon as they find out you are there all the time watching them the stealing stops itself.

Q. That is what you mean by these expressions in your letters, is it?

A. Yes sir, certainly.

Q. That is what you mean when you say you don't prefer criminal complaints and don't bring the parties guilty for stealing for trial in court?

Objected to as not in the letter and misquoting the letter.

Q. You stated Mr. Horn, at least I understand you to state that your business was not that of preferring complaints, laying complaints before the officers and having the parties committing thefts arrested. Do I understand you to make that statement or not?

A. I have not made any statement of that kind, I don't think, I don't know when I made it.

Q. I thought you stated you hadn't preferred any complaints or had people arrested since the Langhoff's were arrested?

A. I think if you refer to the notes, I said it has not been necessary.

Q. The fact is you have not done that, you have not considered it in your line of business or proper to prefer complaints?

A. That comes back again where I can do my work without any expense. The manner I have taken when I have found people have taken my calves; I have taken them away from them and turned them over to my employers.

Q. When you have found people stealing, you took them away and turned them back to your employers, and not filed any complaints in Court. You have not had them prosecuted; you have not had them tried by juries, is that right?

A. That is right, I would like to tell why.

Q. You have not answered the question, if you want to make further questioned answers, go on and answer them.

A. I want to say this same Langhoff outfit referred to previously were notorious thieves to such an extent—I think they were tried in this Court by change of venue—they had taken or maybe some crime they had committed. But that was the time you referred to in 90 or 91—I went in the country at the time, at least when I came they were notorious thieves. As I said before I caught them at 9 o'clock at night. I think I had all witnesses. I was a deputy sheriff in this county at this time; I took them to Laramie and tried them. I took also 7 head of cattle they had, hired a man to haul them in; had the witnesses there and saw these calves and took note of them previous to the Langhoff's killing them; also recognized the calves after they were killed there that night as being the ones they had taken note of when they were alive. Under conditions of that kind I took the whole outfit to Laramie as it was in Albany County. Eventually they were tried there were 6 in the party, 5 of them were turned loose, one of them was sent to the penitentiary and pardoned out very shortly afterwards; and the boss says to me—

Q. Never mind what the boss said to you. I was asking you for an explanation of your business, you gave your business to the jury and I was asking you to explain it, so that they might fully understand what your business caused you to do.

A. Yes.

Q. And you have written these letters to Mr. LeFors with certain expressions?

A. Yes sir.

Q. And you have stated certain things before the jury, and I was asking you to explain what your business expressed. Now then you have referred to the Langhoff case which occurred some years ago, and told the jury that one of the parties were convicted and the rest were turned loose and at that time you were acting as deputy sheriff—

A. No sir, I didn't say I was acting as deputy sheriff, I am under the impression I was commissioned at that time, held a commission, but that was no instigation of mine as an appointment is not necessary in a case of that kind.

Q. You nevertheless had the commission as deputy sheriff at that time?

A. I believe I did.

Q. I was not asking you about the Langhoff case, but you have referred to it three times. I was asking you about your business since that time? I say that your business was not and has not been since that time that of filing complaints or making complaints or reporting to the officials of the kind of stealing or violation of the laws and thus endeavoring to get a conviction before a jury of the people guilty; but you have held yourself in the community in these localities where these offences were committed and endeavored to break up cattle stealing simply by your presence—is that correct?

A. Not simply by my presence. When I would find a man stealing my calf, I mean the people I represented, I would simply take the calf and such things as that stopped stealing.

Q. Go and take the calf and not have the party arrested, not have the party tried?

A. No sir.

Q. And not submit the matter to the judgment of the courts at all, is that right?

A. My preliminary experience weaned me from that.

Q. Whatever that may have been, I understand that you had not faith in courts or juries, is that right?

A. No sir, I had more faith in getting the calf than in Courts. [Laughter]

Q. And because of that fact, your business has been the carrying on the detection of the cattle stealing in that way and not by any process of law?

A. My business from that time on has been to prevent stealing cattle, not the matter of detecting people stealing cattle; identifying myself with the country as to prevent people from stealing.

Q. Your business was remaining in this locality yourself and by your presence preventing cattle stealing?

A. When they know I am in the country; when cow thieves know I am in the country with nothing else to do, that I go at any time at any hour of night or day, I feel inclined—they realize that any time I might say hello.

Q. That you might come in upon them?

A. Yes sir.

Q. Your presence you consider was necessary to prevent the continuing of this stealing? And that you state to the jury was your business?

A. It was not so much that I considered my presence was necessary as it was that people that employed me considered my presence was necessary more than myself.

Q. I said that was the business you were engaged in?

A. That was the method that I used in my business.

Q. If you came across anyone stealing these calves, if you thought he stole these calves, you would go in and take the calf or calves away and not prosecute him according to law, but simply take the calf away?

A. I don't know anything about this A. and B. business, if I caught a man stealing a calf from my employer, I would take the calf.

Q. That would prevent this man from taking any more calves? That is your coming there and catching him in the act of stealing?

A. It would have a tendency preventing him stealing any more and it would also save the calf in question.

Q. You thought that was the only step that was necessary or at least in carrying out your business, you didn't go any further than that since the Langhoff business?

Q. Now at the time, Mr. Horn, when you came over here to Miller's ranch from Coble's ranch, what was the object of your visit over there, was it to see whether somebody had stolen calves, or was it to ride in among people there and inspire terror by your presence or actions, or what was it, why did you go over to Miller's ranch?

A. I understood that Mr. Nickell had moved a bunch of sheep into that country and I heard rumors of considerable kick and growl in that country. If I was asked to say where they come from I couldn't say. I went in there to see if the sheep had been trespassing on any ground belonging to Mr. Coble; also I took a look at some Two Bar ground. I wanted to satisfy myself about it; I had a previous talk with Nickell and he said he would never bother our property by trespassing on our property.

Q. You were not in the employ of the Two Bar outfit at that time?

A. Just at that time, I don't know whether I was or not. I had been previous to that, perhaps up to that time maybe after that time; as to that time I can't say exactly.

Q. Without endeavoring to mislead you, you stated in your Coroner's inquest testimony that your relations with the Two Bar outfit had ceased on July 1st, 1901?

A. My memory was fresher at that time and the probability is my connection had ceased.

Q. At that time you were not working for the Two Bar outfit?

A. That is not my recollection; if I so stated, in all probability that must have been the case.

Q. Then your object in coming over was to look at the Nickell sheep? And not for the purpose of preventing the small ranchmen in that locality from stealing calves, is that right?

A. That was the extreme end of the country that I usually work, as I was in there working all those pastures, being the time of year when I usually do such work, it occurred to me I would just look; I had previously had a talk with Mr. Nickell and he said he would not bother the Coble pasture; he never did, in the meanwhile it occurred to me to ride through the Colcord place; my business was to throw calves between there and the ranch.

Q. Do I understand from your answer that you came over to look after Nickell's sheep primarily, and if you did anything else that was a secondary consideration?

A. It would scarcely be that, because I put two hours looking after Nickell sheep and the balance of the time, ten days, I put in looking over the pastures.

Q. The object of this trip was generally to look after the matter of stealing calves?

A. Not particularly the stealing of calves, but gathering up calves, if I run across any. The country had been previously been gone over by the roundup, if they had any calves I was to get them out of the road, so that nobody would steal them.

Q. So then, you wish to be understood as saying that it would not be stealing calves if these persons were to gather them in after the roundup had passed?

A. People might put different interpretations on the word, my intention and my action shows that my intentions were in case there was any calves there to get them and take them out and brand them and there would be none to steal. Prevention of stealing has been my business.

Q. You must have had some object in coming over there to Miller's?

A. I did.

Q. I was trying to have you explain what your object was, whether it was to look after Nickell's sheep, or whether it was to prevent the stealing of calves, or detecting the stealing of calves?

A. I can tell the jury exactly what I done and let them draw their own inference.

Q. I am asking you to say what the object of your visit was?

A. The object of my visit—I worked the pastures over to see if there were any calves left by the roundup that had previously been there—When I got over to the extreme end of the range where the Nickell sheep were, I took a look to see if the sheep were trespassing on any of Coble's ground and also that of the land of the Swan Land and Cattle Company. On the return home I continued riding through the pastures.

Q. In this testimony before the Coroner's inquest the question is asked "This Colcord Place is owned by the Two Bar outfit?" And you replied yes sir, then the question when you speak of your employers, you refer to the Two Bar outfit as your employers and you answered they were up to the first of July, I referred to them in that manner?

A. Yes sir.

Q. At that time you were at the Nickell ranch, you were not in the employ of the Two Bar outfit?

A. I was not, but if I found anyone with a calf of theirs I would have taken it away, I felt that way towards them.

Q. You stayed at Miller's Monday, Tuesday, and Tuesday night, and left Wednesday morning at 10 o'clock or about 10 o'clock, is that right?

A. It is right that I came there Monday night and was there most of the day Tuesday and left on Wednesday morning, I can't say it was 10 o'clock, it was close there.

Q. You stated on your direct examination that you stayed at Clay's Sunday night?

A. Yes sir.

Q. Was William Clay one of the men whose actions you had to watch?

A. I never considered that I had to watch him, but I worked his pastures just the same as anybody else.

Q. You made William Clay's your headquarters when you were in that country?

A. That is the place I always stopped when I went through the country in that direction.

Q. You looked over his calves and his cattle and his pastures the same as you did everybody else in the locality?

A. Yes, of which he was always aware; they all looked alike to me.

Q. You looked through his pasture three times before you left that section?

A. I rode through them several times, I don't know how many times.

Q. Did you look over his calves; I understood you to say you did, whether everything was all right there Monday morning?

A. I think you misunderstood, but not on Monday morning. I rode through them at various times, but I never said so before.

Q. If you stated in your direct examination that you rode through his pastures, you do not wish to be understood that you did that for the purpose of seeing whether everything was all right with him?

A. I was not doing it for practice. When I was looking around, it was certainly my business to see that everything was all right.

Q. The fact is you were investigating around William Clay's?

A. The fact is I was investigating everywhere I was.

Q. In your examination as I recall your testimony, you said that you went through his pastures Monday morning?

A. Yes sir.

Q. Then you went through them twice again before you left that section of the country, is that right?

A. Everytime I left I went to the ranch, I certainly went through his pastures as he lives in the middle of them.

Q. If you went through these pastures the other times, did you merely go through them as any traveler? Or were you examining the ground there and his cattle to see if everything was all straight or not?

A. I don't think I made the Clay's examination until after I left Miller's ranch coming home.

Q. So that the time you left Miller's ranch, you had made no examination up Clay's?

A. Not of his cattle in particular.

Q. And you had made no examination of the cattle in going from Laramie City to Bosler ranch, or wherever you went from to William Clay's? So that the objective point of your visit was the Miller ranch?

A. You are saying I did not, I told you before that I did.

Q. I do not wish to be misunderstood Mr. Horn, at all; I do not wish you to misunderstand me; I have been trying to have you explain to the jury why it was you went to Miller's ranch; was your object in going to that section of the Country, visiting Miller's in order to look after Nickell's sheep, or did you have some other object in view?

A. I had no object in going to Miller's ranch; the morning of that day if a man would have asked me where I would stay that night, I would have said in the hills or Billy Clay's again. When I finished it was dark; when I got through looking around that day. And then I still wanted to see about his sheep business and I went to Miller's, as far as what my object was in starting out on an occasion of that kind and going for several days, working in one direction and then turning and working and turning back there is certainly an extreme point that you gain; Miller's ranch was the extreme place; it was the only time that I had ever been to his ranch.

Q. You had seen Miller over at the Coble's the week before you arrived at his ranch?

A. If I had seen him the week before, I don't remember anything about it.

Q. You had seen Miller one time before you came there to his ranch? And that was the week before the Monday when you arrived at his ranch?

A. I saw Miller at one time on the ranch on the Laramie Plains, but I am under the impression it was two or three months before.

Q. So that your recollection is that it was two or three months before?

A. I know it was not a week before.

Q. If he testified on the Coroner's Inquest that it was a week before, according to your recollection, he was mistaken in the matter?

A. I should say so to the extent of 5 or 6 weeks.

Q. At any rate you saw Miller at Coble's ranch, two or three months before and then you saw him at his ranch? And you stayed at his ranch as you have indicated here. Now then you went away from his ranch at 10 o'clock. Where were you all day Wednesday from the time you left Miller's ranch, can you tell the jury by looking at the map, whose calves you were looking after and whose pastures you were in, will you turn around and take the pointer?

A. When I left Miller's ranch, I went up the creek after the sheep.

Q. This is Miller's place and this is Nickell's place. Let me ask you this question first to get it clear—did you examine the pastures of August Waechter, John Allen or of Stevens or of Shaffer, or of Berner, during Wednesday after you left Nickell's ranch?

A. I did not.

Q. Then you did not go into this township west of the township where Nickell's lives at all on Wednesday?

A. Yes, but I went in there after sundown.

Q. But during the day time you did not go in there, is that right?

A. This was Wednesday?

Q. I am speaking of Wednesday the day you left Mr. Miller's.

A. I went in there in the evening.

Q. You went in there in the evening at sundown or after sundown?

A. Yes sir.

Q. Up to that time, you had not been in that township on Wednesday?

A. I was not there on Wednesday.

Q. Now this is correct as to the number of people and the location of these people's ranches, is it not as represented on this map, at least approximately. Here is August Waechter's place; here is Allen's place and here is Berner's place, and those are the only places that are west of the Nickell's in this township, is not that right?

A. I could not say they are the only people that live in there; they all live in that neighborhood, I would not say they live in that township.
Q. You know the people pretty well?
A. The country I know to the finish, but the maps I don't know.
Q. You would say these are the people at least approximately that live in that locality?
A. So far as I know they are the only people that live in that locality, there might be others.
Q. By this map, marked Exhibit No. 4, after you left Miller's house where did you go first?
A. I have told you where I went, I won't attempt to find it out on maps, but I know the country.
Q. Here is the schoolhouse and here is Miller's.
A. From Miller's I went right up the creek.
Q. Which is the creek you refer to, this one that has all the branches?
A. The creek that runs in front of his house.
Q. How far up there did you go?
A. I followed the road for 2 or 3 hundred yards.
Q. Then what did you do?
A. I swung off to the left.
Q. Swung off still further to the left?
A. Yes sir, as I left Miller's place I went up the branch he lives on and went in the direction of the beaver dam and crossed from there to the Colcord place.
Q. I understand the Colcord place is over in this direction, you went in this direction?
A. After I got out on the Divide I went in the direction of the Colcord place.
Q. You didn't go past the school house?
A. No sir.
Q. Did you go north?
A. I went right up the creek to the Miller's and turned out on the Divide to the left and from there through the Colcord place.
Q. That is a place of 160 acres?
A. Not to my knowledge.
Q. It is smaller than that?
A. 80 acres.
Q. Then from there where did you go?
A. From there I went on across into Billy Clay's pasture, coming out of the Colcord place, I would come into Nickell's pasture.

Q. Did you go on any of Nickell's land at all?
A. I do not think I went on any of his land, but I went on land he had fenced, I went through Nickell's pasture.
Q. Did you see Nickell himself that day?
A. I did not.
Q. Did you see Apperson or Mahoney or any of those people?
A. No sir.
Q. The Colcord place joins his place or at least his pasture?
A. Joins his pasture on one side I think, and maybe his regular ranch on the upper side.
Q. What time did you get through in the Colcord pasture, about?
A. Sometime after I left Miller's I don't know what time I left Miller's exactly.
Q. In guessing at it you guess it was before noon do you not?
A. I should say it was shortly before noon.
Q. If the other witnesses that were there fixed it at about 10 o'clock, or between 10 and 11, that was probably the time?
A. I would rather you would question me in regard to myself.
Q. Your recollection is, that it was shortly before noon, you didn't stay to dinner on Wednesday?
A. I didn't have any dinner on Wednesday.
Q. You went as you have stated from Miller's over to the Colcord place? I am trying to see if we can find out what time it was you got through at the Colcord place.
A. The way I went from Miller's over there I should not think it was more than 2 or 3 miles over there, maybe 4, it would not take too long to ride over there; I don't remember having done anything except to ride over there; in my own notion, I didn't ride very fast.
Q. Can you give us an estimate of the time when you left the Colcord place?
A. I can make a guess certainly. I cannot say whether the guess will be correct. I would say if I was making a guess I would make that guess from the time I left Miller's, I think it must have been somewheres near 10 or 11, maybe half past 11.
Q. From the Colcord place you went back to Clay's pasture again?
A. Yes sir.
Q. And Clay's house is in the center of Clay's pasture or inside of the pasture?
A. Yes sir.
Q. You didn't, however, go to Clay's for dinner?
A. No sir.

Q. You looked through Clay's calves and his cattle?
A. I commenced that morning, yes sir.
Q. Right after leaving the Colcord place?
A. Previously to this I had seen some of them and not all of them. I wanted to see all of them.
Q. You finished Clay's place after you left the Colcord place; you remained there how long and finished Clay's pasture?
A. When I got through working around there it was very well along in the evening.
Q. So that you confined your time until evening at Clay's pasture, is that right?
A. I don't remember having been out of there from the time I went in after crossing Clay's pasture. On that morning I don't remember being out of them until pretty late along in the evening. Along in the evening I came down the meadow.
Q. And Clay is one of the ranchmen who has a few head of cattle, a few hundred or something like that?
A. Yes sir.
Q. You did not stay away from his ranch because of the fact that you did not want him to know that you were looking at his cattle?
A. I had no particular object in stopping at his ranch.
Q. The fact is you remained away from his ranch and remained in his pasture looking through his pasture until towards evening. Then do you say that you left that township and went over into the other township?
A. I should judge it was. I remember more distinctly the time I left on account of seeing Johnnie Bray come down the flat. I knew he must have done his day's work before he come down and it was night very shortly afterwards.
Q. It was along towards evening or towards night that you saw Johnnie Bray?
A. Yes sir.
Q. When you saw Johnnie Bray you were still on Clay pasture?
A. Yes sir.
Q. After you saw Johnnie Bray it was you went out of that locality? Did you go in the township which is west of that in which Clay's house, Bray house, Nickell and Miller's house are located?
A. I know every hill and branch in that country, but I don't know any townships, as to townships I can't say anything at all.
Q. Well, you can give us some idea where you went after sundown on Wednesday?

A. Yes, I can tell you where I went, so that you can pick it out on the map if you can pick it out on the map; I can tell you where I went.

Q. I am asking you to state it, Mr. Horn.

A. After I left Billy Clay's, I went on down, I didn't go to John Bray's house; I went slightly to one side of it and I headed off across the country to the upper Sybille country that was the country I was headed into.

Q. Let us get the fact before the jury—all day Wednesday from the time you left Miller's until sundown, you were in the vicinity and in Clay's pasture and close to Bray's place, is that right?

A. That is the way I have got it figured out.

Q. Then after sundown, after you saw Bray, how far did you go before you stopped for the night, or didn't you stop for the night?

A. Not Wednesday or any other time, I never went to any of those ranches in that country to get a meal.

Q. How far did you go after you saw Bray, before you stopped?

A. 3 or 4 miles, I should judge.

Q. Was it west, or northwest, or how was it?

A. It was towards the upper Sybille country, headed up the country. All the water made down the country towards the lower Sybille and I was headed towards the upper Sybille.

Q. You had to cross the lower Sybille before you got to the upper Sybille, did you mean that part of the Sybille that is south or north from the main Sybille?

A. The lower Sybille commenced way down.

Q. I understand this is the main Sybille; Sybille creek, running all along in that direction, now what do you mean by the upper Sybille?

A. I mean the heads of it up in here.

Q. Here is Bray's place and you were somewhere in that locality on Wednesday, you say you went 3 or 4 miles before you stopped for the night; you say you were headed toward the upper Sybille, would that be in this direction or this way? Did you turn around and go in this direction from Bray's place, or did you go this way?

A. What is this country here?

Q. That is apparently a level country on the top of some hills, it looks something like a broad stretch of country according to the map.

A. I think that is the country I come through, I would judge from looking at that map, that this may be the same kind of country; I know the country as it is described; as I understand it myself I come across here, I think that is the way I come as far as I can understand the map. A quarter of a mile or a half a mile above Bray's ranch would throw me into this open country that leads out into a succession of broken country. I would judge that on account of this mountain that comes up here from John Allen's place. If you come across here there is a rough patch of hills in there that I don't have any idea what you call them, anyhow, crossing between the Allen and Waechter ranches, as I crossed that, I crossed in below Waechter's that night. I should judge from that somewhere in there was the route I took; whether that is a correct map of the country, I don't know.

Q. I was asking you to explain where you went after you saw Bray, you stated 3 or 4 miles from there when you stopped for the night.

A. Yes sir.

Q. Did you cross these hills between Allen's place and Waechter's place before you stopped that night?

A. Wednesday night, I camped in this country in here; that is from my understanding of the map. The map does not familiarize the country for me.

Q. What time was it about that you camped there?

A. It was about sundown when I left John Bray's and it was a long time after that, about the same time I come into Miller's ranch.

Q. When you got ready to camp, you camped?

A. Yes sir.

Q. At this time you had simply your vest, you had no coat on, no sweater, no slicker or nothing of that kind, is that right?

A. Certainly.

Q. When you speak of camping, I suppose you mean you built a little fire, or simply sleep out on the ground?

A. I built a little piece of fire, brought a couple of pieces of bacon and slept on the ground.

Q. Where did you get the bacon from, from the ranches or take it from Miller's ranch?

A. I left the bacon there as I was going to the Miller's country.

Q. Where did you leave the bacon?

A. Right there by Bray's. In a place I have always called Mud Springs, I don't see anything on the map that indicates; I had a piece of bread and bacon tied in a tree there, that is what I had to eat that night.

Q. When you went to Clay's ranch, you had previously deposited at Mud Springs a piece of bacon and dry bread?
A. I left it there on Sunday when I went in there; I calculated that Sunday night I would stop at Billy Clay's.
Q. When you went in that country, you did take some provisions with you is that right?
A. I took some provisions as far as I would intersect my trail on my way back.
Q. You took some provisions with you?
A. Some bacon and bread.
Q. Did you deposit all of those provisions which you took there at Mud Springs, or only a part of them; did you deposit other portions of your provisions at other parts of your trail? Or where you thought you might want them?
A. I didn't have enough to divide, there was only just a very little of it. That was the only place I left any on that trip. When I go out, if I start on a trip of 7, 8 or 10 days, it is a very common thing for me to take bread and bacon; if I put in my own mind that I am going back through a certain country and have no grub with me and not need any further on, I wrap it up and tie it in a tree.
Q. On this occasion you took your bacon and light bread, did you get that from Coble's ranch when you started?
A. I had never seen any light bread on Coble's ranch.
Q. You got it in Laramie City?
A. I never had any light bread.
Q. I understood you to say light (or rye) bread, or did you say dry bread?
A. Yes sir.
Q. You took it from Coble's ranch?
A. Yes sir.
Q. Did you deposit anything else at Mud Springs?
A. I think only a little piece of bacon and bread.
Q. Anything in the way of clothing; you mean to say that you went out on that trip unprovided with any thicker clothing, any additional clothing than that you had on at Miller's?
A. I didn't have any more because I didn't need any more; it was the middle of summer.
Q. You didn't have anything to put on in the evening in the shape of a slicker, sweater or a coat?
A. No.
Q. You tell the jury on this occasion you didn't have a coat with you at all?

A. I feel very confident I didn't have; I might be mistaken; in the middle of summer I don't carry anything but a little grub.
Q. You slept on the ground that night in the vicinity of Mud Springs?
A. Yes sir.
Q. Didn't you pass the night in the vicinity of Mud Springs?
A. Yes sir. I passed part of it. When I went by it was not night yet. Mud Springs are not more than a mile or two from Johnnie Bray's ranch.
Q. You got your provisions at Mud Springs, but didn't stay in the vicinity of Mud Springs that night?
A. I think that is what I did exactly.
Q. You camped between Waechter's and a place that you pointed out and not in the vicinity of Mud Springs?
A. I think I camped over there on a little spring that runs in the Sybille.
Q. What time did you make that camp, 10 o'clock about?
A. I rode there directly from Johnnie Bray's; it was sundown when I left Bray's about that time, I was not trying to figure out any time.
Q. What I am trying to get at is a kind of estimate what this time was?
A. I would just have to guess at it; you can guess at it yourself, it was three or four miles.
Q. At any rate you camped out somewhere Wednesday night?
A. Yes sir.
Q. You didn't stay at any of these ranches anywhere in that locality?
A. I did not.
Q. You slept out on the ground?
A. Yes sir.
Q. What covering did you have, anything at all except your saddle blanket?
A. That was all.
Q. What time the next morning did you get up?
A. I don't know. It is a great deal owing to the part of the country a man camps in when he gets up. If you camp up where you don't want to be when morning comes, I usually get up earlier. If I camp in some of the larger pastures where cattle are running, I calculate to put in an hour's sleep after the sun comes up; sleeping with saddle blankets is not very comfortable; on this particular morning I don't remember anything in particular as to the exact time I got up.

Q. Was it sometime early in the morning?
A. I should naturally judge it would be; daylight comes between 3 and 4 o'clock; along about that time, I should judge. I don't have any idea now when daylight comes. If I was making a guess I should say somewhere about 6 or 7 o'clock, and it might have been as late as 8 and perhaps as early as 5.
Q. Did you eat breakfast before you went on?
A. No sir.
Q. The only thing you had to eat after leaving Miller's was the little supper you had at night where you camped?
A. Yes sir; when I built the fire that night, I didn't want to build any fire in the morning so I broiled several pieces of bacon and had them to eat in the morning as I rode along.
Q. Beginning now Thursday morning what pastures did you work Thursday, in other words through whose cattle did you pass and whose cattle did you inspect?
A. Probably the Two Bar's and Coble's I think.
Q. Did you go into any of the pastures of the small ranchmen in that vicinity that day?
A. I was already in the pastures of the small ranchmen.
Q. In camping out that night between Jim Allen's and Gus Waechter's place, you were already in one of those pastures?
A. Yes.
Q. You hadn't worked through those pastures that day because you had got there in the evening and you began working those pastures that morning?
A. I didn't work this country that I come through. I didn't work any that night, as having ridden all of them on my way over.
Q. On your way to Miller's?
A. Yes sir.
Q. You had already gone through these pastures when you went to Miller's?
A. Yes sir.
Q. When you went back Wednesday you didn't go through the pastures for the purpose of working the pastures?
A. I was just crossing through there that night.
Q. Now the next morning, it was Thursday morning, was it then you began to work the pastures for the purpose of inspecting the cattle?
A. Not directly there on that prong of the creek.
Q. So you eliminated the working of the pastures of the Allen's and Waechter's?

A. I had previously gone through all those pastures and satisfied myself about that. I considered on that occasion as I was returning towards home, I considered that was country I had already worked; I had satisfied myself as to the condition of it.

Q. As far as Thursday was concerned you hadn't worked those pastures because you had previously worked them?

A. Yes sir.

Q. In the pastures of Allen and Waechter you had no occasion to stay during Thursday?

A. No sir.

Q. You were ready to pull out Thursday morning 6 o'clock or later?

A. That is a matter of guess.

Q. It was somewhere early in the morning as distinguished from a later hour?

A. Yes.

Q. Then where did you go inasmuch as you had no occasion to work the pastures of Allen and Waechter? If you worked anyone's pastures, whose pastures were they?

A. I rode out into the open country like, the larger pastures, getting out of the smaller pastures.

Q. There was no people had pastures in this locality except Allen and Waechter?

A. Between those two pastures, I don't think any small men had pastures.

Q. You see from the indication of this map, this portion is largely on top of a hill; it is somewhat rolling country?

A. You would find it would be one little canyon after another, but not large or deep; a succession of canyons, that is on top of a hill I think that is a divide.

Q. Where did you go after you got up that morning?

A. I headed right out across there.

Q. In a westerly direction in that way?

A. Yes sir.

Q. You think you were up on the top of these hills going in this direction?

A. I know I went across that country up there.

Q. State whether you went up among the small ranchmen on the Sybille that have pastures?

A. Yes.

Q. It was your object was it not to visit these pastures and to inspect their cattle?

A. Not that far down. I was not that far down on the trip. On that occasion I was not as far down as those ranches. All the time I was holding out towards the head of the creeks head of the Sybille entirely.

Q. So that the object was more to get back to Coble's ranch than to inspect cattle in this section of the country?

A. The object was to look in on this divide here in this direction here; I wanted to find out the condition of the country, I calculated that would be my last trip in there.

Q. The fact is that your object was not to inspect these small ranchmen's pastures along this part of the Sybille?

A. I didn't have an definite object I don't think; I just wanted to cover the country, my object was satisfying myself as to the condition of the country, I had no definite object.

Q. So that when you started for Mr. Coble's or Laramie City or wherever you went and around up at Miller's, you didn't have the definite object of inspecting the cattle?

A. Not any particular route or anything of that kind, not any particular person's cattle, only to do the work as I come to it; whatever indicated that needed to be done.

Q. According to this map, we have Plaga's place, Berner's and Burkhart's, Edward Moore, Mary Moore, George Moore, Martin's place, Tom Moore's, Hencke's place and Rudolph Hencke's place and William Taylor's place; those places along there were entirely eliminated from your examination on this trip?

A. They were further down the country than I went.

Q. They were small ranchmen whose operations came under your general supervision in your business, is that right?

A. More or less I should think.

Q. However, that may be, the fact is you threw them off this trip, and didn't go over on to examine their pastures and their cattle?

A. I did not go over on the Chug.

Q. That was the fact in relation to those people?

A. Yes sir, those people on the Chug Water.

Q. What people do you refer to?

A. Anybody.

Q. The Edward's, Latham's and Matheson's?

A. Yes sir.

Q. You eliminated Wedemier's, Matheson's, Kings, Merrifield's as not much of a place?

A. It is a sheep range.

Q. The King Brother's range?

A. I didn't go there.

Q. And these ranches, Widdowman's, Edward's and Wedemier's, all of those were eliminated from this trip?
A. Yes sir.
Q. You didn't have any object in looking over there?
A. That would have been a different trip from the way the country lay.
Q. You could have gone to this country if you wanted to?
A. Yes sir.
Q. You eliminated this stretch of country from your observation, and this country too?
A. I didn't do anything to them.
Q. You threw them out entirely?
A. No sir, I didn't throw them out, I didn't go there.
Q. What observations were made were right around in this section?
A. I think I was ten days on that trip.
Q. I am simply trying to get the fact before the jury to find out the truth of the matter, what section of the country you were over?
A. I can't tell by the map; there is a thousand gulches that is not indicated on the map.

JUDGE LACEY—I think it is not fair to compel the witness to bring it down to a particular place on the map. If the map was in detail it would be different.

Q. I do not want to be unfair Mr. Horn with you, I must point out these locations. So the fact is Mr. Horn you went from the place where you camped Wednesday night, which place you state to be between Jim Allen's and Gus Waechter's you went over the hill in what you would call a westerly or slightly northwesterly direction, you know those directions?
A. That would be about the country in this place.
Q. Now you didn't examine the pastures of Stevens or of Shaffer's, or of Berner on Thursday, did you?
A. I did not.
Q. You did not examine these pastures on Wednesday?
A. I did not.
Q. So that you didn't examine them on your trip entirely, you didn't examine them at all did you?
A. I am mistaken if I didn't; I certainly went through the pastures in going into the country.
Q. I actually don't want to misunderstand you, I thought you said on Wednesday you didn't examine these pastures at all, do you say that now?
A. Yes sir.

Q. On Thursday you didn't examine these pastures at all, do you say that now?
A. No sir.
Q. But in coming into the country from Coble's, you did ride through them, and give them a general look over?
A. I went down on the Berner place; in coming into the country. I come under the rim rock and down through those pastures in a general way that lays on the Sybille, taking as far down as Jim Allen's.
Q. Now when you came into the country, can you remember so that you can tell the jury the route you took? When you arrived at Clay's house Sunday night, where you started from and how you went?
A. I had left the ranch several days before.
Q. And had been in that country for several days?
A. Yes sir.
Q. And you had gone indiscriminately over portions of it, you had not confined yourself to any trail or wagon road?
A. Oh, no.
Q. Whatever route you took, you say now to the jury you didn't examine Berner's pastures?
A. Yes sir.
Q. Did you examine Stevens' pasture?
A. I did.
Q. That is Dr. Stevens of Laramie City?
A. Yes, I come in on that fork of the Sybille that lays off from Bray's and examined every pasture. That is the reason I didn't look at them that night.
Q. You had examined Stevens' and Shaffer's pastures previous to the Sunday you went to Clay's?
A. Yes sir.
Q. You hadn't examined them Wednesday, but previously?
A. Yes sir.
Q. You started out in a northwesterly direction?
A. Yes sir.
Q. You didn't on Thursday examine any of these pastures here on the Sybille?
A. I didn't get that far down.
Q. Now then what pastures did you examine Thursday?
A. Probably the Two Bar.
Q. Probably the large pasture of the Two Bar?

A. Yes sir, and some outside country belonging to Coble, I think it is a sheep range; it is deeded land, railroad land probably.

Q. All day Thursday, we are to understand you didn't examine the pastures of any of these small ranchmen, but you confined your examination to the Two Bar pasture and to Coble's pasture?

A. I was out of the country where the small pastures were.

Q. You could have run over these ranches if you desired to?

A. Yes.

Q. The fact is you confined your operations to what section?

A. At the head of the Sybille.

Q. You speak of this portion up here around in this vicinity at least that portion of the Sybille that is above these small ranches, whose names I have given?

A. I was not down in the country where the small ranches were.

Q. You were up towards the source of the stream?

A. Yes sir.

Q. Did you examine Fitzmorris's pasture Thursday, he is a small ranchman is he not?

A. Yes sir, I don't think I was in Fitzmorris' pasture then.

Q. You didn't examine Hencke's either Wednesday or Thursday or any of the rest of these?

A. In going through there it is a continuation of pastures, between Berner creek and the Sybille, part of it has been ranged by Dr. Stevens, but it is virtually outside for a big pasture. That is just the same as outside country.

Q. You had nothing to do with Berner's pasture or Stevens' pasture on Thursday?

A. I did not.

Q. I was asking in regard to Hencke's and Fitzmorris's and these other small ranchmen, in there on Wednesday or Thursday, were those pastures examined?

A. I crossed that Berner Creek.

Q. He is way down here is he not?

A. Yes, I crossed below the house.

Q. I was referring to the small ranchmen up here?

A. I was not in that country.

Q. On either of those days?

A. No sir.

Q. Now, Mr. Horn how far had you got by noon, or where were you in the morning? Describe it in words or any other description you can give?

A. I am under the impression by noon I was over in this country somewhere. I can give you a general idea. I should say that I had come across this country here, I know I crossed here below the Berner place. I went in those hills. I expect by noon I was in this country somewhere; just what the exact point was I could not state.
Q. Did you get dinner at any of the ranchmen's places here anywhere in this country?
A. There is no ranchmen, only Fitzmorris.
Q. Here is a number of miners close to this place and here is the Swan Land and Cattle Company's place.
A. I don't know whether it was occupied then or not, there was a miner in there.
Q. There is Dick Latham's place and there are three or four miners in that locality?
A. That is further than I went, the following day I went through that country, I didn't get in there Thursday, I went in there Friday.
Q. Thursday you didn't get anything to eat in any of those places?
A. On Thursday, I came across here in this neighborhood, crossed in below Berner's place and went in this direction as far as I can judge from that map, I am under the impression that when Wednesday night come that I was around in here, somewhere perhaps around in that country there.
Q. About how far had you got Thursday noon?
A. I was up in here probably.
Q. Did you eat dinner there in this rough country, or did you go without your dinner that day?
A. I killed a young jack rabbit and roasted it.
Q. That was for your dinner?
A. I can't say it was noon, I killed the jack rabbit and ate it and called it dinner.
Q. Up to that time you had not shot any jack rabibts on this trip?
A. Not that I remember of.
Q. After dinner you continued your course down until where you say you were Thursday night before?
A. It was not down at all it was up stream.
Q. Thursday night did you eat supper out still in the same way and camp out after supper?
A. Yes.
Q. You didn't go to any ranch?
A. No.

Q. You slept out?
A. Yes sir.
Q. Did you still have some of the bread and bacon you got at Mud Springs?
A. Yes sir.
Q. You didn't shoot any jack rabbit?
A. I don't think I ate any supper.
Q. Thursday you were in this section of the country between the point at which you stopped, between Gus Waechter's and Jim Allen's and a point down here somewhere in the vicinity of where I point, which would be south of the center line of this township 20 and range 72.
A. I was certainly somewheres there.
Q. If you were doing it at all, it was not in looking at these small ranchmen's cattle and pastures, but in looking through the Two Bar and Coble's pastures, is that right?
A. Yes sir, that is right.
Q. You saw no one Thursday at all, so far as you know?
A. I don't remember having seen anyone.
Q. Now, in the matter of speaking of this same subject, on the Coroner's inquest, Mr. Horn, I will ask you to state whether or not on that occasion you did not say that on Wednesday after speaking of leaving Miller's this question was asked and this answer given by you—The rest of Wednesday, you were how far away from Miller's house or Nickell's house the rest of Wednesday, to which you replied, "Perhaps 8 or 9 miles, I was in Hencke's pasture and Jim Allen's." This is the official copy of the testimony, now I will ask you if you recall that question and that answer?
A. I do not exactly recall the question and the answer. I recall very distinctly about where I was, I remember at the wind up of the investigation that your deductions from the investigations left you in no doubt as to where I was, it was very plainly stated, I have also read the report since.
Q. You have read this since?
A. Yes.
Q. Do you recall whether you did or did not give this answer to that question?
A. I don't know, but the probabilities are that I did.
Q. If you so answered at that time, was your recollection as to where you were on that occasion better than it is now?
A. My recollection then is the same as it is now.

Q. Now in regard to where you were Thursday, on the Coroner's inquest do you remember this question being asked you—"Thursday, how far were you all day from Nickell's place," to which you answered, "I do not suppose all day Thursday at any time I was as much as a dozen miles from there. I don't think at any time I went up the divide. I think I was most of the day within 7 or 8 miles."—do you recall that?

A. I recall very distinctly having described the country I was in, and you asked me about the distance, I didn't know what the distance was and I don't know what it is now. I told you the exact country I was in. Then there is also quite a lot to me what is confusion in that report, but at the same time I say that there was no misunderstanding between you and me as to my whereabouts as on the 13th page where you were making a final deduction and summing up as to exactly where I was, it was settled definitely as to where I was, that will show very clearly and distinctly. There was no misunderstanding about it at that time.

Q. Is there any misunderstanding now?

A. All through that report, or in several places there has been days that were called Tuesday that should have been Wednesday or Thursday or something of that kind and it is mixed up to some extent. As I say there was not apparently any misunderstanding at all, for the simple fact that on the 13th page you will find that the deductions were finally made by yourself as drawn from the statement I give you and will show that I said on that examination that I was exactly where I told you I had been now, and that the distances are approximated or something, I don't know what, 7 or 10 miles.

Q. In regard to this matter let me read you a little more at this inquest—there was no map of this character?

A. There was a map that I knew just about as much as I do with this one, there was some kind of a map.

Q. You were on this divide on Thursday to which you replied—not until Thursday evening, that is the way it appears in the report, what divide do you refer to?

A. I think it says the divide between the Chugwater and the Sybille.

Q. Can you point out that divide on the map?

A. I don't think it shows there.

Q. Speaking of your testimony before the Coroner's inquest, when you gave your testimony at that time, you had as full a knowledge of the circumstances as you have now, or have you refreshed your recollection as to those circumstances?

A. I have refreshed my memory as to those circumstances, because at the time I was called in here, I just come in from work and I didn't have any time to figure out to a certainty where I was. Since that I have had time to study out in my own mind where I was exactly.

Q. You have a copy of this official report and have pursued it a good deal, studied it over?

A. Certainly, yes sir.

Q. So that you can speak more clearly as to where you were than at that time?

A. I certainly can, because I have had several things to refresh my memory. The simple fact of your questioning me so closely; the fact of having been arrested for this murder; the fact that I was associated with it in the minds of some people at least before I was arrested has certainly had a tendency to refresh my mind on the subject.

Q. Your recollection is that you were not in Hencke's pasture on Wednesday or you did not go into any of those small pastures on the Sybille?

A. Perhaps I went through Allen's and Waechter's pastures. As I went through naturally some of those pastures at that time; I told you what I told you now as to my route and I say there is some little misstatements in the final wind up of the examination it is clearly defined and clearly put by you and taken down by the stenographer as to my exact whereabouts as I say.

Q. That is as you described it in your own language without pointing it out on any map?

A. I really didn't have any idea what you were going to ask on that occasion as you asked a question here and there. I was beginning to place myself and to know and remember where I was; and I really didn't know when I came in the Courthouse until after I had talked the matter over with you in the court and I defined my route as I have stated all the way through.

Q. This is your statement after having refreshed your recollection, aided by the copy you have been pursuing since your arrest?

A. Aided principally by the examination in person before the Coroner's Jury something like a month I presume after I made the trip or perhaps less, maybe twenty days.

Q. You slept that Thursday night the same as you did Wednesday?

A. Yes sir.

Q. Your statement is that you didn't have anything to eat Thursday night for supper. Now Friday what time did you get up and continue your journey?

A. On Friday morning I don't know exactly as to the time; but I can draw a closer guess as to the time from the nature of the country where I was at; in the country where there was no one where scattering cattle would naturally be rough country, and being no one around and no particular occasion to hurry I would not shove out as soon as I would as if I was down in the pastures of Allen and Waechter. I think I would naturally move out of there sooner than I did before. I have no definite idea as to times I was at any particular place, that I started anywhere or arrived anywhere.

Q. You have a sufficient recollection of the facts to give us a kind of approximate idea when you started out Friday morning?

A. I will say somewhere in the neighborhood of seven o'clock; it might have been six or half past five.

Q. Did you eat your breakfast before starting out?

A. Yes sir.

Q. Did you have any fresh game or still have a piece of bacon?

A. I still had a piece of bacon.

Q. Describe where you went Friday?

A. I turned back down by the Fitzmorris place Friday, from the Fitzmorris place out across towards where those mines are. The Fitzmorris place don't look exactly right to me but I guess it is right. I can't tell much or exact from the map.

Q. You are a pretty good judge of that country, as good an authority on it as anybody?

A. Yes, day or night.

Q. You have been called a traveller and know a good deal about maps as a matter of fact?

A. I know all about maps when they are clearly defined and every gulch in the country is taken in a topographical way. Where you give the main creeks and there are a thousand and one gulches between—look at that Wedemier country. All the country is like that. If the smaller ones were defined like the larger ones you could define it. You can't tell by this map about that. To me as far as I know maps there is nothing defined than the main lines; they are designed principally to be in fact smaller creeks.

Q. Of course we have to make these maps on a small scale; the whole world is sometimes made on a few inches of paper. You get some idea of the general features of the country?

A. Yes sir.

Q. And sufficiently to talk intelligently to the jury?

A. Here is the Two Bar fence running along there that I have not noticed before. I know very well on that Thursday I don't remember of having crossed above that fence.
Q. That is you hadn't got to this way from the fence?
A. I don't remember of having got over it although I said in my report I was out on the divide. I didn't say about going through that fence. It didn't occur to me that I did; that is the first time I located that fence; I can locate that country better than by the roads say where it crosses Berner Creek.
Q. So that when you look at the map you find that there are little streams and fences sufficiently accurate to help some anyway to locate places?
A. I can judge more accurately from that Two Bar fence than anything else on the map.
Q. Before you saw the Two Bar fence you pointed out this part of the country where you were Thursday night?
A. Yes sir.
Q. I am asking Thursday where you went from that point?
A. I went down the ridge here and down into the Fitzmorris country.
Q. Around Fitzmorris' ranch?
A. Yes sir.
Q. Thursday you had not been at Fitzmorris' ranch as you pointed it out before?
A. I come down within two or three miles, but on Friday I was down on the creek.
Q. In passing along Thursday you were riding over the country without regard to trails, roads or paths, or anything of that kind, just looking through the pastures I understand?
A. That is all, on pasture.
Q. You had no object in following any particular trail?
A. There is not any particular trail running through the country unless you want to take the trail down the creek. You always find a trail going in the direction you don't want to go; they are principally trails made by stock; I don't know of any wagon or horse trails in the country.
Q. Now, where were you all day Friday?
A. I was around the principal part of the day around Fitzmorris' ranch.
Q. When you say the principal part of the day what do you mean?
A. I camped several miles off from there the night before and I rode down there sometime in the middle of the forenoon. I stayed around there until the middle of the afternoon and maybe a little

before the middle of the afternoon, and then I went on out towards the Blue Grass country.
Q. What did you do in the vicinity of the Fitzmorris' place Friday until the time you left did you go in his pasture and examine his cattle or didn't you?
A. I did not go into the pasture and examine his cattle.
Q. Did you examine anybody else's pasture in that locality?
A. It is all Two Bar pasture there.
Q. The Two Bar pasture is in that vicinity outside of that fence you pointed out?
A. That is all Two Bar pasture; Fitzmorris lives in the Two Bar pasture.
Q. On both sides of that fence?
A. Probably on the upper side.
Q. So that when you examined the Two Bar pasture you were examining it in the vicinity of the Fitzmorris place?
A. Yes sir.
Q. You were not examining Fitzmorris' pasture or Fitzmorris' cattle?
A. Fitzmorris has no cattle; he keeps cattle in summer time; they are run out with the Two Bar cattle.
Q. So that his cattle are mixed up with the Two Bar cattle?
A. Yes, so many of the small ranchmen are.
Q. The Two Bar and Fitzmorris were running together in the vicinity of his ranch?
A. Yes, and a great many Coble cattle also.
Q. You were up in the morning looking around this pasture of the Fitzmorris place?
A. You talk as if you could see the edge of the pasture; that Two Bar pasture is a day's ride; what is called Two Bar pasture is perhaps twenty miles wide and maybe fifty or sixty miles long; there are dozens of little ranches inside of this pasture. In place of calling it a pasture speaking of it in a general way you would consider it outside as it has been only a year or two that it has been fenced.
Q. I think I understand that you have referred to closed pastures and all of these other pastures?
A. That gets back into a district where it is all small ranchmen.
Q. You say Friday you were around the Fitzmorris place. I ask you if you examined Fitzmorris cattle on his pasture?
A. On Friday I was around Fitzmorris' place. Information came to me that Fitzmorris had been dogging all the cattle that came

in through there to water, or drifted in that direction; and it occurred to me to take a look at it as I went through which I did and didn't see anything of the kind.

Q. So that you were all day Friday until the middle of the afternoon between the place you camped Thursday night and Fitzmorris' house in that section of the country?

A. I was in that section of the country. I was on various sides of the Fitzmorris house in that country.

Q. Where did you go after the middle of the afternoon of Friday?

A. I struck off up the divide and headed in what we call Blue Grass country.

Q. Did you eat your dinner at noon, or did you have dinner on Friday?

A. I don't remember of having eaten anything at noon at all. No, when I got away up the gulch there, I should judge quite a spell after the middle of the afternoon, after I left Fitzmorris', you understand, I run across a nice comfortable place in the canyon. I roasted and ate the rest of the grub I had there.

Q. That was in the afternoon after you left the Fitzmorris place?

A. Yes, along towards evening.

Q. Along about sundown?

A. I should say an hour or two?

Q. Where were you at sundown that day?

A. I was up in the Blue Grass country.

Q. Where is this Blue Grass country, how far from the Fitzmorris place, and in what direction from the Fitzmorris place?

A. It must be over in here.

Q. Off up in this direction. Going up some of these streams is called Blue Grass, or what do you mean by Blue Grass?

A. I am under the impression that it heads up in here, the stream.

Q. How far from the Fitzmorris place?

A. I should say five or six miles.

Q. In a northerly direction or northwesterly direction?

A. From the way those gulches lay, from the way this main gulch lays it lays up in there. I should say it was across in here somewhere. I should say from its location it is that gulch going in there from Fitzmorris'. I went out this way because I remember it was very close to that place where I ate my lunch. I know that gulch on the map on account of its coming in below Fitzmorris'. It's coming in here would make it where I camped in this direction here.

Q. After having eaten your piece of bacon did you remain there, did you camp there that night?
A. No sir, I went on several miles after that; that was along there; it was a couple of hours before sundown when I went there.
Q. In what direction did you continue to go?
A. Right up the divide.
Q. Up towards Coble's Bosler ranch?
A. That would throw me out on the edge of the Plains like; so that you could go in any direction you wanted to, to Coble's ranch; you would head in the direction of Coble's. It is all good travelling after you get up on this divide after you get out there you begin to run in on the edge of the plains; that lets you out of this rough country in here.
Q. When you get out of this part that is indicated by these little ink marks on the map, would you strike the Laramie Plains?
A. You notice they come in there; I think that was the country I come into.
Q. It is your recollection that you were somewhere in this country where you camped Friday night?
A. That is like the map I know; I know that hill; I would say that I slept that night on this mesa here. I can tell this map because there is section lines; I came off of this round mesa there.
Q. This point is Coble's ranch here?
A. Yes sir.
Q. You slept about here on this mesa at night?
A. Yes.
Q. You had eaten the last of your bacon; you had not obtained any clothing from the time you left Miller's up until Friday?
A. I did not have any Friday night either.
Q. What did you do Friday afternoon between the time you left Fitzmorris' place in the middle of the afternoon until you camped out at night?
A. I just crossed over in there.
Q. Did you examine any pastures there then; was there any pastures to examine?
A. I was in a pasture all the time continuously from the time I left Fitzmorris' until I got down to this point here. All the time I was up in there I was in this Two Bar pasture.
Q. Friday night you slept—you had eaten the last of your bacon along in the middle of the afternoon, did you eat anything more Friday?
A. I didn't have anything more to eat Friday.

Q. You slept out Friday night; on Saturday morning what time did you get up?
A. I think I got up rather early Saturday morning along after sun-up; I got up at daylight. When you sleep out in the night, even in the summer it is moderately cool. There is not any place where you can camp and stake a horse and find sufficient grass to last him the entire night; so that it comes very handy if you have a saddle blanket; you let your horse go; that is the way I worked on this occasion.
Q. You did not impede your movements in carrying anything with you in the shape of an extra blanket, or a coat, or anything to put on you?
Q. You simply used your saddle blanket as I understand you?
A. Yes sir.
Q. What did you do Saturday morning after you got up? Did you attempt to make breakfast out there or did you ride immediately into Coble's ranch?
A. I went right straight into the ranch.
Q. As soon as you could saddle your horse you went into the ranch?
A. Yes sir.
Q. How long did you take to get into the ranch, how many miles did you have to go, not over 12 or 15? Nor as much as that would be?
A. I expect by that map twelve or thirteen miles.
Q. You rode in there on the same horse?
A. Yes sir.
Q. You didn't have anything to eat until you got into the ranch?
A. No sir.
Q. You did not get anything to eat until you got in the ranch at noon?
A. That was not long.
Q. It was the time they had a noon meal?
A. I suppose so.
Q. In the meantime you changed your clothes?
A. I changed horse and I changed clothes; I wrote some letters, I sent off a telegram and attended to a little business I had to, done several things. Went out in the pasture and got a horse also.
Q. But your object was to go to Laramie City, and to change the clothes you had on this trip having been sleeping out around as you had they had gotten more or less dirty? It was the latter part of the week and you thought you would go to Laramie City and wanted a change of apparel, is that right?

A. I change clothes sometimes anyhow. [Laughter.]
Q. You did it on this occasion?
A. Yes sir, I did it on this occasion. [More laughter.]
Q. You left your rifle and your field glasses there at the ranch, at Coble's ranch?
A. I did.
Q. On this trip all the way along you had your rifle and your field glasses?
A. Yes sir.
Q. Your rifle was the 30-30 Winchester soft nosed bullet?
A. Yes sir.
Q. You had the field glasses?
A. Yes.
Q. Did you have a six-shooter?
A. I didn't take a six-shooter with me.
Q. Nothing tied on your saddle?
A. Nothing that I remember of except a little grub when I left the ranch.
Q. What time did you leave Coble's ranch to go to Laramie City?
A. I got my dinner first, right after dinner.
Q. So that you got into Laramie City at what time?
A. I got there as soon as I could ride there. I went along a pretty good gait into town. It occurs to me it's somewhere near twenty miles, I believe; just exactly twenty miles, maybe twenty-two. I was riding Coble's bay horse, he was pretty fast and I let him go; the road is pretty level there.
Q. In going down did you meet anybody on the road from Coble's ranch that Saturday?
A. I don't remember having met anyone.
Q. During your whole trip in going from Miller's back to Coble's ranch that time you hadn't seen anyone except Bray?
A. I saw a man working in the field, and also working on the wire fence at Fitzmorris'.
Q. Outside of seeing somebody working at Fitzmorris' place, working about the ranch, you saw no one except Bray?
A. I don't remember of having seen anyone.
Q. On your trip from Coble's ranch to Laramie City you didn't see anyone?
A. I don't remember of having seen anyone.
Q. You are sure this was Saturday; you haven't any question about the day of the week being Saturday?

A. I know to a certainty it was Saturday.
Q. You know to a certainty you did not go into Laramie either on the 18th or 19th?
A. From the evidence produced here it would be evident if I would have went into Laramie it would be for the purpose of proving an alibi. Certainly would have proved it to a certainty. I was not there until Saturday evening.
Q. That is an inference of yours from this testimony. As to your recollection and statement of the fact you have to say that you were not in there on the 18th, and you were not in there on the 19th?
A. And I was not there until the afternoon of Saturday.
Q. On this Saturday did you meet Mr. Irwin when you went in? If you had met Mr. Irwin on Saturday you would have remembered that fact?
A. I would.
Q. You know as a matter of fact that you did not meet Mr. Irwin on Saturday, on Friday or on Thursday?
A. I don't think I met Irwin at all.
Q. You will say that on the 18th and 19th, or even Saturday the the 20th, you were not on this road anywhere, or any of these cross roads leading down into Laramie City as described by Mr. Irwin?
A. I will say to a certainty that I followed this main road here. There is exactly the road I come out going to Laramie, consequently I would not have been in that country at all.
Q. You say now to this jury you did not go there?
A. I do.
Q. And that you didn't see Irwin?
A. He didn't see me anywhere except on that main road.
Q. That you didn't have tied on back of your saddle wither on any of these days, Friday, Saturday, or Thursday any bundle or clothing of that kind?
A. I don't remember to a certainty; I didn't have a sweater.
Q. You say that you didn't have a dark sweater on the 16th of June tied on your saddle?
A. I will say that I didn't have a dark sweater on the back of my saddle; I never owned one or had one.
Q. You heard the testimony of Lyman Murdock on that subject and you say that he was mistaken as to the sweater?
A. I understood him to testify that he thought I might have had a sweater. The only sweater I had at that time—I remember very distinctly having met him on this divide on the occasion he re-

ferred to but I didn't have any sweater at all at that time. In fact the only one I have had for three or four years I remember is a yellow buckskin tan colored kind of sweater, and I have not worn that; Duncan Clark has worn it all the time.

Q. Did you have on your straw hat in riding from Coble's ranch down to Laramie City on July 20th, or do you remember how you were dressed?

A. I don't remember.

Q. You do remember distinctly that you did not see anyone on the way down?

A. I don't remember distinctly that I didn't see anyone; I don't remember of seeing anyone.

Q. Do you remember of meeting Mr. Titus in Laramie at any time previous to the 21st of July?

A. As regards that occasion I don't remember having met Mr. Titus any particular time although he lives very close to town and I usually see him every time I go into town.

Q. You stated to the jury you did not see him there on the 19th?

A. I certainly did not on the 19th as I was not there.

Q. You went to Denver on the 28th of September to attend the festivities of the Mountain and Plain Festival?

A. I left Friday at noon. I can refer to the calendar and tell. I left on Saturday I believe to the best of my recollection. I cannot be absolutely certain, but I think it was Saturday, October 26th.

Q. You mean September?

A. Undoubtedly I left here on Saturday, September 28th.

Q. At Laramie either on the 18th, 19th or 20th did you leave a bundle of any kind in the shoe shop where George Powell and Matlock were?

A. I could not have done that because I was never in the shoe shop. The only shoe shop I was ever in was Mr. Pete Rauner's. I would not go to a stranger because I know many merchants there.

Q. You left no bundle and had no conversation such as testified by them?

A. The only time I remember ever having seen them was when they were on the stand.

Q. On September 28th, you left Cheyenne for Denver and were there to take in the festivities of the carnival—is not that correct?

A. Yes sir, I think I must have left Saturday the 28th. I know it was Sunday morning I got into Denver about sun-up, at the Denver stockyards.

Q. Is it a fact that you met these three gentlemen that testified here as to conversations they had with you, or which you had in their presence in the Scandanavian Hotel or house or saloon?
A. It is a fact that I never met, or spoke or saw them, or heard of them, I heard of them through information. The papers, the witness papers that I had a copy of is the only way I had any idea; it is the only intimation that I had they were in existence. As far as seeing them or speaking to them I never saw or spoke to them, not any occasion in the world.
Q. You say that you didn't speak to them at any time on this trip?
A. I did not.
Q. You say that you did not say to Mr. Mullock any of those things he has testified to?
A. I say I never met him or spoke to him about anything. I never knew him.
Q. You never said any of those things testified to by Mr. Cousley?
A. I did not.
Q. You never said any of those things testified to by Mr. Campbell?
A. I did not.
Q. Do you say that you did not say; or do you say you do not remember saying; which way do you wish to say it to these gentlemen?
A. I wish to say to the jury that at the time those gentlemen say I spoke to them I was laid up in the doctor's care, and my head was in plaster paris. The only way I had was to write. I couldn't answer the doctor. I had to write; he bound up my head and said, "Don't attempt to talk any more."
Q. Throwing aside anything as to when it was, state to the jury what the fact is; did you have any conversation with them at all at any time whatever?
A. I had no conversation with them at any time in the world.
Q. That is the way you wish to be understood?
A. That is the way.
Q. You do not wish to say you might have had a conversation of that character, but you were in such a condition you do not recall what it was?
A. I wish to say that I never saw, or spoke or heard of them until they took the witness stand.
Q. Now, it was a fact, was it not, you were hurt shortly afterwards in Denver?
A. On late Sunday night or Monday morning.
Q. That is a fact you were hurt?

A. Yes sir, it is.

Q. At that time, I am not asking to reflect on you in anyway, were you in a condition to remember whether you had these conversations with these men or not?

A. I remember everything that occurred to me in my life.

Q. You have never been so much under the influence of liquor as to not remember what you said?

A. Not if I could talk.

Q. So that you have a clear recollection of things that have occurred to you?

A. On this particular occasion I have a very distinct recollection; I have cause to have a very distinct recollection.

Q. They testified as to your saying you were the best shot in Wyoming?

A. Yes sir.

Q. Now, you got into trouble on account of saying something similar to that telling what a good shot you were?

A. I am under the impression that I got into trouble because a man called me a liar.

Q. You got into trouble at any rate during this week; and up to the time you got into trouble you say that you hadn't seen these people and talked in anyway; and you say because you remember you did not talk to them, and not because you say you may have talked to them and been in a condition not to remember?

A. I do not wish to be understood as saying anything of the kind I was not in a condition on that occasion that I would not have remembered any occurrence of that kind. More than that from other details of the statement the man Mullock made on the stand everything indicates that I could not have possibly had anything to do with him, neither did this alleged conversation take place.

Q. You were hurt in Pennington's saloon? Not many blocks from the Scandanavian house?

A. It was not near there.

Q. In your conversation with Mr. LeFors, at the time of his confession you had the utmost confidence in Mr. LeFors?

A. I had no particular occasion to have any more confidence in him than anybody else.

Q. You had sent him a telegram on January 11th that you would be down that night?

A. I presume it was January 11th, to the best of my knowledge, although I would not be exactly certain as to that, but I think that is the date.

Q. At the time you sent the telegram you were fully cognizant of the fact that you had been asked for in Montana, and you were on your way to so accept the job?
A. Yes sir.
Q. And you were going to have an interview with Mr. LeFors concerning that job?
A. Yes sir.
Q. And that is how you sent him the telegram, and you inquired for him in town before you finally found him?
A. I might have asked somebody if he had been around.
Q. You came across him ten or eleven o'clock that morning of Sunday?
A. I should say somewhere from nine to eleven o'clock, or it may have been eight or half past eight, somewheres along there; somewhere in the morning anyhow.
Q. This was a bona-fide job and the people were bona-fide people?
A. I think as far as I knew it was.
Q. When you went up to Mr. LeFors your object was in talking with him about these people was it not to ascertain the kind of people you were going to work for?
A. There were several reasons, that was one of them.
Q. In that conversation did you say, I don't want to be making reports to anybody at any time; I will have only one report to make and that will be at the finish; if a man is compelled to make reports all the time, they would catch the wisest son-of-a-bitch in the world?
A. Don't give me too much at a time, I think I made that remark; of course, I don't know as that is the exact language and those oaths being used; but in all probability I used them, as I am given in a natural way to profanity; I would naturally suppose I did while I don't remember the exact words that occurred during that conversation; but I would naturally use words anyhow to that effect, for the simple reason that when you go into a country where you are a stranger you want to get everything behind you. I am giving only my idea, because if you have to go out and write letters to this boss or that boss, when you are on a mission of that kind, if you are in a neighborhood they will about locate you.
Q. You will admit using that language at that time?
A. If I did not use that I used something very similar to it.
Q. Either that language or the substance of it?
A. Yes sir.

Q. Did you say in the same connection "if a fellow goes to shooting they won't get scared?"
A. I said that every time you go in a country.
Q. The question is did you use that language at that time to Mr. LeFors?
A. I did. I would like also to explain that.
Q. Certainly, and answer my question first, and then explain.
A. To the best of my knowledge and belief I used that language, I naturally would.
Q. You do not claim that you were so intoxicated that you did not know what you said?
A. I know to a certainty I know what I was saying. I had not been to bed the night before; I had been up visiting, drinking, having a good time; I knew perfectly well what I was saying.
Q. You used this language what I am saying or the substance of it?
A. I used that language or the substance of it.
Q. When Joe LeFors said, "No, they are not afraid of shooting," did you say, "That is right, I don't want them to get scared if I go to shooting; I want to make those people know I am all right, I will protect the people I am working for; when it comes to shooting you know me." You used that language?
A. I think I used that language or very nearly so.
Q. You knew what it was at the time, no question about that?
A. I did. I would like to explain in connection with that. Every time that LeFors and myself have ever met, the conversation has generally been about shooting someone or killing someone. As a matter of fact I do not remember to have talked with Mr. LeFors about anything else more than somebody he had killed, or somebody I had killed. I think we were telling one another such stories at nearly every occasion we had met previous to this time.
Q. He had your complete confidence in all matters of that kind; you did not mistrust or distrust him in any way; you thought he was entitled to your confidence?
A. I had no occasion to mistrust or distrust him; he is like anybody else to me.
Q. You did talk to him about shooting?
A. I don't remember of having talked to him about anything else, only this particular occasion about going to Montana.
Q. Did you talk with him previous to that on August 14th, previous to Frontier Days?

A. At the time I was examined here before the Coroner's jury, or inquest, whatever it was, I talked to him either that night or the following night. I also talked to him one night during Frontier time, and another time between Christmas and New Year's last, as I remember. Those are the three occasions I remember. I would remember any others that would be called to my attention.

Q. You told him on those occasions of your own accord of your shooting?

A. Perhaps so, I think so.

Q. In his conversation following the same answer, did you say at that time, "I give protection to the people I am working for, but I know I shoot too God damned much"?

A. I don't think it occurred in exactly that manner. I always consider I have to protect the people I am working for, and the protection comes in this manner. If you allow anyone to steal your calf and they get away with your calf, and you have them arrested and prosecuted, they are turned loose. You are at the expense of the prosecution and the man goes loose just the same; there is a very little satisfaction to the man that has to protect his stock.

Q. I will ask you to state to the jury whether or not that was said or the substance of it was said by you at the time?

A. If the words were not exactly said the substance of that would have been said. When I start to work for a man I certainly work to this best interest in any manner that I think will benefit him.

Q. In the same answer further on did you say, "I have never got my employers in trouble yet over anything I have done; a man cannot be too careful because you don't want no God damned officer to know what you are doing"?

A. I did, I said that for the simple reason that a man, more especially a man like myself has to be very careful, or the numerous reports that are following a man with the reputation I have gained —I don't know why, but the reputation I have I know it necessitates my being extremely careful all the time; and I am naturally careful to protect the interests of the people I work for.

Q. You said it at that time and you said it for a reason?

A. Yes sir.

Q. In that conversation did LeFors say at the time, "I know you are the best man to cover up your trail I ever saw; in the Willie Nickell killing I could never find your trail, and I pride myself on being a trailer"?

A. That is where the orange blossoms come; he commenced to throw boquets at me; and I naturally returned the compliment; I commenced to rig myself up.

Q. Now, you say the orange blossoms commenced to bloom?
A. Yes, I noticed the first boquet was tossed there.
Q. When he said in the Willie Nickell case I could never find your trail and I pride myself on being a trailer, you considered that a compliment?
A. That Willie Nickell conversation emanated from a previous conversation I had with Mr. LeFors regarding this Iron Mountain trouble in June.
Q. In the previous conversation you had with him about the Iron Mountain trouble you told him you were the man that shot five times at Kels Nickell?
A. I told him decidedly that I didn't see why anyone should connect me with the killing of Willie Nickell, when to a certainty after the officers had made an investigation, they found I was not there; and they also investigated in connection with the shooting of Kels Nickell, and I was a hundred miles from there at that time, and had not been in the country for two or three weeks, that is what I told him.
Q. Did you not in Hynd's saloon on August 14th, say, that you were the man that shot Kels Nickell, shot at him five times, and explain to him in that conversation why your shots went wide of the mark?
A. I had a conversation with him regarding that, not in Hynd's saloon I think it was down in Tom Heaney's saloon. We were down there talking for two or three hours that night and Joe LeFors says, "Tom, if you will throw in with me we can cinch that damned outfit out there." That is about the substance of the statement he made to me on that occasion.
Q. Do you say that you did not in Heaney's saloon, or in Hynd's saloon, on August 14th, tell Joe LeFors voluntarily, that you shot at Kels Nickell five times?

Judge Lacey: I object to these questions. What are we trying here. The witness has answered two or three times and stated where he was, but regardless of that are we trying the defendant for an assault and an attempt to commit murder on Kels Nickell. There is no doubt we can show where we were when that case comes up; we object to the interrogation of the witness in this matter.

Mr. Stoll: The witness himself volunteers the information that he talked to LeFors about this matter, and he tells himself what the matter was.

Judge Lacey: We object to mixing all this up.

Mr. Horn: I would like to answer that.

By the Court: Pass on with your examination, I will consider the matter.

Q. (By Mr. Stoll) In this conversation in the Marshal's office with LeFors in reply to what LeFors said, did you say, "No, by God I left no trail, the only way to cover up your trail is to go barefooted." The question is did you say that or that in substance?

A. I think I said that, or that in substance.

Q. You knew at the time you said it what you said perfectly well?

A. I did for the simple reason that I was not there, and I could not have left a trail.

Q. You state to the jury that you were not there at the time of the killing?

A. I was not.

Q. Notwithstanding that fact you did use this language to Mr. LeFors?

A. Yes sir, I would have used anything else.

Q. That was the language that you used at the time and you knew the language you used, you were in perfect possession of your faculties at the time?

A. I was.

Q. I will ask you if this language was not asked you, "Where was your horse," to which you replied, "He was a God damned ways off." Did that conversation occur at that time?

A. It did and the horse was a long ways off at that time; and I was with the horse also.

Q. You did not either say or imply in the language that you used at that time that you and your horse were separated?

A. I just allowed him to draw any inference he wanted to make.

Q. The fact is that you and your horse were both a long ways off; and notwithstanding that you did say what I have read here?

A. Yes.

Q. You knew perfectly well what you said?

A. I think I did.

Q. Did LeFors reply, "I would be afraid to leave my horse so far away, you might get away from him," to which statement you said, "You don't take much chances, there people are unorganized, and anyway I depend on this gun of mine; the only thing I was afraid of was that I might be compelled to kill an officer. I would do everything I could to keep away, but if he kept after me I would kill him." Did you use that language—were those statements made at the time? And do you know what you said?

A. I think I made those statements at the time, and I am sure I knew what I said; also I would have said anything else that pleased him. I felt very nice that morning; I felt peaceful, I would have told a dozen more lies if he felt inclined to think that way.

Q. I will ask you if this was said, by LeFors: "Tom, I never knew why Willie Nickell was killed, was it because he was one of the victims named or was it compulsory?" To which you replied, "I think it was this way: Suppose a man was in the big draw at the right of the gate, you know where it is, the draw that comes into the main creek below Nickell's house where Nickell was shot. Suppose a man was in that and the kid started to run for the house, and the fellow headed him off at the gate and killed him to keep him from going to the house and raising a hell of a commotion, now that is the way I think it occurred." Did you use that language?

A. I think I used very much that language, for the simple reason that at the preliminary examination I did not know the details of the killing of the boy, I did not know he was on the road going to Iron Mountain. I supposed the circumstances of killing the boy were, he was prowling around the hills and run on to somebody else, I got this in my mind, I never knew any of the details and he began to question me about that, I just told him what I had to. Had I known the boy was going to Iron Mountain I might have told him I run on to him going to Iron Mountain, I would have told him anything that fitted the case that was sprung on me. I didn't know about the details of the killing, it didn't fit what seems to be the facts of the case. It was no fault of mine because I didn't know what the facts were in the case.

Q. So you gave him the facts as they came into your mind not knowing about them?

A. Imaginary facts, that is all.

Q. You didn't know the boy had made a break and started to run home as a matter of fact?

A. I got the impression that the boy was in the hills and run onto somebody. I heard there was thirteen shots fired at him. I thought there was a great many more shots than developed at the preliminary examination. I was under the impression that he ran crazy or was running away. I don't know how I got this impression, I can't tell now, anyhow I had the impression that he run onto somebody. A party of people or one man; anyhow I understood there were thirteen shots fired in place of three.

Q. You had the impression in your mind that at the time you were doing your talking to Joe LeFors that thirteen shots had been fired at the boy?

A. A great many anyhow.
Q. And yet you didn't know any of the facts in the case, and you didn't tell Mr. LeFors of this impression that was in your mind? Why did you not say to him that you had been informed that there were thirteen shots or a great many shots fired at the boy?
A. I talked that over previous to that time and there never was any intimation at any previous conversation between Mr. LeFors and myself that I was connected with the kind of killing, previous conversations had always been a desire by him to throw in with me and help convict somebody else.
Q. He was trying to find out who did the killing?
A. I suppose he wanted to use me to help him, there is no question about that.
Q. This information had been given to you by somebody and you did not impart it to him at the time?
A. I did not, I did not go into details any more than what would occur to me at the spur of the moment.
Q. You were not then trying to help him ferrit out who it was that committed the crime?
A. No sir, I was not.
Q. You were interested in the matter of stopping cattle stealing, and in your business did you limit yourself to cattle stealing, or were you willing to help ferrit out murders as well as cattle thieves?
A. That would not come directly in my line of business. To make an explanation of that it would necessitate going into the origination of the trouble over which this boy was killed.
Q. Whatever it may have been, the fact is you didn't give him the information you possessed?
A. There was no occasion for it, it was not even asked. The talk I had with LeFors had never been for the matter of developing any legitimate information, it was to job somebody and get information in that manner, it was never a question as to legitimate information.
Q. So far as your knowledge of the actual facts were concerned you had not any knowledge of it?
A. I hadn't at that time, and I haven't now.
Q. Who gave you this information about a large number of shots being fired?
A. It occurs to me I got it from the newspapers.
Q. If it is a fact that the people only knew of 2 or 3 shots being fired your inference is wrong?
A. Yes, I don't think it was known only 2 or 3 shots were fired.

Q. Had you investigated anything about the case to know that the boy received but 2 wounds?
A. I heard that he only received 2 wounds.
Q. You knew the Coroner's inquest was in session? And had been in session day after day and all the people in that locality had been brought down to testify?
A. I did.
Q. It had been generally understood that three shots had been heard and not more than three?
A. I never heard the amount that had been fired, I heard two had struck, but as to the amount of the shots fired, I never heard those enumerated. I got the impression from someone that it was more.
Q. You didn't know whether the boy had been headed off at the gate, you didn't know as a matter of fact whether he was making a break for the house or not?
A. I didn't, only what I heard from rumors and newspapers.
Q. You gave this simply as your opinion?
A. I did, I stated it all along, that I thought that is the way it occurred.
Q. You didn't know that the boy was going on the Iron Mountain road?
A. I say now that I didn't know that he was.
Q. You said a while ago that you didn't know that the boy was going to take the Iron Mountain road?
A. That he was traveling on the Iron Mountain road. My impression always was before I was tried at the preliminary examination that the boy was wandering around in the hills. I do not remember hearing of his going to any place being said anywhere.
Q. You were not expecting the boy to be going to Iron Mountain? From what you know of the boy he was looking around of the pastures and attending to work about the house?
A. I didn't know anything of him, I didn't know there was a Willie Nickell, I never saw him or heard of him before. If I ever saw him it never could have been more than one occasion and that was a cold winter day and I spoke and asked him where his father was, I am not certain whether that was him or not. It is the only occasion I spoke to anybody about the Nickell house beside Nickell himself.
Q. You never saw him about his business at the ranch?
A. I never saw him but on one occasion and that was in his father's corral.
Q. You said a while ago you didn't know about his going on the Iron Mountain road?

A. I had not heard from the reports that he was going on the Iron Mountain road on this mission when he was killed.

Q. In answering Mr. LeFors as you did, the whole matter was a matter of supposition, that supposition being based on what you understood the facts, is that right?

A. Yes sir. On that occasion he commenced to hint to me that I was the man, intimating that I was the man that killed Willie Nickell.

Q. This conversation of his with you at the time?

A. I think another part impressed me as though—in fact he was insinuating—you killed him, and I know all about it. He didn't say it in those words but that was his regular way of talking when he and I would be conversing. I never killed anybody, and I don't think LeFors did, if he did I never heard of it. I did hear about his killing a man in the Hole-in-the-Wall, I don't think there is anything in it.

Q. So that you knew perfectly well at the time of this conversation that you and LeFors were not killers at all?

A. I knew that I was not; if LeFors was, I never heard of his being a killer. On this occasion in the Hole-in-the-Wall, that was not very creditable to him. I would not have mentioned it.

Q. That is why you mentioned it as you did concerning the killing of Willie Nickell?

A. Yes sir.

Q. Did LeFors say to you: "Tom, you had your boots on when you ran across there," to which you replied, "No, I was barefooted" —LeFors said: "You didn't run across there barefooted," to which you replied, "Yes, I did"—Do you say those words were used or a substance?

A. I think those identical words were used or the substance.

Q. You say you understood them fully at the time?

A. I did, I felt at the time it was a pretty ridiculous statement to make.

Q. He replied: "It surely must have hurt your feet, I know I could never do it," to which you replied, "I did," were those words used likewise?

A. Yes sir.

Q. You knew them and their importance fully at the time?

A. Yes sir.

Q. You knew them and these words: "How did you get your boots on after cutting up your feet?" to which you replied, "I generally have ten days to rest after a job of that kind."?

A. Yes sir.

Q. Those words were used?

A. I think that ten days was used on account of a previous conversation. He had been questioning me very close as to the length of time I was in Laramie. I told him when I went to Laramie that time I stopped about ten days. In that conversation he referred to this ten days several times that I stopped in Laramie, to such an extent that it began to get old fashioned you might say; so when he made that remark about cutting my feet bad, I just says to myself—that it occurred to me first about my being in Laramie so much—and I told him that I cut them up pretty badly but it didn't make any difference.

Q. You put those two events together your staying in Laramie shortly after this occurred and the fact that you had ten days generally after you did a job of that kind to rest up?

A. He asked me I presume half a dozen times about these ten days I stopped in Laramie, he asked me several times what I done these ten days. I hadn't done anything—it occurred to me when he said you must have used your feet pretty bad, it occurred to me then that a man could not have run across there without using his feet pretty bad and I just said, a man has to lay off a week or two. I had some intimation about these ten days before, he asked me about the ten days I stopped in Laramie. I never could exactly understand why, before the developments in this trial, I did understand officers had been there, Pete Warlaumont and a sheriff of our county had been making an investigation just subsequent to the killing of this boy as to the exact time when I come into Laramie; of course I knew that investigation would develop the fact that I come in there on Saturday.

Q. So you wished him to remain under the belief you did the job, and for ten days after doing the job, you rested?

A. I kind of wanted to leave that impression, I didn't care particularly what he thought about it.

Q. Did you say: "Do you remember the girl" in the same answer?

A. Yes sir.

Q. To which he replied, "Who do you mean"—to which you said "The school marm, she was sure smooth people, and she wrote me a letter as long as the Governor's message—telling me in detail everything asked by the Prosecuting Attorney—Stoll thought I was going to prove an alibi but I fooled him, I had a man on the outside keeping me in touch, before I showed up, with everything that was going on—I got this letter from the girl the same day I got the summons to appear before the Coroner's inquest"—you said that?

A. I think I said that.

Q. Or the substance?
A. Or the substance.
Q. Was that all a josh or the facts which you stated to him?
A. I had a letter informing me of this and as to the investigation so far as that was concerned. Then it was that the conversation took a turn that showed that he was trying to implicate me; previous to that he always wanted me to help him job someone else. He inferred all the time I had done the job. I didn't want to disappoint him. I would have helped him out in any manner.
Q. These words were used and you knew what they were at the time; they were not said under the influence of liquor or intoxication or anything of that kind?
A. I had been drinking considerably of course, but as far as that influenced anything I had to say, I knew perfectly well what I was saying.
Q. Exactly. Then did he say this: "Did the school marm tell all she knew?"—to which you replied, "She did, I wouldn't tell an individual like her anything, not me, she told me to look out for you and she said look out for Joe LeFors he is not all right, look out for him, he is trying to find out something—I said what is there to this Joe LeFors matter, she said Miller didn't like him and said he would like to kill the son-of-a-bitch if God would spare him long enough"—now the question is was that said there?
A. I think it was.
Q. Did you say: "There is nothing to those Millers, they are ignorant old jays, they can't even appreciate a good joke, the first time I met the girl was just before the killing of the kid, everything you know dates from the killing of the kid." Was that said there?
A. I think it was.
Q. You knew perfectly well what it was that was said—what reason did you have for saying, everything you know dates from the killing of the kid?
A. An event of that kind in the country or any other event of any importance marks that part of the country as an eventful day like in the spring when the roundup starts, you will say before or after roundup started. That was an event in that country, the shooting of a boy, and naturally they count back and forth before the boy was killed.
Q. Did LeFors say: "How many days was it before the killing of this kid?" to which you replied three or four days, maybe one day, damned if I want to remember dates—she was there at this time and of course we soon paired ourselves off" was that the language used?

A. I think it was.

Q. During the entire conversation you were thoroughly cognizant of the language that was used?

A. I was.

Q. Did LeFors say: "Didn't Jim Dixon carry you grub" to which you replied, "No, by God, no one carried me grub," to which LeFors said "How can a man who weighs 204 pounds go without anything to eat" to which you replied, "Well I do sometimes, I go for days without a mouthful, sometimes I have a little bacon along." Was that language used, do you remember distinctly that language being used or the substance of it?

A. I remember distinctly the language being used, I remember it made an impression on my mind. He is not grabbing these stories he don't hardly believe me, he knows I am lying, and he wants me to understand that he knows I am lying, that is what I inferred from that.

Q. Then was this language used: "You must get terribly hungry," to which you replied, "Sometimes I get so hungry I could kill my mother for grub, but I never quit a job until I get my man."

A. I think it was. There was not a time but what everything had a tendency to show and every impression was that such as would be used between men that had talked as much about killing people as LeFors and I.

Q. This question was asked: "What kind of a gun have you got"—to which you replied, "I used a 30-30 Winchester"—to which he replied, "Do you think it will hold up as well as a 30-40?" to which you replied, "I like to get close to my man, the closer the better."

A. I think it was.

Q. For the same purpose?

A. Yes, in the same identical strain, the whole business.

Q. This language "How far was Willie Nickell killed?" to which you replied, "About 300 yards, it was the best shot I ever made and the dirtiest trick I ever done, I thought at one time he would get away."

A. I thought there had been 13 shots fired in place of three. The intimation I had in regard to the killing of the boy was that he had been fired at continuously and was about to exit and escape when he was killed. I had drawn that inference from about what I had heard about the killing of the boy. In all the talk I had with LeFors regarding the whole business, when it comes down to defining the actual manner in which the boy was killed, it never was stated by LeFors as if he knew himself.

Q. Then if you never knew it, why did you say the boy was killed at a distance of 300 yards, and that it was the best shot you ever made?

A. I was just bluffing. I was under the impression that in place of having said that, I thought I said that I thought he was going to get away or something like that. The only thing in his entire conversation and I heard it read and repeated many times—the only thing I don't remember having said, or ever having had occasion for saying, was that it was the best shot I ever made and the dirtiest job I ever done, I don't remember of having used that language. I do believe also that the young gentleman Charlie Ohnhaus, who took down the conversation in short hand, I have every reason to believe that he took it down as accurately as he could, and he didn't make any mistake that I know of, and I certainly don't think that he made an intentional mistake, and as he read that in his notes, I consequently think I must have made that remark. But a remark of that kind I never remember to have made before in my life on any occasion in my life.

(The next six typewritten lines of the testimony are torn and could not be read).

Q. So that unless it had been a fact, there was no occasion for your saying it was the best shot I ever made and the dirtiest trick I ever done?

A. Had it been a fact, there was no occasion to say it.

Q. However, it was said?

A. I think it was to the best of my knowledge and belief.

Q. You did know sufficiently about the circumstances of the boy's killing, however, to have been impressed at all times with the idea that the shot was a good one and the trick was a dirty one—that impression was always in your mind?

A. It was.

Q. You had no hesitation in connecting yourself as the author of it so you said, it was the best shot I ever made and the dirtiest trick I ever done, is that right?

A. I think to the best of my knowledge I said it, yes sir.

Q. I will ask you if this conversation was had: "How about the shells, did you carry them away?" to which you replied, "You bet your God damn life I did." Was that said?

A. To the best of my knowledge it was.

Q. Then was this said: "Tom, do you need any more money for this trip?" to which the reply was made, "No, if I get a pass I will not need any more money, if I have to buy a ticket, I must have some all right, but today is Sunday and I will wait until tomorrow," do you think that language was used?

A. I don't remember that any more than anything else, I think it was used.

Q. Then this language: "Well, it is afternoon and I will go home and see you again this afternoon or this evening when we can talk this matter over"—to which you replied, "All right I will be back, I want to know all about these people before I go up there," was that language used?

A. I think it was to the best of my knowledge.

Q. And then this question: "Let us go down stairs and get a drink, I could always see your work clear, but I want you to tell me why you killed this kid, was it a mistake?" to which you replied, "Well, Joe, I will tell you all about it when I come back from Montana, it is too new yet."?

A, Yes sir.

Q. That language was used?

A. Yes sir.

Q. You remember using the language?

A. I was afraid to go any more into details of the shooting of the boy because I could see that he knew more about it than I did.

Q. He merely asked you questions and you answered them?

A. We were talking.

Q. You hadn't given him the information you had obtained as to the 13 shots being fired, or whatever information you may have had?

A. That was not discussed, I don't think.

Q. If he knew more about it than you did, there was no reason why you shouldn't tell him what little you did know?

A. I didn't really know anything and I was guessing and I saw that my guessing was not coming up to what he actually knew; it occurred to me from the way of the conversation.

Q. There was no reason for saying it is too new yet?

A. I thought before I went any more into the details I had better post myself more about the details of the killing of the boy that is what I thought at the time.

Q. In the afternoon session, was not this language used: "We have only been together about 15 minutes and I will be thoroughly sure that some people are saying what are those son-of-bitches planning now, and who are they going to kill next; we have come up here because there is no other place to go, if you go to the Inter-Ocean to set down and talk for a few minutes, someone comes in and says, let us have a drink and before you know it you are standing up talking and my feet get so damn tired it almost kills me," was that language used?

A. I think the language was used and I think it was used at that very time.

Q. Although you were not a killer and although LeFors was not a killer, yet you said on this occasion that you supposed that people after seeing you together 15 minutes would be talking about your killing somebody.
A. Yes sir.
Q. Now, you remember that conversation was used, do you?
A. I don't remember particularly, I think the conversation was used all right.
Q. You were in a condition to understand it then?
A. I was, I didn't happen to have a stenographer to take it down, from then consequently I didn't know it or take it down word for word as the stenographer did that was placed there.

(Recess for 10 minutes)

Q. Mr. Horn, you state that you had several conversations with Mr. LeFors previous to this one, with relation to the killing of Willie Nickell, will you state how many and where such conversations were had?
A. I don't believe I can state as to the exact number, or the exact places, but I can state any how several of them.
Q. Approximately, how many?
A. As I remember now, three certainly.
Q. Where were these conversations, where did they take place?
A. I don't know of one of them that didn't occur in a saloon or very close proximity to a saloon.
Q. And in Cheyenne?
A. Yes.
Q. You testified at the Coroner's inquest August 9th, 1901, and this conversation took place with LeFors January 21, 1902, between those two dates you say you had three conversations with Mr. LeFors relating to the Willie Nickell killing?
A. Anyhow, that many, I say.
Q. There were at least three?
A. I think there were.
Q. They were all in Cheyenne?
A. I think they were all in Cheyenne.
Q. Can you fix about the time the first one occurred?
A. I can fix it so that you can find out, I don't know the dates; the first one occurred before I appeared before the Coroner's jury, that night or the following night, or within two or three days of that time; while I was in town on that case any how.
Q. Where did that conversation occur?
A. The principal part, I think, occurred down in the Tom Heany's saloon standing at the bar.

Q. Which one of his saloons, the Tiviola?
A. Yes sir.
Q. It was not at the 17th street saloon?
A. Not if it was at the Tiviola.
Q. When did the second one occur?
A. The second one, if I remember now, on the second night of Frontier days a year ago.
Q. The 2nd day of Frontier day, 1901?
A. Yes sir.
Q. Where was that?
A. I talked with him in Hynd's saloon and also out in front of the saloon I think.
Q. About what time of day was that the second conversation occurred?
A. It was no time of day, it was night.
Q. It was sometime during the night of that day?
A. Yes sir.
Q. The conversation was both in the saloon and outside?
A. As I remember now, yes sir.
Q. That was in Hynd's saloon?
A. Yes sir.
Q. Was there any one present, that is in immediate presence of you and LeFors, that could hear the conversation?
A. There were many present that could have heard the conversation when it first started, and he asked me to step out on the sidewalk with him; he said he wanted to talk about that affair, and we stepped out on the sidewalk.
Q. About what time of day was it the first conversation occurred, was it night?
A. It was night.
Q. Who was present at the time?
A. No one.
Q. These two conversations both occurred so far as this killing was concerning between yourselves and not within hearing of anyone else?
A. There was no one talking with us.
Q. Now where did the third one occur and when?
A. The third one occurred in Hynd's saloon, it was in the night between Christmas and New Year's. I know because I had been to Omaha with beef cattle and it was on my way home. I locate the matter because it was on Christmas week; I was in town and it was during that time.
Q. That was one night also?
A. Yes sir.

Q. And you and LeFors had a conversation between yourselves?
A. Yes sir.
Q. Was that inside of the saloon or outside?
A. It was inside.
Q. In these conversations, each of them the subject of killing of Willie Nickell, was the matter that was discussed?
A. It was not so much the subject of the killing of Willie Nickell, as it was the subject principally consisted of his asking me to go in with him and furnish evidence from the country to convict somebody in the country.
Q. Anybody in the country?
A. One particular party.
Q. It was however for the killing of Willie Nickell?
A. Presumably not for the punishment of the crime of killing Willie Nickell. The talk was generally to get me to go in with him and we would make a thousand dollars reward and we would cut it up between us.
Q. What was that for, there was no reward except for the murderer of Willie Nickell?
A. There was a party in the country he said with my assistance he could convict of the murder of Willie Nickell. The question of the killing of Willie Nickell was not discussed so much as to how we could job this man, fix it up so as to convict him; in fact the principal gist of the conversation was that. I could not go into any details without having it recalled to my mind in some manner, but the main part of it was that he could handle the sheriff and prosecuting attorney here in town and all the witnesses to carry on the case, he could get in town, but it would be necessary to have some witnesses from the country to convict this party and he thought I could furnish those witnesses.
Q. Whatever may have been said as to that matter, the matter concerning which this arrangement was talked about was the killing of Willie Nickell, was it not?
A. It was the thousand dollars reward, making this money was the way it was usually put; there was not so much talk, in fact very little talk, regarding the exact killing of Willie Nickell you understand, but the talk was principally about how we could fix up and bring evidence sufficient to convict a party in the country for this murder and get the thousand dollars.
Q. It was the conviction of the murderer of Willie Nickell?
A. That was what it was for.
Q. That was the subject talk between you and he in each of these three conversations?

A. He told me what a bad man he was and I told him what a bad man I was. I don't think there was any other conversation occurred between us except something about this crime and something about someone he had killed and some others I had killed.

Q. Now you fixed three times when you had conversation with him between August 9th and the 12th of January. A while ago you said you had previous conversations about the killing of Willie Nickell previous to this one on January 12th?

A. Yes.

Q. Now, I will ask you if the subject of killing Willie Nickell was not mentioned at each of the three conversations you have referred to?

A. It was mentioned.

Q. All turned around and hinged around that one matter?

A. Yes sir.

Q. So you wish to be understood as saying before the jury now that in each of these three conversations that was the main topic of conversation?

A. I don't want the jury to understand that the talk of the killing of Willie Nickell was the main part of the conversation, the main part of the conversation was wanting me to stand in with him and putting up a job on a certain party out in the country. The killing of Willie Nickell was not mentioned, only as something to do with this.

Q. However, the killing of Willie Nickell was the basis of the whole conversation?

A. It was.

Q. You wish to be understood that the killing of Willie Nickell was talked about?

A. I want the jury to understand that Joe LeFors wanted me to bring evidence against a party in that country for the killing of Willie Nickell. The details of the killing of Willie Nickell were never discussed between us. He was the boy killed. I knew it and he knew it; there was never any details talked as to how he was killed or even why he was killed, definitely, until he asked me on January 12th—when he inferred that I had done it.

Q. So that the mere fact of the killing of Willie Nickell was assumed as a fact in each of the conversations?

A. Yes sir.

Q. That is what I am trying to get out?

A. It was, but from the general tone of the conversation at least a person that would have overheard would have thought it was the least part of the conversation, the actual killing.

Q. Those are the three conversations which you fix as the conversations to which you referred to a while ago when you say you had previous conversations with LeFors about this Willie Nickell killing—that is right?

A. That is three of them. I don't remember talking with him any other date that I could come near specifying.

Q. Now referring to the conversation at the marshal's office, I will ask you to state whether this language was used? "I am 44 years, 3 months and 27 days old, and if I get killed now, I will have the satisfaction of knowing that I have lived 15 ordinary lives; I would like to have somebody who saw my past and could picture it to the public; it would be the most God damned interesting reading in the country, and if we could describe to the author our feelings at different times, it would be better yet; the experience of my life, or the first man I killed was when I was only 26 years old, he was a coarse son-of-a-bitch;" now, was that language used?

A. I think it was.

Q. There is no question about your knowing what you said is there, Mr. Horn?

A. There is no question about my knowing the exact words, to the best of my knowledge that conversation occurred.

Q. Now, instead of referring to any fact, was that mere fiction, that there had been nothing in your past that could be used as the basis of any such assertion?

A. There was certainly not, I never killed a man in my life.

Q. I will ask you if this language was used: "How much did you get for killing these fellows, in the Powell and Lewis case, you got $600 apiece, you killed Lewis in the corral with a six-shooter; I would like to have seen the expression on his face when you shot him," to which you replied, "He was the scaredest son-of-a-bitch you ever saw," was that language used?

A. I think the language was used; I know to a certainty that something very much like that was said. If he would have asked me if I killed him with a double barreled gun or gatling gun, I would have said yes.

Q. Just the same?

A. Just the same. Anybody that investigated or knew anything about the killing of that man Lewis knows I was summoned before the Grand Jury here at the investigation of the killing of Lewis. I was in Bates Hole, Natrona County, at the time the killing occurred and the summons was served on me by the sheriff of Natrona County to appear here which I did, and reported to

Col. Baird, who was then Prosecuting Attorney. I got an intimation from some one that I was being investigated as to the killing of William Lewis and I told the Prosecuting Attorney at the time, I told . . .

Q. Never mind that.

A. I just simply told where I was and the Grand Jury was adjourned several times until they found where I was, and that was all as far as I was concerned.

Q. You did use this language and LeFors used this language at this place, and you understood fully its importance at the time?

A. Yes sir.

Q. There is no getting around the fact you knew what you were talking about while there?

A. There might be a way of getting around it, I can't say that. I know it was talked about. If he would have said he was killed by anyone else, I would have said yes.

Q. There was some fact there as well as fiction?

A. He might have had some facts, I don't know.

Q. With relation to this particular language, I understood you to say a while ago that it was all a josh?

A. Yes sir.

Q. Several times you stated inferentially it was more or less fiction these things you referred to. You stated, for instance, you did so and so with relation to Willie Nickell—now in regard to this language there was something referred to that was a fact, for instance Lewis and Powell were known to have been killed?

A. The killing of Lewis was a fact, certainly, he was a man that I never knew or saw at no time in my life.

Q. The killing of Powell was a fact?

A. Powell had also been killed.

Q. So that when you referred to those matters you referred to something that was well-known so far as the method they departed this life was concerned?

A. It was generally supposed they were shot certainly.

Q. But it was not a fact that you got $600 apiece for shooting them?

A. Oh no, if he had said I got $17,000 I would have told him yes.

Q. If you got $50.00 apiece you would have told him the same?

A. Yes, or $1.25. [Laughter]

Q. Whatever you say about it, the fact is that was stated as in this report?

A. That was said undoubtedly.

Q. And you knew it at the time it was said?

A. I knew it was said, yes sir.

Q. Was this language used: "I have known everything you have done for a good many years," to which you replied, "I was paid this money on the train between Cheyenne and Denver." LeFors said, "Didn't you get two 100 dollar bills and the rest in gold," to which you said, "Yes, this is where I learned to take care of my shells; I left five 45-90 shells there after I flashed powder in them to make them smell fresh and the damned officers never found them." Now that language was used at that time was it not?

A. I think I remember very distinctly of its having been used; he was telling me how smart he was and I didn't want to look like a farmer entirely.

Q. This language as given in this report was the language used at the time?

A. To the best of my knowledge it was the language used.

Q. You understood fully at the time?

A. I did.

Q. When you referred to the fact, "I flashed powder in them to make them smell fresh and the damned officers never found them," you used that conversation?

A. Yes sir.

Q. So far as the fact is concerned, you never did anything of that kind?

A. I never did it.

Q. So far as receiving this money is concerned, that also is a falsehood?

A. Yes, that is a falsehood.

Q. Then was this language used: "Why did you put the rock under the kid's head after you killed him, that is one of your marks isn't it"—to which you replied, "Yes, that is the way I hang out my sign to collect my money for a job of this kind," was that language used?

A. Yes, I think it was used.

Q. You think it was used?

A. I think it was used.

Q. You understood it fully at the time it was used?

A. Yes sir.

Q. There was nothing about your mental condition to deprive your ability to comprehend it at the time?

A. In fact, I think otherwise, I realized at the time he made this remark, about there being a stone under the boy's head I never heard of that before either, and it occurred to me that he knew a great deal more about the details of the killing than I did, that was information to me that the boy had been turned over and there was a rock under his head. Had he said, why did you lay him on a cot or hang him up on a tree, I would have given him the same reason for it. I remember very distinctly that part of the conversation having occurred.

Q. You had quite a distinct impression in your mind even at the time of the conversation as to the situation of the boy there in the road, there didn't you?

A. Not so much as I did of the impression that he knew more about the killing than I did, and I had better be careful how I talked, or he would know I was lying to a certainty.

Q. That is the reason that you replied as you did?

A. Yes sir.

Q. Then was this language used: "Did you ever have an agreement drawn up," to which you answered, "No, I do all my business through Coble, he is the whitest son-of-a-bitch in the country in a job of this kind," was that language used?

A. I think it was.

Q. You understood it fully at the time?

A. Yes sir.

Q. You referred to the killing of this boy?

A. Any kind of killing.

Q. This was the job referred to in a job of this kind?

A. This was the one under discussion.

Q. Was this language used: "In the Powell and Lewis case, did Coble put in toward your pay?"

A. I think it was.

Q. You understood it fully at the time?

A. Yes sir.

Q. And to which you replied, "No, I wouldn't let him, he fed me and furnished me horses and has done more for me than any man in the country"?

A. Yes sir.

Q. Was this language: "Did you ever have any trouble to collect your money?" to which you replied, "No, when I do a job of this kind they knew they had to pay me. I would kill a man if he tried to beat me out of ten cents that I had earned," was that language used?

A. I think it was.

Q. You understood it fully at the time it was used?

A. I did for this reason, that anything that occurred when we were talking to one another, anybody that done anything that we didn't like, we talked about killing.

Q. As a matter of fact, you didn't kill a man or do a job of this kind?

A. There would have to be an initiation, I never did kill anybody. It would be questionable as to what I would do, I never killed anybody, nor contracted to kill anybody.

Q. You want to say to this jury, you would not kill anybody, still you said you would kill a man for doing a job like that?

A. I would not talk to this jury as I did to a man like LeFors.

Q. At the time that you were talking to LeFors, you wanted LeFors to understand you would kill a man if he tried to cheat you out of ten cents after you done a job of this kind?

A. He knew different. LeFors is very much the same kind of a man I am for talk.

Q. Did you use this language: "Have you got your money yet for the killing of Nickell?" to which you replied, "I got that before I did the job."

A. I think so.

Q. You understood if you realized fully at the time you used that language?

A. Yes sir.

Q. It was not a fact that you got any money for the job; in other words you told him what was not true with relation to that matter?

A. I thought I would sooner lie than disappoint him.

Q. Was this language used: "You got $500 for that, why did you cut the price?" to which you replied, "I got $2,100," was that language used?

A. I think it was.

Q. You have no question about its being used and its being fully understood by you at the time it was used?

A. Just as to the $2,100 I could not say exactly, I might have said $2,500 or $1,500, anything that would have occurred to me I would have said.

Q. Was this language used: "How much is that a man?" to which you replied, "That is for three dead men and one man shot at five times, killing men is my specialty, I look at it as a business proposition and I think I have a corner on the market." The question is, did you use that language and was that language used at the time?

A. I think it was.

Q. And you understood it fully at the time?
A. Yes sir.
Q. In the language three dead men and one man shot at five times, I will ask you if the three dead men referred to there were not Powell and Lewis and Willie Nickell?
A. I think they were enumerated.
Q. And the one man shot at five times was Kels Nickell?
A. I think that is the way it was reckoned, was understood if it is not enumerated, I think that is the way it was understood anyhow.

REDIRECT EXAMINATION BY JUDGE LACEY

Q. Where was it that you got the revolver which you carried into Laramie?
A. I left my revolver at the ranch and took it at the ranch.
Q. When these insinuations were made against you for killing Willie Nickell and other people why was it that you didn't deny them?
A. Nobody ever insinuated that I had done the killing, anything directly. Joe LeFors is the only man and the only man who tried or said in my presence that I had anything to do with the killing. Well, I am always of a rather generous disposition, I would rather lie than disappoint him; when he said I done the killing I would go along with Joe and other people like that?
Q. All the men that you ever did kill were in these friendly talks with Joe and other people like that?
A. As far as actual killing is concerned I never killed a man in my life or a boy either.

MONDAY, OCTOBER 20

With the resuming of the trial, both the Defense and Prosecution were vigorous—this was to be the final week.

Charles L. Miller was the last witness for the Defense. He was cross-examined by the State to prove that Frank Stone, witness for the Defense, had been in Laramie before July 21. A file of *The Laramie Republican* containing a personal item relating to Stone being in Laramie on the 19th of July was introduced and exhibited to the Court. The witness testified that he did not know whether he was there or not.

The Defense rested at this point and the Prosecution began offering evidence in rebuttal.

The first testimony was the introduction of surgical appliance for taking the measurements of a wound.

Joe LeFors, was again called to the stand. The Prosecutor asked him if during his conversation with Horn on Sunday, January 12th, any mention was made of the $1,000 reward offered for the apprehension of the slayer of Willie Nickell. He was also asked if he and Horn had attempted to fix the blame on other parties.

The Deputy U. S. Marshal told the Court that he met the accused during Frontier Days, 1901. He recalled that at that time Tom Horn asked him what had been done in the Coroner's inquest in the killing of Willie Nickell. Horn, LeFors said, intimated he had a friend on the jury that would keep him "posted" on what was being done.

LeFors concluded his testimony by saying statements were made by Horn, himself, and he was clear and sober at the time.

When cross-examined LeFors was asked if he had not joined the Defendant in saying that James Miller could be convicted on the evidence Horn had. LeFors replied with a heated "no!" The next question was to the same effect and regarding Victor Miller. Again an emphatic "no!" was the answer. The witness began to squirm a little.

Walter Stoll, Counsel for the Prosecution, vigorously objected to such questioning. The Court sustained the objection and ordered the Jury to retire while the issue was argued. The Counsel for the Defense was quick to challenge the action. Judge Lacey argued for the return of the Jury. The Court sustained his position and the Jurors were ordered to be returned.

Thus, Joe LeFors continued his testimony. He testified that on August 14, 1901, he met Tom Horn in the Tivolia Saloon in Cheyenne. They talked of the shooting of Kels P. Nickell. LeFors said he asked Horn why he had not killed Nickell. The reply was stated to have been, "The shoot'n was done early in the morning, when the light was bad and the sun shone so on my sights that I could not fire well." LeFors said Horn described Nickell as running and yelling like a Comanche Indian when fired upon.

Peace Officer Leslie Snow was the next person called to the stand. He testified that he was in the room adjoining the room where LeFors and Horn held their conversation on January 12th. He said although he did not see Tom Horn during the talk, he heard his voice and judged from the tone of it that Tom was sincere, truthful, and was not "joshing."

The next series of witnesses testified for the Prosecution as to the veracity of Otto Plaga's testimony, made the day before (Friday, 18th). Plaga had testified that he had seen Tom on July 18, 1901, between eight and nine o'clock in the morning, and at a distance of 25 miles from where Willie Nickell was killed.

Granville Faulkner of Mud Springs and formerly of Sherman, was the first witness. He testified that he had known Otto Plaga for nine years and had heard him to be a notorious story teller.

Attorney Burke asked Faulkner, "Who had said that Plaga was not truthful?" "Ed Finfrock," replied the witness, "he declared he had no confidence in anything that Plaga said."

C. H. Edwards told the Court that he had known Otto Plaga for nine years and his reputation for truth and veracity were very bad. He added, "I would not believe him under oath."

H. M. Davidson stated that he had known Plaga for twelve years and he considered his reputation for truth and veracity very bad.

Thomas Moore of the Sybille country testified he had known the man whose testimony was being questioned for the entire fifteen years he had lived in the county and his reputation for truth was not good.

Richard Fitzmorris corroborated the testimonies of the five men before him by adding that he had known Otto Plaga for thirteen years and his reputation was bad.

Joe D. McArthur, part owner in the Michigan Mine and one who had been a resident of the Sybille country for a long time testified, "Plaga's reputation is not good, in fact he could hardly be believed under oath."

McArthur's testimony concluded the Prosecution's attempt to question the important "Horn time and place" testimony.

The next witness was E. B. Davies, Marshal of Laramie City. He testified that Frank Stone, one of the witnesses for the Defense, was in Judge Grant's police court held in Laramie on October 6, 1902. While in the Court Room, Marshal Davies said Stone remarked in presence of a number of persons that he (Stone) was in Laramie the 19th of July, 1901, and that he was in Snowy Range on the 18th working for a cattleman and that he came to town on the 19th and met Tom Horn. The Marshal continued, stating Stone had remarked that he and Horn had a drink together. The witness said Stone was sober when he made the statement in the Court Room.

On cross examination by Mr. Burke, Davies testified Stone made his remarks voluntarily. Stone said he had been asked to come to Cheyenne and help prove an alibi for Tom Horn, and had added, "He'd be damned if he would do it!"

Judge Grant was called to the witness stand. His testimony corroborated that of Marshal E. B. Davies.

Upon the conclusion of Mr. Grant's testimony the Attorneys for the Defense began their rebuttal. The first group presented testified as to the reputation of Otto Plaga for telling the truth. In this group were some of the best cowboys ever to mount horses in Wyoming. Many of them had felt the dynamite of Steamboat—the greatest bucking horse of all time.

The first witness called was Thorton Biggs, foreman for Ora Haley's Two Bar ranch. The cowboy was dressed fully in western regalia. His appearance caused considerable comment throughout the Court Room. He stated his business was being a cow puncher, and that he had known Otto Plaga for fifteen years and Plaga's reputation was good. On being cross examined he admitted to his knowledge that Plaga's reputation for the truth had never been brought into question in his hearing at least.

Henry Mudd was next to testify. He said he had lived on the Sybille for ten years and he had never heard of Plaga's truthfulness being questioned. Ranchman Ed Hoffman testified that both he and his brother, Fred, thought the cowboy's reputation was good.

Court was then recessed until afternoon.

When Court convened, the testimony of Otto Plaga was still the subject.

Sam Moore, the manager of the Swan Land & Cattle Company, was the first of the afternoon session to be called before the Court. He testified that he had never heard the character of Otto questioned. Adding that he had known him for years.

Perry Williams, William Clay and Frank Ferguson all expressed opinions in their testimonies that Otto "Pleger's" reputation for telling the truth was good. Duncan Clark's testimony also supported Plaga.

With the conclusion of witnesses favoring the testimony of Otto Plaga, Judge Scott declared all evidence had been received and presented and that the case was closed. The Jury would receive their instruction.

TUESDAY, OCTOBER 21

The trial opened with Judge Scott delivering instructions to the Jury. One of the major points in the Judge's address was circumstantial evidence.

He said the circumstances must be such as are consistent with the guilt of the Defendant and inconsistent with the guilt of any other person.

Another point in the case cited by Judge Scott was the admission of Horn's confession as evidence. The fact that the Defendant might have been intoxicated would affect the weight of the evidence, he continued.

The Court then instructed the Jury as to three material allegations: (1) Willie Nickell was murdered (2) The scene of the crime was in Laramie County and (3) The Defendant was in some way the criminal agent.

The Jury was instructed in regard to Tom Horn's own testimony. Since he was admitted as a witness they should give his testimony whatever weight it was entitled to. The latter concluded Judge Scott's address.

Prosecutor Walter Stoll opened for the State with a review of the crime. "The crime," Stoll shouted, "is similar to others committed in the state, and that the failure to punish for such crimes was one reason they continued to happen!"

He gave the details of the Defendant's trip to the scene of the crime and carefully analyzed Horn's testimony.

In regard to the Court's instructions to the Jury as to the three material allegations, Mr. Stoll argued that the first and second were conclusively proven and that he would show that the third was true.

He summarized evidence and stated the only new fact was that the distance claimed by witness Otto Plaga was 25 miles. Stoll said it was 12 miles.

Tom Horn's whereabouts on July 18, 1901, was the next subject brought up by the attorney. He said it had been proven that the Defendant was at the Bosler Ranch around noon on the 20th of July —so couldn't have been in Laramie. Therefore, he continued, Horn must have been in Laramie either on the 18th or 19th. The Prosecutor exhibited the Elkhorn Livery Barn entry books covering July 18, 19, 20, and added that they were hardly dependable.

Horn's confession in Denver was carefully analyzed. Although Horn was drunk, Stoll said he knew what he was talking about. He cited Horn's statements to LeFors as being exactly the same as those made in Denver. Thus the corroborating, all evidence, the linking up of facts, would have been impossible had the accused not committed the crime the attorney emphasized.

In his summation, Stoll gave the Defendant a verbal lashing in effective legal language. The surgeons that had expressed opinions upon the wounds and the calibre of the bullets were also criticized, as was the testimony of gun maker Peter Bergusson.

Mr. Stoll concluded his address at 5:30—the Defense would have their day tomorrow.

As the crowd filed out of the Court Room, many felt that the State's case was materially strengthened by the Prosecutor's brilliant and factual address.

WEDNESDAY, OCTOBER 22

The Court Room was crowded shortly after the opening of the doors; all were anxious to hear the Defense present their final arguments.

Clyde M. Watts, who had been assisting Walter Stoll with the Prosecution, made a brief speech and was followed by Waldo Moore, who spoke eloquently. However, neither brought out new evidence.

At 10 o'clock, Attorney Burke began the opening speech for the Defense. His powerful address lasted over three hours. The Attorney's primary subject was the testimony of the State, rather than that of the Defense. He attempted to break down the chain of evidence the Prosecution had established. Horn's whereabouts and frequent visits to the Nickell vicinity were emphasized. He stressed the logic of Tom Horn's alibi, which he claimed was fully proven. This he labeled "doubt number one."

The Court's instructions to the Jury regarding the motive for the crime was the Attorney's next topic. He attempted to show that Horn had no motive. This was called "doubt number two."

He then reviewed the time the Defense had established that Horn rode into Laramie. He said that the evidence submitted by the Defense was more conclusive than that of the State.

Burke spent considerable time before the Jury concerning the confession that Horn was said to have made in Denver. It would have been impossible for the Defendant to have done so, Burke said, because he had a broken jaw and was hospitalized at the time. The language and exactness of the two confessions as paralleled by the Prosecution was made possible only because Denver papers copied the story from the Cheyenne papers he stated.

In speaking on the wounds of Willie Nickell, the keen Attorney said that Dr. Conway, Dr. Johnston and Dr. Barber had all testified at the Coroner's inquest—before anyone was aroused, and they all stated that they thought the wound was made by a larger calibre bullet than a 30-30. During this address, Burke was at his "best," the crowd was spell bound. To emphasize a point he would repeatedly walk up to the table of the Attorney for the State and pound his fist vigorously, demanding to know if the Prosecution was attempting to hang an innocent man on a lie, or were they merely trying to support a theory! An interrupting voice from the crowd shouted, "Yes! Yes!" This was followed by an outburst of both yeses and noes from the spectators. Judge Scott rapped for order in the Court and warned the audience against such violations of the Court. Attorney Stoll remained unmoved by the charges.

With order restored in the Court, Attorney Burke resumed his address. "A confession," he said, "must be seriously, willingly and purposely made! And statements to LeFors were not a confession! It was drawn out by the skill of LeFors and was without purpose." In reviewing the confession he pointed out factors that he cited as being absurdities and points that had been emphasized by the Prosecution.

Attorney Burke concluded his address by making a vigorous plea to the Jury not to hang an innocent man merely on circumstantial evidence. "Tom Horn," he said, in a somewhat modified voice, "like you and I (to the Jury) has an aged mother; he has three kind sisters —they are anxiously awaiting to hear of his acquittal."

Judge Lacey took the floor and began his super-charged address at 4 o'clock. He followed much the same course as had his colleague. He reiterated and re-emphasized the former's statements. "Tom Horn," he said, "was drinking all night before the alleged confession to LeFors. Although he was not drunk, he must have been under the influence of alcohol." Lacey brought chuckles from the gathering when he adlibed that he never saw a drunken man that would ever admit later that he had been drunk. The Attorney related that he was positive that under the confession circumstances, Horn would have admitted he had murdered his entire family if Joe LeFors had insisted on such. He then tried emphasizing that the accused was drunk at the time and had to be put to bed.

The latter statement concluded the Defense arguments in the case for the day—tomorrow they would have another chance. Judge Scott thumped his gavel and shouted "Court's adjourned." The events of the day's session had been trying indeed.

THURSDAY, OCTOBER 23

This was the next to the last day. The Court was closer to a verdict than most realized. The Court Room was again jammed within a matter of minutes after the doors were opened. All Cheyenne was there, also in evidence was the aroma of the corral and sweaty horses. Men apparently had hurried to the Court after doing early morning chores. The Attorneys for both sides would make their last momentous efforts. Everyone seemed to be near exhaustion, except Stoll, and he was said to have been tireless.

Judge Lacey again took the floor for the Defense as soon as Court procedure would permit it. He reviewed Stoll's arguments point by point and attempted to disprove each. Several times he urged the Jury not to condemn Tom Horn because of circumstantial evidence and the mere fitting of facts.

He discussed the matter of the print of a shoe found near the gate. This print was a size six or seven. Then he shouted, "Only one witness could have worn that shoe!" In a lowered voice Mr. Lacey added, "this witness was not called by the Court to testify!"

Judge Lacey then discussed the many points presented by the Prosecution in an attempt to show how each could not apply to the case. A comparison of witnesses was made. He challenged the testimonies of M. M. Grant and Marshal Davies stating they must have been falsified as they conflicted.

In his concluding statements, Judge Lacey made a dramatic and impressive appeal for the life of Tom Horn.

Walter Stoll was quick to the floor. This would be his closing address to the Jury.

He made no mention of the vociferous attacks made by the Defense. He referred to the points he had brought out about the Denver confession, emphasizing that they had not been disproven. The circumstance of a confession is not important so long as it was a fact he shouted. Then pausing, he picked up the jacket worn by Willie Nickell at the time of his death. With his fingers protruding through the holes torn by the bullets, Stoll reiterated, "The calibre, size of wounds and angle of the shots was of little importance—the fact that they were fatal is the paramount concern."

Continuing his address late into the day, Walter Stoll made his most bitter attack on the Defense.

FRIDAY, OCTOBER 24

The Court Room was again crowded—many were standing on the outside waiting to have word relayed to them. Sometimes they could catch a word or two as the brilliant and experienced legal minds of Lacey and Burke fought the unrelenting Walter Stoll in the battle of words for the life of their client. This was the day and the hour. The verdict was close at hand. All in the Court Room strained for the tip-off clue, but no quarter was asked—none was given. Today, some thought, perhaps Horn would weaken—maybe he would tell all.

Walter Stoll took up his argument from the day before as though the Court had returned from but a fifteen minute recess. He tore into Horn's alleged confession with a tirade of legal vernacular. The confession and evidence supporting it were reviewed at great length. Then graphically he portrayed the scene of the crime step by step to the attentive Jurors. Horn was even said to have been impressed as he displayed a considerable concern as the Prosecution reconstructed the crime as they believed it happened.

The thoughts running through the mind of Tom Horn at this moment are purely speculative; in his mental processes, he could have followed the Prosecution step by step to Iron Mountain—a 30-30 rifle—the damp and dreary morning of July 18—the gate—"the Kid" —no doubt he marveled at the brilliance of Stoll. Wondering how in the hell he could have pieced the details together with such accuracy. Perhaps Tom couldn't have done any better himself. Or maybe Horn's impulse was to jump up and shout, "You're wrong! LeFors trapped me! Otto Plaga is right! I didn't do it! No, Hell, no!" Or possibly his eyes might have strained through the audience in search of John Coble. Where was John? He was his best friend. John knew! Perhaps Tom was just day dreaming, not mentally defending himself —just recollecting. All the good times; Frontier Days; the steaks he and Coble had eaten; the jokes, all the cussing, bunk house fights, and gettin' busted by broncs. How he longed to climb on a good horse just once more, to smell saddle leather, and feel the chill of a Wyoming breeze against his face. Yet, Tom Horn, irregardless of his inner thoughts was passive and expressionless—displaying casual concern intermittently. Self control was something he had mastered from the Apaches, perhaps he even excelled them.

The introduction of letters written by Horn-LeFors-Smith by the Attorney Stoll could have made him angry inside. But maybe he didn't care any more. Maybe it was hard for him to realize this was October 24th, he was Tom Horn, and 44 years, so many days, so many seconds old, and that he was on trial for his life. Perhaps the Prosecutor disturbed him with his eternal shouting. Damn his hide Tom shouted from his brain! Now Stoll was in his face again—pointing, he roared, "Tom Horn was not joshing in his conversation with Joe LeFors! These letters are conclusive evidence of his guilt!"

Walter Stoll, studying each Juror, concluded his address with a burst of eloquence. He said the prolonged case had cost Laramie

County heavily—but the people had done their job—now it remained up to the Jury to do theirs. That was to find Tom Horn guilty of murder in the first degree!

The tired Jury filed out at exactly thirty minutes after eleven. All eyes were on the group as they shuffled from the Court Room. Collectively they held the fate of the Defendant in their hands.

The Counsel for the Defense relaxed. They talked in confident tones, but perhaps underneath it all they were uneasy. They assured Horn that he would be acquitted. Tom was perfectly calm but visibly pale—he was noncommittal. Walter Stoll near prostration would hang on until the verdict was given, it was only a matter of a few long hours. He didn't know . . .

Thus an air, thick with anxiety, settled down over Cheyenne. Men congregated about the Courthouse, on the streets, and in noisy bars over nickel beer. Bets were hot, heavy and numerous. Friends had made elaborate plans to celebrate the freedom they were sure Tom Horn would acquire shortly.

And the verdict as published in *The Cheyenne Daily Leader*, Saturday, October 25, 1902:

HORN GUILTY!!!

JURY BROUGHT IN A VERDICT YESTERDAY AFTERNOON AT JUST 4:37 O'CLOCK

Punishment Under the Law Will Be Hanging—Horn Hears Fatal Words Which Sealed His Fate Without a Trace of Emotion—Motion for New Trial Will Be Made.

At 4:37 o'clock last evening the jury in the Tom Horn case brought in a verdict of guilty of murder in the first degree. The imposition of the death sentence and the fixing of the date upon which this sentence will be carried out will probably occur Monday, although Judge Scott may postpone the last step he will take in this great case until later.

While Court Clerk Fisher was reading the verdict of the jury, carrying with it, as it does the ignominious death of hanging, Tom Horn, the cattle detective, the defendant for whose life the brightest attorneys in the state have been battling for two weeks, sat unmoved with his impassive face showing not the slightest indication of the emotion aroused by the verdict.

COURT ROOM CROWDED

It was just 4:20 o'clock when the bailiff sitting at the foot of the stairs which lead up to the jury room, was summoned by a voice calling from above:

"We have arrived at a verdict."

It was the voice of the foreman of the jury and the bailiff went down stairs, notified Judge Scott, who immediately proceeded to the court.

At that time not over half a dozen persons were in the room, but like wild fire the news spread. Within ten minutes people were flocking to the courthouse from all directions. Within fifteen minutes after the announcement was made by the foreman of the jury that a decision had been reached, the court room was crowded.

It was just 4:30 o'clock when the jury filed into the court room.

Tom Horn was sentenced to be hanged by the neck until dead between the hours of 10 a.m. and 3 p.m. on January 9, 1903. Sheriff Edwin Smalley was ordered to carry out the death sentence.

"THE KID"

Taken from the painting of Willie Nickell by Paul Gregg of the Denver Post Staff.

(Courtesy Denver Post)

PART THREE *The Last Mile*

My foot's in the stirrup, my pony won't stand
Goodbye Old Paint, I'm a-leavin' Cheyenne.
Goodbye Old Paint, I'm a-leavin' Cheyenne
Goodbye Old Paint, I'm a-leavin' Cheyenne.

—*Old Paint* (Author Unknown).

OCTOBER 29th

The Attorneys for Tom Horn wasted little time in filing a motion for a new trial in the District Court. Judge Scott refused to consider the motion because Prosecuting Attorney Walter Stoll was ill and thus unable to argue the matter before the Court.

However, the plea for a new trial began in earnest on November 8th with both the Prosecution and Defense represented. Attorney Burke presented the arguments for the Defense. Twenty-three reasons were put forward for a new trial.

The most prominent reason cited by Attorney Burke was that the Jury had been unduly influenced by a conversation they had overheard in the Inter-Ocean Hotel. The Attorney maintained that this conversation was held expressly for the purpose of influencing the Jury—especially for the benefit of one Juror.

Mr. Burke dwelled considerably on the language of Prosecutor Stoll. He said Stoll had been abusive when addressing the Jury. The part considered abusive was quoted to the Court. He read:

> "You gentlemen must do your duty. You need have no fear of blood guiltiness on your head. If you should make a mistake there is the Supreme Court that will do its duty, and then the Governor and he will do his duty. But if you make the mistake of freeing the defendant, he may do as another man, who was tried in this Court and because of the contrariness of three Jurors was acquitted; in three weeks killed a whole family in Montana. . ."

The Attorney then maintained that the Court had refused to give the Jury one instruction, to-wit: If there was any doubt in the minds of the Jury that if the wound in the boy's body was made by a 30-30 bullet the Defendant should receive the benefit of the doubt.

Burke also maintained that the Court had erred in allowing Joe LeFors to testify in regard to the "confession" Horn was to have made, and though it was later stricken from the Court Record, it no doubt unduly influenced the Jury.

The Attorney for the Defense concluded his rebuttal and rested.

The Prosecution successfully blocked the motion for a new trial. The Defense then filed a petition of error in the Supreme Court of Wyoming on December 31st. The higher Court's decision was to authorize a stay of execution until the case could be heard and determined by it.

Tom Horn was immediately notified of the action. It was reported the he displayed little concern over the news. Apparently he had been assured that such was thc due course of law by his attorneys.

The Legal action was based on the laws of Wyoming providing for the granting of a stay of execution in capital cases. A petition of error filed was all that was necessary, leaving the Court with no other alternative.

The Supreme Court was then to decide whether or not the judgment of the Trial Court was valid. If the verdict was termed valid then the Supreme Court was to select another date for the carrying out of the execution; if not it could grant a new trial.

Thus, Tom Horn was assured at least six more months of life at the minimum. The ruling gave the defense sixty days in which to file their brief on the legal questions involved. The Prosecution was given forty days to file its brief, after which the Defense was given sixty more days to file a counter brief. Following this action the entire case was to be heard by the State Supreme Court, and then the decision rendered after a period of advisement.

The time and delay factors made the Defense and the Defendant view the final outcome with a great deal more optimism. Tom Horn was not pleased at the thoughts of spending several more months in jail. He was said to have become very sullen and moody about it all.

The news was received in Cheyenne and surrounding country with the "I told you so" attitude. Most were somewhat tired of it all. Taxpayers were ever conscious of the drain the case had made on county funds. Laramie County couldn't afford another such trial.

JANUARY 1903

James P. Miller, formerly of Iron Mountain, was reported to have disappeared. He had moved into Cheyenne during the fall of 1902. Upon the missing report being made public, the Attorneys for Horn made insinuations that Miller had left the country because he feared new information had been discovered that would implicate him. The Defense censured the Court for having acquitted the ranchman and his son, Victor, upon the testimony of school teacher, Gwendoline Kimmell at the Coroner's inquest.

News of Horn's plan to break jail caused a considerable amount of excitement. The plans were exposed by the *Cheyenne Tribune* to the chagrin of law enforcement officers.

The break was well thought out and had it not been for one weak link—perhaps Horn would have gained his freedom.

The scheme began in the sentencing of a cowboy by the name of Herr to jail for theft of a saddle. Herr had his instructions. Once in jail he communicated with Horn, giving him the information he had been told to. Tom's friends were to dynamite the east wall of the jail, while the latter was taking his daily exercise in the hallway between 6 and 6:30 p.m. Once outside the cell block, Horn was instructed that he was to pass through the doors that were to have been "fixed," then on to the alley behind St. John's Hall, where a horse and gun awaited him. The escapee was to ride west via a relay of horses.

The plot was planned to perfection by the two inmates. Their communication was carried on by writing on toilet paper.

A fresh snowball was to be placed on a designated step of the building across from the jail. This was the signal to Tom that all was ready on the outside. Horn was then to signal he was ready by lighting a cigarette as he stood in a certain jail window, during his exercising period.

Two months had elapsed since the initial plans were made; then everything was ready.

In the meantime Herr, loaded with a message from Horn to John Coble, was released from jail; having served his time. Broke, hungry, and with nothing to do but brood, he became despondent. Herr feared that he would end up on a mortician's "slab" irregardless of the outcome. Jail officers, he thought, probably had observed his cordiality with Tom Horn during the short "stretch." Perhaps they had suspected him anyway. What if he was arrested and the message he carried found? Combining all, Herr suffered a severe case of "cold feet." After another restless night he conceived the idea that he would make a "deal" with the *Wyoming Tribune*. That was it! Herr would give them a terrific story in exchange for transportation to Utah and perhaps a little cash.

With the plan well in mind, Herr approached William C. Deming, publisher of the *Tribune*. After stammering and stuttering before the impatient Deming, Herr put his plan across—supporting it with the "toilet paper" message. Deming immediately realized the headline potential of the story. And so the nervous "kid" and reporter John Charles Thompson were ushered to seclusion. Herr poured out his heart and the plot to Thompson. He also gave up the message addressed to John Coble. Once he had the story, the reporter was quick to clasp a train ticket to Ogden, Utah, in Herr's hand and then beat it to his paper. This was the young reporter's big break—his first exclusive.

However, the story was withheld from publication for twenty-four hours as was agreed. Then on the morning of January 21st it was "spread" in bold headlines on the front page of the Tribune. Immediately it was a sensation. The entire Horn-Coble plot was revealed. All over Cheyenne, excited people heard the news and rushed to buy their copies.

Within a matter of minutes Sheriff Smalley bolted into Thompson's office screaming "fake," and asking, "what the hell?" in consecutive gasps. The "toilet paper" message, shoved across Thompson's desk, was the only reply. Smalley immediately recognized the handwriting, and became more furious.

And so—a failure. The big exposé only resulted in increased vigilance, and curtailment of Tom Horn's exercise periods. "Damn that Herr," Tom said as he paced back and forth in his cell, "damn him!"

Horn's attorneys in all probability were stunned when they learned of the plot. This didn't improve the situation. Too many ideas, too many workers, too much money... The Defense then decided to postpone the appeal as long as they could before filing a brief for a new trial. They had to make amends.

MARCH 31

The Defense filed a motion for a new trial with the State Supreme Court. The lengthy brief set forth their reasons in requesting the new trial for the condemned Horn. The document was complete in every detail. The Attorneys for the State had sixty days in which to file their brief.

MAY 1903

This month found President Theodore Roosevelt "strutting" in Cheyenne. The "Old Rough Rider" was wined and dined by Wyoming's big men—perhaps he heard about Tom Horn.

JULY 1903

At this point the case seemed to bog down. It was almost ninety days before further action was taken. The Wyoming State Supreme Court postponed the taking of the arguments for a new trial until after August 20th.

The news was apparently not welcome to Tom Horn. Since the plot, he had become increasingly irritable and restless; always smoking and pacing in his cell. He was completely isolated from the other prisoners.

As the hot and dry summer wore on, new twists were printed almost daily on the case. Horn's past was probed for something revealing, but little was found. Tom was sick of everything. "God, to get it over with—one way or the other," he mused.

Then came August and Jim McCloud. The latter was also in death row. Tom Horn liked McCloud, he was different—maybe he had "guts." They made plans.

AUGUST 10—THE BIG BREAK

The long "expected" jail break came on a hot and peaceful Sunday morning. Good Christians were worshipping in church. "Indulgees" were recuperating from the night before. But the majority of Cheyenneites were just piddling, taking advantage of the beautiful weather on their day of rest. Thus the hour of the break was timely.

The two prisoners were almost alone at the county jail, Richard Proctor was on duty. Deputy Leslie Snow was basking in the sunshine on the Courthouse steps. Sheriff Smalley was at his home adjoining the area.

The escape had been planned by the two prisoners well in advance. Jim McCloud had laid the initial ground work by feigning a stomach illness for several days. Water was required with each dose of his medicine.

Mr. Proctor was in the habit of handing McCloud his water through a door leading into the corridor of the two prisoner's cells. On this morning the attendant mounted the ladder to the upper cell block, as usual. He entered upon the narrow gang-way through a steel door. Proctor had filled the glass unusually full, McCloud had been complaining that he hadn't been receiving enough water. Thus the jailer was fully occupied in attempting to avoid spilling any of the water as he unlocked the steel door—his eyes were not on the prisoners. The instant the lock was released, the two large men hit the door. Proctor was knocked backward by the jolt. Immediately he dropped the water and lunged back at the door. It was too late, the prisoners were on him. A fierce fight followed on the narrow gangway as the two men tried to overpower the law officer. Proctor fought with superhuman strength. He succeeded in knocking McCloud half way over the railing with a solid punch, but in an instant Horn was at Proctor's throat with his powerful hands. As the Deputy twisted at the hands about his neck, McCloud regained the railing and began smashing away at him. Near strangulation, the jailer sank to the floor; Tom relaxed his grip, and color returned to Proctor's face as McCloud began tying his hands with window blind cord.

Horn and McCloud, then removed the jailer's keys and headed for the Sheriff's office and guns, pushing Proctor ahead of them. They were told by Proctor that the guns were locked in the safe. However, McCloud found a loaded Winchester repeating rifle on the top of a wardrobe. In the corner of the same room was a closet filled with weapons, but neither of the desperadoes noticed it.

Once in possession of the gun, McCloud pushed the muzzle of the rifle against Proctor's head while Horn held him, demanding that the safe be opened. Proctor stalled for time—feeling that help would surely arrive any minute. He succeeded in convincing the two that his hands would have to be untied to enable him to work the safe combination. As he fumbled at the combination, McCloud sensed the stall and jammed the gun muzzle in his back and shouted, "open the safe or I'll blow your G—— D—— head off." As Dick Proctor began opening the safe door, he told McCloud to look in the closet for an inside key. At this time, Tom Horn was with his eyes away from Proctor, watching the windows in case anyone started to come into the jail. Les Snow was still basking on the steps just outside the door. Once Jim McCloud turned his head and was off guard to pick up the key, Proctor jerked his rifle away from him and had it in his back. An instant later Tom Horn was on him. The three men again rolled over and over on the floor. The two were unable to get the gun away from the Deputy. Twice the jailer fired the gun, but each time the men managed to twist away from the deadly line of fire.

McCloud finally succeeded in twisting the rifle from Proctor's hands, but at the same time Dick lunged for the safe and grabbed a revolver. Horn was on him again. An instant later Les Snow, still not having heard either the shots or the commotion, concluded it was time to feed the prisoners and entered the office, only to have the muzzle of the rifle McCloud held shoved in his face. Snow quickly whirled and ran.

As Les Snow fled, McCloud seized the opportunity to gain his freedom and left Horn still grappling with the officer.

The fight raged on a few minutes longer. Then the prisoner managed to twist the Belgian made revolver around behind Proctor's back, almost tearing off a finger through the trigger guard. Proctor realizing he was "bested" said, "Well, if you want the gun, let go my arm and I'll give it to you." As Horn turned loose of his arm, Proctor snapped the automatic on safety and handed the weapon over to Tom Horn as he said he would.

The instant Horn had control of the gun he pointed it at Proctor.* He found that he could not work the firing mechanism. At any rate, thoroughly confused, Tom Horn turned and ran out the door, left open by the fleeing McCloud. Once in the court yard, Tom looked for a horse—McCloud had taken the only one. Leaving the barn he ran around the Courthouse and into the alley at the rear of the jail.

In the meantime Les Snow had succeeded in giving the alarm by firing his gun and shouting; church bells and the firing of more guns made the alarm general. Church congregations immediately dispersed and citizens poured from their homes into the Courthouse area. Chaos and confusion reigned! All the while Horn and McCloud continued their break in separate directions.

Tom Horn, running up the alley had been observed by O. A. Aldrich, a merry-go-round operator. Aldrich immediately sensed the situation, took pursuit with his six-shooter in hand. At the corner of Twentieth and Capitol, two blocks from the jail, Aldrich overtook Horn. The latter's ignorance of the safety mechanism was perhaps all that saved Aldrich's life. The carnival man fired once at Horn, grazing the top of his head, then he used his gun as a club. About this time police officers, Ahrens and Stone arrived, whereupon

*Whether Horn would have killed Proctor at this point, had he been able to work the gun has often been a point of speculation. Opinions have been expressed to both effects. Tom Horn could have choked the Deputy to death a few minutes before.

Tom Horn surrendered, and was escorted to the jail with "half" Cheyenne following. When near the jail, Deputy Sheriff Les Snow rode up on horseback and dismounting he directed a heavy blow at the captive's head with his rifle butt. Sensing the action, Officer Stone threw up his arm and blocked the blow, but in doing so suffered a broken arm.

Back to Jim McCloud: He had secured the only horse from the Courthouse barn. As the desperado was mounting the animal in the alley, Sheriff Smalley, having heard the alarm, started for the jail with his gun when he saw McCloud and took a quick shot at him. McCloud then dodged behind the animal and retreated down the alley with the horse serving as protection. Smalley fired again, McCloud still trying to get on the horse feigned as he had been hit, swung under the horse and came up on the opposite side and mounted the animal and was on his way. Emerging into Eddy Street from the alley he ran into one Patrick Hennessey, a mail clerk. Hennessey was armed with a double-barreled shotgun, and had also heard the alarm and at this instant was on his way to the center of the excitement. However, Hennessey did not know McCloud and so hesitated. Afraid of Hennessey, the mounted man shouted, "Tom Horn has escaped! Have you seen him?" The armed man lowered his shotgun and answered, "No." Then he asked, "Which way did Horn go?" McCloud whipped and spurred the mare past the confused Hennessey and turned into the alley at Twentieth and Twenty-first streets on the dead run with a host of possemen in hot pursuit. The alarm was general by now and Cheyenne an armed camp. The rider entered an alley only to find it blocked at the other end. Jumping from his horse he sought refuge in a small barn.

Policeman John Nowlan and a youth named Oscar Lamm, saw him dart into the barn. Both men were fully armed. Not realizing he had been spotted, McCloud stuck his head out of the barn door to size up the situation, whereupon Lamm shouted, "Move and I'll kill you!" McCloud ducked back in, shouting, "Don't shoot! I'll surrender!"

The two men then escorted the near-trembling McCloud back to jail where they turned him over to Sheriff Smalley.

By the time the prisoners were being returned all of Old Cheyenne was in a high state of excitement. Mob violence against the escapees was mounting. Distortion and rumor was being voiced. It was reported that both Horn and McCloud would die because of wounds and that Proctor was seriously injured. Men keenly interested in the case were cussing and criticizing Sheriff Smalley—demanding he punish the offenders. Kels P. Nickell began haranguing the mob—urging action. However, he was quickly silenced by Sheriff Smalley who threatened to put him into the same cell with Tom Horn.

AUGUST 20

The Counsel for the Defense had filed a petition in error for a new trial. Again they were embarrassed by Tom's break with McCloud. Damn it all! Public sentiment was against them for sure. God, what could they do? Nevertheless, Judge J. W. Lacey opened for the Defense, followed by T. F. Burke, United States District Attorney from Wyoming. The Prosecution was represented as usual by the unrelenting Walter Stoll; he was assisted by the able J. A. Van Orsdel.

The grounds for the trial were purely technical in nature, as the plea that new evidence had been obtained was not received. The basis for the Defense arguments was on the admission and rejection of certain testimonies. The rejection of the testimony of Victor Miller was one of the major contestations. The case was argued at length before the Court. It would be at least a month before the higher Court would render their opinion on the verdict of the lower Court.

Thus, the fall of 1903 saw the epoch enter its final and most furious stages. The Counsel for the condemned worked feverishly to find a "legal loop-hole," while Horn's friends made vows to free him through violence if necessary. The accused man seemed to "become alive" again, confident that he would gain his freedom—one way or the other.

In Cheyenne and contiguous areas an assortment of rumors were freely circulating. A frontier street duel between LeFors and Horn was depicted by many, should the latter gain his freedom.

Whether or not Tom Horn was going to talk before his execution was also a major topic of conversation. No doubt, some Horn men were becoming increasingly uneasy. Kels Nickell believed that the man in the death cell would reveal all about his employers; in fact he made public statements to that effect. The *Cheyenne Tribune*, September 2, 1903:

> "Kels P. Nickell believes that Tom Horn will weaken and give up the names of his employers if the finding of the Supreme Court is adverse and he realizes that he is really

to be hanged. Nickell knows that the testimony of a condemned criminal is not permissible evidence, but says that revelations which Horn may make will aid in fastening upon the right parties the conception of the crime for which Horn bids fair to pay the penalty. Nickell no longer has the slightest doubt that Horn is the murderer of his son and disowns any suspicion concerning other parties at the time of the murder suspected."

OCTOBER 1

The Lower Court's Verdict Affirmed

The long awaited verdict of the State Supreme Court was rendered. The High Court handed down an opinion affirming the verdict of the Lower Court that had adjudged Horn guilty of the murder of Willie Nickell. The execution date was affixed at November 20th.

The Higher Court's opinion was read by Justice C. N. Potter. The opinion required two hours to be read, and covered the entire case in detail. The decision was concurred on by Chief Justice Corn and Justice Knight.

The condemned man was sentenced to be hanged by the neck until dead on the James P. Julian gallows. The same as those used for the execution of Charles Miller in 1892.

The Attorneys for the condemned man gave notice to the Court that they would file a motion for a review of the case. Few conceded to the idea that the Court would reverse itself. Tom Horn and his attorneys had a conference the following morning.

MID OCTOBER

Almost one month from the day he was to be executed, Tom Horn wrote a letter of appeal to a Denver man who he said had perjured at the trial. He pleaded for him to tell what he knew. The letter was published as follows:*

"Cheyenne, Wyo.

"Mr. ——————:

"Dear Sir—I am writing you this letter with the sentence of death hanging over me. I'm to be executed Nov. 20 if something is not done to show up the fact that this testimony was all wrong, and that the ones that testified against me did so influenced by either Stoll or LeFors, or maybe both of them together.

**Laramie Boomerang*, October 20, 1903.

"A great injustice has been done me, and you can if you will rectify it so that I will not be hung.

"I wrote Billy Loomis to come and see you, and if you will consent to help me now I will have my friend, Mr. John C. Coble of Bosler, Wyo., come down and see you. If you done as you did at the instigation of the prosecuting attorney and deputy United States marshal THEY AND NOT YOU ARE RESPONSIBLE.

"Mr.——— ———, you can do me a service now such as few men have a chance to do in a lifetime. You can just open your mouth and save my life.

"WILL YOU DO IT?

"You may write my attorney, Mr. T. F. Burke, Cheyenne, Wyo., or better still if you feel inclined to do anything for me, write to Mr. Coble at Bosler and he will come down to see you personally.

"There will necessarily be some expense attached to making out the necessary papers, and I am sure Mr. Coble will pay all expenses. Please write to HIM anyway.

"I wrote Billy Loomis to go and see you. Words cannot express the feelings of one in my position—condemned to die as I am, and after once more asking your assistance and hoping that you will comply with my request and save my life I will close. Yours truly,

"TOM HORN.

"Please write to Mr. J. C. Coble, Bosler, Wyo., as I am not in position now to carry on a correspondence.

"T. H."

With the execution drawing near, rumors of another jail break plot made its rounds. *The Denver Post* created a sensation when it printed a feature on how six desperadoes backed by certain Wyoming cattlemen would storm the Laramie County jail in an attempt to free the condemned man.

Sheriff Smalley, cognizant of what the supporters of Horn might do, had a Gatling gun mounted into the building. The weapon was obtained from the Army authorities at Fort D. A. Russell. A Sgt. Mahon, a gunner, was given the operation assignment; Mahon was quartered in the jail.

When interviewed by a reporter from the *Cheyenne Leader,* Smalley stated, "I do not expect an attack, but am acting upon the theory that the best way to prevent one being made is to take such precautions as to make the failure of the attack almost certain." The Sheriff went on to say, "We have received warnings from many different sources of plans to free Horn and believe there are many people who would risk their lives and fortunes to get him out. With this condition of affairs staring us in the face, we will leave no stone unturned in providing against such an emergency. The defenses of the jail are now complete and unless the Courts or the Governor interfere, Tom Horn will be executed on the date set."

The weapon was given a large amount of publicity. It was advertised to have the capacity to fire up to 250 .30 calibre steel jacketed bullets per minute, with velocity enough to penetrate a brick wall. In the machine gun, Sheriff Smalley found an effective weapon and a great deal of security.

OCTOBER 29

An affidavit was filed by the Defense with Governor Fenimore Chatterton. The document was purported to have been written by the "real" murderer of Willie Nickell, and said to have contained a complete confession of the crime.

This was the first in a series of startling developments.

Secondly were the charges brought against Victor Miller by Glendolene Irene Kimmell, the former Iron Mountain school teacher. She had lived with the Millers.

Miss Kimmell, with the Defense Attorneys, appeared before Governor Chatterton for a hearing.

An affidavit made by Jack Martin of Laramie was also presented by Attorney Burke. In part the affidavit read:

> "That he, prior to the arrest of Tom Horn, had two separate conversations with said Joe LeFors in reference to the killing of Willie Nickell; that the said LeFors told affiant in one or both of the said conversations that he (LeFors) had been investigating the killing and that he dug around so close to Jim Miller that Miller gave to him five hundred dollars to cease the investigations as against the said Miller and his family, and the said LeFors saying at the time that the said $500.00 given him by Mr. Miller was a part of $600.00 which the said Miller had then recently received.

That the said LeFors further said to the affiant that there was a $1,000.00 reward for cinching somebody for that murder, and that Tom Horn was always claiming every man that had been killed within four hundred miles of him and had a bad reputation it would be easy to cinch Horn, and the said LeFors asked affiant to go in with him and help furnish evidence to cinch the said Horn for the purpose of getting the reward."

Mr. Burke then related to the Governor that how he had been the administrator of an estate, in which the deceased had money to loan. Just prior to the murder of Willie Nickell the amount of $600 had been loaned to James Miller. Of this amount Burke said only $100 had been accounted for. It was then inferred by the Attorney that $500 must have been paid Joe LeFors to leave the Millers out of the investigation.

Mr. Burke read the following petition from the condemned Horn in which he asked for a commutation of his sentence to life:

"Cheyenne, Wyo., Oct. 29, 1903.

"To His Excellence, Fenimore Chatterton,
"Governor of the State of Wyoming.

"Sir: I, the undersigned, Tom Horn, your petitioner, beg to show to your excellency that I have been convicted of the crime of murder in the first degree; that I have carried my cause to the Supreme Court of the State of Wyoming, which has affirmed the judgment and sentence against me and has fixed Friday, the 20th day of November, A.D. 1903, for the carrying out against me of a capital sentence.

"I do hereby most solemnly assert my innocence of the crime charged against me, and do express my confidence that within a few years at most my innocence will be made apparent to the entire community by the full disclosure of facts showing that another and not myself committed the crime for which I have been sentenced. Personally I do not know who committed the crime. I am informed that affidavits have been procured from different persons by my attorneys indicating that another has confessed the crime. I have not read said affidavits, or any of them, nor do I know, except in a general way, their contents, and as far as I do know the contents the facts shown were not known to me at any time prior to my appeal to the Supreme Court for the reversal of the judgment and sentence against me in this cause.

"To the end that full justice may be done, I hereby respectfully petition your excellency to grant a reprieve and substitute as a penalty against me imprisonment in the state penitentiary in the state of Wyoming for the period of my natural life instead of the capital sentence which has been pronounced against me.

"Presented most respectfully,
(Signed) "Tom Horn."

Attorney Burke then made a lengthy appeal for the life of his client. He emphasized that the prisoner had asked no more than life in prison which Burke said was the penalty in many states.

Judge Lacey followed Mr. Burke. He too made a plea for the life of the condemned Horn.

Miss Kimmell was presented to the Governor by the Attorneys. They stated that she had voluntarily traveled from Kansas City to appear in behalf of Horn. Following the introduction, Governor Chatterton and the former school teacher had a long conference in the Chief Executive's office.

Attorney General Van Orsdel represented the Prosecution at the reading of the affidavits. He asked the Governor to establish the time when the State could file its counter-affidavits. Mr. Chatterton accordingly set Thursday, November 5 at one o'clock for the hearing. Prosecutor Stoll was in Laramie City on another case at this time.

NOVEMBER 3

Attorney Walter Stoll retaliated against the affidavits of the Defense with surprising action when he filed complaint of perjury against Miss Kimmell. The complaint was filed with Justice of the Peace Trump in Cheyenne. Upon receipt of the complaint, a warrant for Miss Kimmell's arrest was issued.

At 2 o'clock Miss Kimmell appeared before Mr. Trump with Attorney T. F. Burke. Attorney Burke defended his client, pleading that she be set free upon the ground that Mr. Stoll's charge was not a legal complaint. Attorney Van Orsdel, representing Walter Stoll, declined to defend the latter's action; however, he suggested that Miss Kimmell be held until the Prosecutor could appear in his own behalf.

Mr. Burke then filed a demurrer to the complaint which was overruled. Mr. Trump held the Defendant under bond for the amount of $2,000 "to insure her appearance on Saturday morning at 10 a.m. for the preliminary hearing." The amount of the bond was put up by Mr. T. T. Clark and Mr. John Coble.

On this day Governor Fenimore Chatterton invited the Prosecution to present its side of the case on Thursday (November 5th) at 2 o'clock in the afternoon. He refused to give reporters his decision deadline date.

The turn of events caused considerable speculation throughout interested areas. Kels Nickell was a witness at the hearing before the Governor—on one occasion was cautioned against interrupting the proceedings with outbursts of his opinion. The return of Marshal Joe LeFors from South America added to the growing tenseness of the situation.

Thus all awaited the decison of the Governor. Would he succumb to the great pressure exerted on him by Horn's backers? Public opinion? A decision either way might affect his political future.

NOVEMBER 4

A stack of affidavits was presented to the Governor by persons anxious to save Tom Horn from the gallows. The new evidence tended to implicate the James Millers—clearing the condemned.

Albert W. Bristol of Horse Creek swore that he had held a conversation with either Victor or Gus Miller (stating he could not tell them apart) and that this person said Tom Horn had not killed Willie Nickell and implied that he knew who did. The alleged conversation was to have taken place during October, 1902.

Sheriff Cook of Laramie made an affidavit to the effect that Jack Martin of the same city had told him of a "deal" between Joe LeFors and James Miller. Cook swore that Martin said LeFors told him how James Miller had paid the Deputy Marshal $500 to stop investigation in the Miller direction.

Deputy Marshal Yund, also of Laramie, made an affidavit supporting Sheriff Cook.

During the evening of the same day Clerk of the District Court T. J. Fisher, received the mandate of the Supreme Court ordering that the execution of Tom Horn be carried out. The date had been set for Friday, November 20th, between the hours of 9 a.m. and

3 p.m. The mandate was delivered by Sheriff Smalley to the condemned Horn.

Late in the evening Victor Miller arrived in Cheyenne, in preparation for his appearance before the Governor. He was escorted by Sheriff Smalley, who had presented him the appearance notice.

The lad told the officers how he had been approached south of Wheatland on the same day by two horsemen and told that conclusive evidence had been filed with Governor Chatterton implicating him of the murder. They suggested that he leave the country immediately. Almost terrified, the boy rode on home where he met Sheriff Smalley. At first sight of the officer he thought the men were correct and he was to be arrested. Soon he learned the truth of the ill-conceived plan.

NOVEMBER 7

Victor Miller was summoned to the Capitol to appear before Governor Chatterton. The results of the meeting were not made public. Later in the day the boy was provided with a police escort as it was feared he might be threatened or intimidated.

The presence of an unusual number of cowboys in Cheyenne caused some speculation as to a probable "break." A message marked 11-11-11 was tossed into the jail yard by a horseman and intercepted by officers. The note was interpreted to have been directed to Tom Horn. Meaning an attempt to save Horn would be made on November the eleventh month, the eleventh day and the eleventh hour.

In the meantime Sheriff Smalley took additional protective measures at the county jail. Armed guards maintained vigilance by being strategically stationed about the Courthouse. A large arc light was placed near the building thus eliminating fear of a surprise night attack. Loitering in the immediate Courthouse area was prohibited.

NOVEMBER 10

Shortly before mid-day Judge Richard Scott issued a bench warrant for the arrest of the dark and shapely Miss Kimmell. The grounds for the arrest were perjury. Prosecutor Attorney Walter Stoll filed the charges.

The former teacher's affidavit had charged Victor Miller with the murder of Willie Nickell. Accordingly Police Officer Nowlan escorted the parents, Mr. and Mrs. James Miller, to Cheyenne from their Iron Mountain ranch. They were prepared for the ordeal.

Miss Kimmell was placed under a $2,000 bond. The American Security Surety Company held the bond through Riner & Schnitger. Attorney Burke argued for a smaller bond.

NOVEMBER 11

Governor Chatterton set 10 o'clock Thursday, November 12th as the day he would hear the arguments of the Attorneys for the Prosecution. He indicated his final decision was not to be delayed.

The affidavit of Jack Martin of Laramie was considered the strongest. The evidence charged Joe LeFors of conspiring with James Miller in conducting the investigation—clearing the latter.*

The Wyoming Tribune of November 11, 1903 noted John C. Coble's appearance in Cheyenne as follows:

COBLE IN LARAMIE

"John C. Coble, of Bosler, the close friend of Tom Horn, who has been in this city since the appeal was made to the Governor, is now in Laramie watching the struggle between Frank Stone and Steamboat. Coble offered Stone $250 to ride the horse without spurs, and to whip him at every jump."

NOVEMBER 12

This day marked the opening of the Prosecution's reply to the affidavits by Miss Kimmell, Martin, Shaffer, Plaga and others. Kels P. Nickell and John Coble were vitally concerned onlookers.

Before the Prosecution began its rebuttal testimony, another affidavit was presented the Governor by the Attorney for the Defense. The affidavit was that of William Fitzmorris. The affidavit read:

"The State of Wyoming, County of Laramie, ss.

"In the Matter of the Application of Tom Horn for Reprieve.

"AFFIDAVIT

"William Fitzmorris, being duly sworn upon his oath, does depose and say: I live at the present time at the ranch of John Shaffer on the Sybille, in the County of Albany and State aforesaid, and am 17 years of age.

"I remember that on the fourth day of July, 1901, that I met Willie Nickell at a dance at my father's ranch on the

*Considerable curiosity was beginning to be evinced at this time as to who would be invited to attend the execution should Horn not be granted a reprieve. The law provided that Sheriff Smalley could invite twelve witnesses. The condemned Horn was allowed six. Thus a total of eighteen men could witness the execution.

Sybille, and Willie Nickell told me that him and Victor Miller had had a quarrel and Victor had threatened to kill him; he did not say just when the quarrel was, but that it was just a few days before. The same day Victor Miller, who was also at the picnic and dance, told me that if the damned kid (meaning Willie Nickell) bothered him he would kill him, and if he did not look out he would kill him anyway. I went to California in March, 1902, and stayed there till November, 1902. I was well acquainted with Willie Nickell and Victor Miller and knew both boys for many years and ever since we were little boys.

"WILLIAM FITZMORRIS

"Subscribed in my presence and sworn to before me by the said William Fitzmorris on this eleventh day of November, A. D. 1903. And I certify that the said affidavit was written by me out in the hills near Iron Mountain, Wyoming, from statements voluntarily and personally made to me by the said affiant, and in as near his exact words as possible, and that I read said affidavit over carefully to the said affiant before he signed it and said affiant then solemnly swore that the statements are true. I further certify that my commission expires on June 29, 1903.

"D. W. ELLIOTT,
"*Notary Public.*"

In his casual, eager and confident manner, Walter Stoll slowly began. He attacked those presented by the Defense—and read affidavits for the Prosecution. The first few presented were merely introductory.

The first was that of a Mrs. Simpson of Laramie. She made an affidavit that she had seen Tom in Laramie on July 19, 1901. Another was by James Daugherty, also of the same city. The latter declared that Horn had been seen by him in Laramie on July 18, 19, 20; part of the time in Allen's Saloon. Steve Frazer made an affidavit corroborating that of Mr. Daugherty.

Attorney Stoll pointed out such an abundance of evidence of this type would have been impossible to have secured at the time of the trial because the affiants were afraid to testify.

VAN GUILFORD'S AFFIDAVIT

The Prosecutor read the affidavit of Van L. Guilford regarding the sweater found in the Laramie Shoe Shop which was believed to have been Tom Horn's. Mr. Guilford's affidavit stated that Tom Horn had entered Max Meyer's store several weeks before the murder and asked for the sweater. Mr. Meyer, he stated, had told him later that he (Meyer) had supplied Horn with a sweater which he procured from another store.

W. F. MULLOCK'S TESTIMONY

Mr. Stoll then presented the testimony and refuted the evidence given in the affidavit by W. F. Mullock. The latter had testified that it was Horn who had made a "confession" in regard to the Nickell murder at the Scandinavian Saloon in Denver during October, 1902. The Attorney exhibited correspondence refuting Mullock's reversal. In the letters to Stoll, Mullock congratulated the Attorney on his victory in conducting the prosecution. Mullock had written that he had other evidence corroborating what he had testified. He affirmed that he had seen "Roberts" the bartender in the Scandinavian Saloon, while in St. Louis, and this person had told him the check Tom Horn had tried to cash was one signed by John C. Coble and for the amount of $200.

THE $500 ALLEGEDLY PAID JOE LEFORS

The Attorney made quick work of the charge that $500 had been paid Joe LeFors by James E. Miller to direct the investigation away from the Millers. Evidence was presented to the effect that the money had been borrowed from the firm of Riner and Schnitger. Vouchers covering the expenditure of the entire amount to various Cheyenne merchants were exhibited by the Prosecution.

JACK MARTIN'S REPUTATION

The reputation of Jack Martin for telling the truth was considered in a large number of affidavits.

Mr. M. N. Grant, Police Justice of Laramie, stated in his document that Martin's reputation for the truth was bad.

Frank Irwin, also of Laramie, indicated in his affidavit that Martin was known to "stretch" points. He said on one occasion Martin had told him he was one of the Younger brothers (Missouri outlaws) and that Martin had shown him a picture of himself and Jesse James.

Charles W. Settelle's affidavit stated Martin's reputation for telling the truth was poor. He also said Martin had indicated to him that he was one of the Younger brothers.

The affidavits of S. C. Downey, Frank H. Eggleston and George E. Eggleston also mentioned that Martin's reputation for veracity was bad.

An affidavit by Joe LeFors denounced all the statements made by Martin as false. LeFors stated that during the Posse hunt for the Wilcox train robbers, Martin told him that he was in contact with the Curry Gang. The Deputy United States Marshal also stated that Martin wore a white handkerchief around his arm during the "chase," so Martin would not be fired on by the outlaws should they corner them.

Judge Lacey in turn presented affidavits of E. J. Bell, Ora Haley, E. A. Williams, W. H. Frazee, N. K. Boswell, John W. Connor, A. Whitehouse, and R. H. Homer. All stated that Jack Martin's reputation for telling the truth was good. Several of the affiants stated that Martin had been employed by them at various times.

THE SENSATION OF THE DAY!

The sensation of the day was the affidavits of "Chris" Lund and Charles Fletcher. They were introduced by Attorney Stoll. Lund swore that he saw Tom Horn a short time after the crime had been committed. Fletcher stated that he saw the condemned Horn fire the shots that killed the boy.* The Prosecution said that this evidence was in his hands at the time of the trial, but as Fletcher was in prison in Colorado for calf theft, he decided not to submit it to the jury.

HORN WAS SPYING

Claude Draper's affidavit was read in which he says that while fishing he saw Tom Horn emerging from the brush near the Nickell ranch. This was stated to have taken place a few months before the death of Willie Nickell.

STOLL VS. MISS KIMMELL

In referring to the affidavit of Glendolene Kimmell, Attorney Stoll said that he had met her when she visited Cheyenne shortly before her trip East and that she had not made any reference to having important evidence regarding Tom Horn.

*Perhaps the affidavit of Charles Fletcher was presented by Stoll as a counter move; in an effort to emphasize the fact that absurdities obviously were being sworn to.

Mr. Stoll stated that he had written a number of letters to Miss Kimmell at Kansas City. None of them were answered he added. The affidavit of W. B. Ross who went to Kansas City and attempted to induce Miss Kimmell to come to Cheyenne and testify was read. Ross, Stoll said, failed to get Miss Kimmell to return with him.

The Prosecution made no attempt to impeach the sworn statements of Miss Kimmell. The only denials were those affecting James E. Miller and his son.

MILLER AFFIDAVITS

The affidavit of Victor Miller was introduced next. His statement denied all the charges made by affiants for the Defense that he had killed Willie Nickell. Stoll mentioned Joe LeFors, and that LeFors in his affidavit denied that he had made statements implicating the Millers in a conversation with Attorney E. T. Clark during a ride from Sherman to Cheyenne.

The affidavits of James, Dora, and Victor Miller were then jointly introduced, in regard to the attempt that had been made the week before to induce Victor Miller to confess to Governor Chatterton that he was guilty.

The affiants stated that Charles Irwin, formerly with the Coble ranch, and Neil Clark, the present foreman, came to the James Miller ranch and told Mr. and Mrs. Miller that Cheyenne officers were on their way out to Iron Mountain to arrest Victor, and that the best thing for them to do was to have Victor go into town and confess—he would be making it easier on himself by doing so, the men were to have said. The two men, according to the affidavits, left in haste when they learned Victor was in Wheatland. The lad was intercepted at Clay's ranch. At which time Irwin was said to have taken Victor behind the barn and repeated the arrest story urging him to ride into Cheyenne and confess to the crime. The lad, it was stated, replied that he was not guilty and intended to return home even if there were a dozen officers waiting there.

Stoll reiterated the affidavit of Victor Miller was conclusive proof that he was in Cheyenne at the time he was to have made his alleged confession to Albert Bristol. This was to have taken place at the Iron Mountain ranch.

Attorney Stoll, then in a relaxed manner, spoke on the preparation of the case by the Defense. He pointed out and analyzed each of the four major alibis (as he called them) that the Attorneys for Tom Horn had followed. Primarily that they sought to prove that Otto Plaga had seen Tom Horn on July 18th, 1901, at a distance too far away from Iron Mountain for Horn to have committed the crime. This was refuted by another testimony Stoll added.

Last and bitterly contested was the affidavit of Clarence D. Houck. He stated that Alex Sellers had told him that John C. Coble gave him a letter addressed to Attorney T. F. Burke. He took the letter to Mr. Burke's office; the latter then opened the letter and let Sellers read it. Mr. Sellers told Houck the letter stated that the bearer would testify that Horn was at his ranch on the night of the killing. The Attorney then asked Sellers if this was true and the ranchman replied it was not. The two men then went to the office of Mr. Lacey who in turn asked Sellers if the letter was true and reply was the same —"no." The two, according to the affidavit, then asked Mr. Sellers if there was anything that could be offered that would induce him to change his mind and swear that Tom Horn was at his ranch, and he replied there was not.

At this time the hearing was reaching the boiling point. Both Mr. Burke and Mr. Lacey were on the floor strongly denying the affidavit of Houck. Mr. Stoll was asked by Judge Lacey if this evidence was introduced to asperse the reputations of the Attorneys in the community. To this Mr. Stoll replied that all through the case it had been intimated in various ways that he had been using unprofessional methods in conducting the Prosecution. He stated he had simply introduced the evidence to show the degree of developments.

The affidavit stated that it was contrary to Mr. Houck's desire to connect himself with the case. However, he felt in view of the statements sworn to by witnesses for the Defense he thought it his duty to appear in behalf of the State.

One of the most excited spectators at this hearing was Kels P. Nickell. He practically lived every word of the tense situation. He, no doubt, felt the outcome of this hearing would be the "cincher"—Horn would be executed. Several times, it was reported, he interrupted the proceedings. On one occasion he became so upset that Judge Lacey asked that he be removed from the room. Then Governor Chatterton requested him to remain quiet.

UNDERCURRENTS OF THE CASE

M. M. *Grant, right, Laramie, Wyoming; W. D. Smith, center, Miles City, Montana; and E. Davies, Marshal of Laramie, Wyoming. Mr. Smith corresponded with LeFors in regard to the Montana job for Horn.*

(Courtesy Rocky Mountain News)

DUNCAN CLARK

Leathery cowboy, foreman for the Iron Mountain Cattle Company. Tom was his friend.

(Courtesy Denver Post)

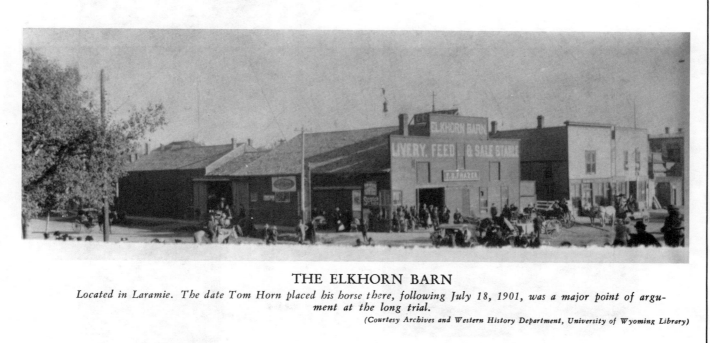

THE ELKHORN BARN

Located in Laramie. The date Tom Horn placed his horse there, following July 18, 1901, was a major point of argument at the long trial.

(Courtesy Archives and Western History Department, University of Wyoming Library)

FRANK STONE ON NEVADA

He was a witness at the long trial.

(Courtesy Archives and Western History Department, University of Wyoming Library)

"STEAMBOAT"

A solid contemporary.

(Courtesy Archives and Western History Department, University of Wyoming Library)

PRESIDENT THEODORE ROOSEVELT AND
DR. AMOS BARBER

The President visited Wyoming May, 1903. Perhaps he learned about Tom Horn.

(Courtesy Archives and Western History Department, University of Wyoming Library)

FRONTIER DAYS WAS BORN DURING THE SAGA OF TOM HORN

Charles Irwin with branding iron, R. M. Carey with flag, and R. S. Van Tassell judging.

(Courtesy Archives and Western History Department, University of Wyoming Library)

JUDGE C. N. POTTER

(Courtesy Archives and Western History Department, University of Wyoming Library)

JOHN CHARLES THOMPSON

As a young newspaper reporter, he covered the case in its entirety.

(Courtesy John Charles Thompson, Jr., Rawlins, Wyo.)

SALOON AT 1719 BLAKE STREET, DENVER

Here Tom Horn was said to have bragged, "The killing of the kid was the longest shot I ever made and the dirtiest trick I ever done."

(Courtesy Rocky Mountain News)

GLENDOLENE M. KIMMELL

The dark little school "marm" from Iron Mountain. "Smooth people," Tom called her.

(Courtesy Archives and Western History Department, University of Wyoming Library)

GOVENOR FENIMORE CHATTERTON

"I do not believe that the law and justice would be served by the interposition of executive clemency."

(Courtesy Archives and Western History Department, University of Wyoming Library)

TOM HORN

"Keep your nerve John, for I'll keep mine. You know Tom Horn."

(Courtesy Archives and Western History Department, University of Wyoming Library)

THE "BIG" DAY

November 20, 1903. The day of Horn's execution. Armed troops helped keep the crowd orderly.

(Courtesy Archives and Western History Department, University of Wyoming Library)

JAMES JULIAN

Mr. Julian, a noted Cheyenne architect, designed the gallows that Tom Horn was hanged on. His death-taking device was a weird classic in "Rube Goldbergism."

(Courtesy Archives and Western History Department, University of Wyoming Library)

T. JOE CAHILL

"Joe," said Horn, "they tell me you're married now. I hope you're doing well. Treat her right . . ." Those were Tom's last words.

(Courtesy T. Joe Cahill, Cheyenne, Wyo.)

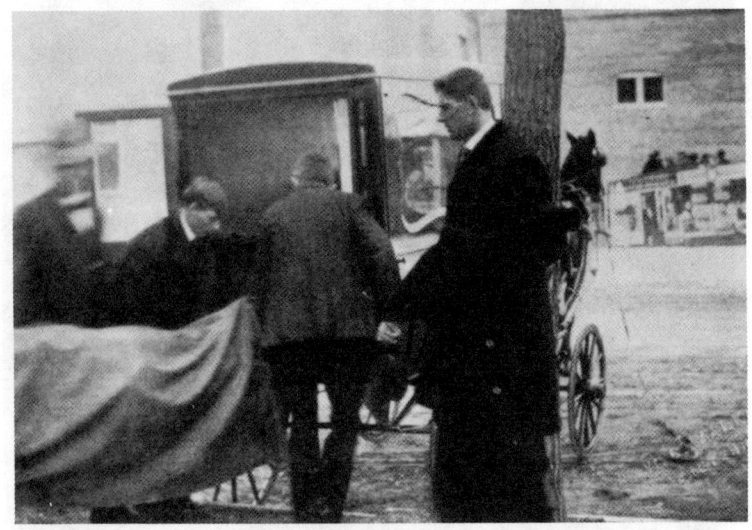

TOM HORN'S BODY

Charles Horn looks on. The funeral was held in Boulder, Colorado.

(Courtesy Archives and Western History Department, University of Wyoming Library)

THE DEFENSE HAS THEIR LAST CHANCE

Attorney Lacey began the defense by discussing the affidavit of Jack Martin's character.

He then read the affidavits of T. Clark and Charles Irwin. Both qualified statements to the Miller family during their recent visit, by swearing that they had said if Victor were really innocent they would certainly not expect him to make a confession.

Next Judge Lacey presented affidavits from a large number of persons living in Kansas City and St. Joseph, Missouri, who knew Miss Kimmell. The documents were all complimentary, lauding her fine character and family.

The Attorney dwelled on the arguments for the Defense, adding that he was no longer engaged as Tom Horn's attorney, but was participating because of his past connection. Mr. Lacey reiterated the points he previously called weak in the Prosecution's testimony and affidavits. Judge Lacey concluded his long and untiring efforts in the case by making a final plea to Governor Chatterton by dramatically stating, "Governor, prevent an irrevocable wrong. Commute the sentence from death to life imprisonment, so that our client, when vindication came, might enjoy his liberty. . ."

Attorney Burke then took the floor. His appeal reviewed the stronger points for the Defense. He said the Defense had only one more affidavit to present. Before closing Mr. Burke asked that Mr. Sellers be brought to Cheyenne to appear personally regarding the charges of bribery. He said he had the original letter from Mr. Coble which Alex Sellers brought to him. Mr. Burke stated the letter referred to the whereabouts of Tom Horn after the shooting of Kels Nickell; not Willie Nickell.

The hearing was over shortly after 2 p.m. As the pageant of personalities filed out of the Governor's office, many were displeased, others laughed. The Defense was uncertain; Stoll confident; Kels Nickell, no doubt angry; and Governor Chatterton mentally and physically exhausted. He anticipated more affidavits, hearings, pressure and more sleepless nights.

NOVEMBER 13

Perhaps because this was Friday the 13th, the superstitious believed something would surely break. Maybe Governor Chatterton would commute the death sentence to life. Maybe Tom would break down—some "big" men were said to have become increasingly restless. Desperation plots and plans were thick in Cheyenne's heavier smoked-filled atmosphere.

But little happened to alter the course of events. Attorney Burke presented the Governor with a lengthy affidavit—this was supposed to help "blow the lid off the works." It was made by Philander D. Killiam, in Tom Horn's behalf. It read:*

> "I reside at the corner of Twenty-fourth and Garfield streets in the city of Denver. My occupation is that of dairyman, which occupation I have pursued for a year past; previous to that time I was in the employ of the John Evans estate office at room No. 19, Evans block, Denver. I am well acquainted with Frank Mullock and Robert Cousley and have known them since the year 1897; that some time in October, 1902, to the best of affiant's recollection Robert Cousley in a conversation with affiant held in the hallway in the Evans block, stated to affiant that he, Cousley, and Mullock were on to a scheme whereby they could make some money out of the Horn case; that by going to Cheyenne and testifying they could make money; that he was broke and that this was the only scheme he knew of to make money. He said that he and Mullock had fixed up this scheme and loaned him money in order to prevent the necessity of his doing this, and Cousley agreed not to do it. Affiant says that he did not see Cousley again until after his return from Cheyenne, when affiant had read in the newspapers that he had been a witness in the case of the State of Wyoming against Tom Horn; that said Cousley on the day of his return told affiant that he went to Cheyenne because he had to have some money and that was the only way he could get it; and in said conversation he said, 'You know as well as I do that my evidence was a damned lie;' that affiant charged him with having given evidence concerning the location of the Scandanavian saloon, which was altogether wrong, and Cousley said 'I took Mullock's word for that.' He said further, 'You know as well as I know that I never saw Horn before this trial, neither did Mullock.' Affiant states that he asked Cousley what had become of the money which he had previously told affiant he could make by testifying in the case and he replied, 'Campbell got away with

**The Wyoming Tribune*, Cheyene, Friday Evening, November 13, 1903.

the money.' He said further, 'If these lawyers had questioned me they would have got me sure.'

"Affiant further states that he had a conversation with Frank Mullock, which said conversation occurred, to the best of affiant's recollection, a month or so after the trial of Tom Horn at Cheyenne, in which conversation affiant remarked, 'You fellows done wrong to make money out of that Horn case; you know that you lied about it,' to which he replied, 'It was easy money, but we only got witness money out of it because Campbell got away with the money.' In the course of the conversation I said, 'You fellows made a mistake about the location of the Scandinavian saloon.' He said, 'I never was in the Scandinavian saloon and at the time I testified I didn't know exactly where it was but since I got back you bet your life I looked it up.' Then he said, 'I never saw Horn until I saw him at the trial.' Affiant says that he related these facts to a friend, Fred Hecht, several days ago, and Hecht advised him to make known these facts; that Hecht stated that he knew Judge Lacey, Horn's attorney, and that affiant told Hecht that he had his permission to write Judge Lacey if he wanted to do so.

"That he makes these statements freely and voluntarily in order that injustice may not be done and for no other reason.

(Signed) "PHILANDER D. KILLIAM."

Thus another affidavit was added to the stack of evidence that the Governor was sifting. Perhaps he had made up his mind long ago —the decision was withheld.

The affidavit of Jack Martin and the refutal of it by Joe LeFors in his appearance caused considerable interest and comment throughout the state. When approached by a newspaper reporter after the hearing in regard to some of his statements, Martin became rather incensed about it all.

When questioned about the story that he was really John Younger and a former pal of Jesse James, he was non-committal.

In regard to Joe LeFors' statements to the Governor about Martin's connection with the Wilcox train robbers, he was very emphatic. LeFors had stated that Martin had worn an arm band to identify himself with the outlaws should there have been a shooting scrape. Martin said he had never worn such a mark. In speaking of the chase he said that had telegraphed "Ed" Dickenson from Glenrock that the robbers would be in the hills south of Casper and attempt to cut across the bridge there at about 2 o'clock on a certain morning. This was not followed up he intimated.

He continued his story to the reporter that he then met Joe LeFors, Sheriff Miller and United States Marshal Frank Hadsell and others at the Tisdale ranch and started upon the trail of the robbers once more.

With Phil Hausseaux, Martin said that he went into the Hole-In-The-Wall country and saw, at Billy Hill's ranch, the saddles and horses ridden by the robbers. He rode back eight miles to notify the rest of the party of the fact, but Mr. Wheelan, a Union Pacific man was in charge, and said the robbers had been located upon a certain mountain and were being watched to prevent their escape.

Martin said he could prove by a number of people that he arranged with Hadsell that he should go through LaBonte Canyon to the Douglas road to see whether the robbers had taken the route to either Douglas or Casper. Hadsell and his party were to go through Bates Hole and thus save forty miles and rendezvous with him in Casper.

Once they discovered the robbers tracks did not go into Douglas, Martin stated, his party headed for Glenrock, that place being the nearest telegraph station. Upon their arrival he said they saw the lights of the train comfortably carrying the posse back to Cheyenne.

Then the interviewed man added, "If it hadn't been for Joe LeFors and a few other 'hoodoes' like him we would have made a better showing in that chase."

"As to my character," said Mr. Martin, "I was trusted by Mr. N. K. Boswell and the State Board of Charities and Reforms to make all the shackles for the prisoners when they were moved from Laramie to Rawlins, and to put them on and take them off and I did it with credit."

Martin arrogantly remarked: "I am both Prophet and John Younger, I shall go to the World's Fair and expect to make a fortune exhibiting myself."

"I hope," said Martin in concluding the interview, "that I can meet Joe LeFors someday, and have a pleasant talk with him, and a good drink, and then settle up all these little differences. . ."

NOVEMBER 14

This was the dawning of the day that sealed the doom of Tom Horn—although the condemned Horn wasn't to learn of it until the 18th. A large crowd gathered around the Capitol building early in the morning awaiting the Governor's decision. Some thought it would not come on this day, but they would wait anyhow. Perhaps a few cowboys boasted that the Governor wouldn't dare hang Tom. Many were just curious. They had followed the drama since the curtain was raised almost twenty-two months before—the end was near and they didn't want to miss any of it.

More affidavits were presented the Chief Executive by the Prosecution as soon as he arrived at his office:

Van L. Gilford swore that he met John C. Coble in the Paxton Hotel at Omaha and Coble told him that he had secured an affidavit from Miss Kimmell stating Victor Miller was guilty of the crime. The affiant added that John Coble said that he had to get the affidavit and have her throw the crime on Miller to save Horn's neck. Two more affidavits completed the "stack."

The big story broke at 3:30 in the afternoon. The Governor's decision was announced in the form of communications to the attorneys. Horn must hang! The Chief Executive in his lengthy review of the case refused to set aside the judgment of both the lower and higher courts.

The Governor's communication set forth his reasons for the decision. The affidavits, he stated, should have been presented at the trial as evidence—not to him at this late hour. He upheld the State Supreme Court's decision regarding Horn's alleged confession in the Scandinavian saloon in Denver. This decision read: "In view of the remainder of the testimony in this case, we believe there is sufficient evidence not to justify a reversal even if the Denver testimony—so called—should be entirely disregarded."

He pointed out that the two affidavits submitted by the Attorneys for Tom Horn claim that no confession was made in the Scandinavian saloon. While those of Mullock and Roberts claim that it was made by Horn's double. These Mr. Chatterton cited, were contradictory, incompatible and rendered all of the evidence of no weight.

The testimony of Joe LeFors was rendered to have been immaterial and could have been disregarded as there was sufficient evidence to warrant a verdict of guilty. He cited criminal law as a well-established rule that a bare confession supported by proofs of corpus delecti was sufficient to justify a confession because Tom Horn admitted the confession in question.

The decision set forth that none of the affidavits presented the Governor by the Counsel for the condemned would be competent or admissible in a Court of Law. Therefore, he stated, should a new trial have been granted, none of this evidence would have been accepted by law; a second trial would have been based on the same evidence as had been presented during the first. Thus, Horn's conviction for a second time would have been a certainty.

In the lengthy document Mr. Chatterton expressed only one doubt, and that concerned the affidavit of Miss Kimmell. He stated, "The one question in my mind is whether or not the Kimmell affidavit is true. I have considered this question in all of its details; I have checked every statement made with every other statement and with all the evidence of the Coroner's inquest and the trial of the case and with Miss Kimmell's correspondence. From my investigations, confirmed by the affidavit of H. A. Mendenhall, I do not believe the statements made in the Kimmell affidavit are true.

"My investigations have led me to believe Miss Kimmell, at this stage of the proceedings, was willing to present theories to save Horn, intending after the commutation of the sentence to exonerate Victor Miller of the insinuation cast upon him."

Governor Chatterton concluded his lengthy decision by stating: "I do not believe that the law and justice would be served by the interposition of executive clemency."

And so all hope for the life of Tom Horn through the proper legal channels was gone. The death watch was set. The execution would be carried out between 9 a.m. and 3 p.m. on November 20th.

NOVEMBER 17—THREE DAYS OF LIFE

The fatal hour was drawing closer with each movement of the clock—all could not help but admire Tom Horn's display of nerve. While his jailers were becoming increasingly nervous, the doomed man was said to have kept his appetite and slept very well. During his waking hours, Horn wrote a great deal. The guard around the jail was increased almost daily.

On this day, Prosecutor Stoll, now confident that Tom Horn would be executed, announced that he would press his perjury charges against Miss Kimmell to the maximum.

When interviewed by the press concerning the matter, Mr. Stoll said, "I most certainly shall prosecute her. The action of the Governor in no way influences any action I may take. I have not singled out Miss Kimmell more than the others, but will take action against all the rest of those perjurors. I have an abundant evidence to make me feel certain of securing their conviction."

Miss Kimmell, under heavy bond, had become increasingly upset at the turn of events and possibly longed to return to Kansas City.

Governor Chatterton again made public his statements about the affidavit of the alleged sweetheart of Tom Horn:

> "... For my investigations, finally confirmed by the affidavit of H. A. Mendenhall, Sheriff of Wyandotte County, Kansas, I do not believe the statements made in the Kimmell affidavit. My investigations lead me to believe that Miss Kimmell at this stage of the proceedings, was willing to present theories to save Horn, intending after commutation of Horn's sentence, to exonerate Victor Miller of the imputation cast upon him by her affidavit."

NOVEMBER 18—TWO DAYS UNTIL...

Perhaps Tom Horn arose early this morning, he had spent a somewhat restless night. Half awake he could have stumbled over to his cell window, leaned against the bars, and watched the sun come up. He had done it before. Then Tom vaguely recalled the many times he had slept out in the open—recalling how hard it was to start a fire with damp wood and numb fingers—that the sun felt so good when it did come up. Now he didn't care; perhaps he wished he could stop the sun—and everything. Maybe Tom chuckled to himself as he remembered the time he was alone down on Rock Creek, bent down to "cup" his early morning drink. Suddenly he had lost his footing and fell headfirst into the ice-cold creek. God, it was "frio." Tom had danced and stomped around for an hour or more trying to get dry. The boys would have laughed if they could have seen him. . . especially Coble.

Tom continued his gaze out the window. It was cold and clear, with a slight breeze blowing from the north as usual. The trains down at the depot were doing their usual morning chores, bumping and blowing—they never quit. He noticed smoke was beginning to spiral up from most of the houses that he could see. Then Tom gave the bars a squeeze and jerk, whirled and went to his "sack" and rolled a cigarette. He guessed they would have mush for breakfast again—mush—damned old, cold, sticky mush! Then he saw Jim McCloud, his jail mate coming out of it. "Mornin' Jim," said Tom, "Whatcha say, Tommy," replied McCloud. Tom added, "Wonder what the boys'll try to pull today?" Then he shouted at the slumbering man on the death watch, "Hey, wake up! Horn's gotta gun!" The two inmates laughed at the aroused and embarrassed sentinel.

In the mid-morning mail, Tom received an unusual letter. He read it several times, rubbing the stubble on his chin all the while. Then he called out to Dick Proctor, and asked him to deliver the letter to his Attorneys.

The letter read:

"Laramie, Wyoming, Nov. 17

"Tom Horn, Cheyenne, Wyoming.

"I killed Willie Nickell, tell them I do not want to see an innocent man hung.

"I will confess if they will not hang me.

—."

The communication was presented to Governor Chatterton.

District Court was opened this day and the docket was read. There were a great many cases up for trial. The case against Miss Kimmell would not start until the following week. Nothing seemed to be of great importance for within a few hours Tom Horn was to die.

That afternoon Jailer Proctor appeared before Tom's cell—in a way Dick hated himself for what he had to give Horn. Despite the circumstances there was a bond between them. Tom could have killed Dick during the jail break last summer, and hadn't. "Tom," said Dick, "here, read this," and the Undersheriff handed him a newspaper containing the Governor's decision.

Tom Horn read the account through just once, then turned to the editorial comments and other items in the paper relating to his case. He folded the paper neatly, as he always did papers, then calmly handed it back to Proctor and remarked, "Well, Dick, I guess I've reached the end of my trail. I'm not surprised at the Governor's decision, because the Courts had already attended to my case, but it does seem rather hard, after all. Well, I'm ready any time now. I'm not afraid to die. . ."

In a matter of hours it would be all over, he thought to himself. "Better luck next time, Tom," he said half aloud. Then methodically, as always he began calculating how much time he had left. How he would spend each hour, how many smokes he could have. . .

NOVEMBER 19—THE LAST FULL DAY OF LIFE

This was the last daylight to dark "stretch" for Tom Horn. After the day had passed he would never see the sun set again.

Tom hadn't slept too well, neither had "Old Cheyenne." He had heard most of the activity that went on during the night. The challenging by sentries, movements of troops, and the continuous flow of traffic. There had been some excitement about a rocket being sighted north of town. During the pre-dawn hours, the restless man had heard someone shout from a distance, "We'll save you, Tom!"

After his breakfast tray was taken away and he had assured Dick Proctor that he didn't want anything other than a few cigars, he would get busy—so much to do and so little time. Horn's activities and attitude indicated he was fully resigned to his fate. Tom hoped he could see John today before he . . . He thought also of his personal effects; he had to dispose of them. A couple more letters to write. There were the preachers, they would be in again. Tom wondered if he would hear from his brother Charley today.*

Horn decided to give a few of his personal effects to John Coble, including the manuscript of the story of his life prior to coming to Wyoming. The neat autobiography was written in pencil.† Then there were Frank and Charley Irwin, damn good friends. The Irwins would be back in town soon, they had been circulating petitions throughout the state in an effort to get Governor Chatterton to commute the sentence. He wanted to give them something. And T. Joe Cahill, the young County Clerk. Tom liked him, and had asked him to assist with the . . . instead of Les Snow. The doomed man also

*Charles Horn was the older brother of Tom. Charles was born at Chautauqua, Ohio, January 1, 1852. Tom was born in 1861. In 1874 Charles Horn married Elizabeth Blattner. They moved to Boulder, Colorado, in 1890. Mr. Horn was engaged in the teamster business. He passed away in 1932. Tom Horn had a sister, Mrs. E. W. Prosser, who resided in Briggsdale, Colorado.

†The manuscript was published by John C. Coble in 1904 by the Louthan Book Company of Denver. The title of the work is the *Life of Tom Horn*, "A Vindication." In the book Tom Horn tells about his life up to the year 1894 before he came to Wyoming. "From this time on," Horn states in his book, "the people of Wyoming seem to know more about my affairs than I know myself and there would be no occasion for me to dwell upon my career."

thought of Ed Smalley and Richard Proctor, they had treated him well. Possibly there were several others Tom didn't want to forget—maybe Otto Plaga, Harry Hynds, Sam Moore, "Stony," "Dunc" Clark, Frank Meana, the Clays, young "Bud" Gillespie, Thorton Biggs, the Danks boys, Jim and Clayton. Yes, Tom thought, lots of real friends—mostly cowboys he had worked with on roundups.

During the afternoon Attorneys T. F. Burke and J. W. Lacey received an affidavit from Alex Sellers, a rancher. Sellers had received a considerable amount of notoriety as a result of the affidavit submitted by Clarence D. Houck. In his affidavit Houck stated that Sellers had told him that he had delivered a letter from John C. Coble to Mr. Burke, in which the sender had stated that Mr. Sellers would testify that Tom Horn was at his place on the night preceding the murder of Willie Nickell. When Mr. Sellers informed the attorneys that this was not true they asked him if there was an inducement they might offer to have him testify to that effect.

The affidavit of Houck was a direct charge against the attorneys of attempting to bribe Mr. Sellers to give a perjured testimony. In his affidavit Sellers admitted that he had delivered a letter to Mr. Burke, but emphatically denied the other statements made by Mr. Houck. He swore that neither Mr. Burke nor Mr. Lacey asked him if there was any inducement they might offer to have him change his mind as desired.

Shortly after four o'clock, Architect James Julian and a crew of carpenters were admitted into the jail area to erect the gallows,* and to install the water operated trap springing mechanism. The timbers for the scaffolding had previously been fitted together. A curtain was placed between Tom Horn's cell window and where the work was being carried on. The scaffolding was constructed on the same level as the cell. As the workers began, Horn was reported to

*The gallows, a classic in Rube Goldbergism, were designed by James P. Julian, noted Cheyenne Architect in 1892. Julian's theory was that the condemned man automatically hanged himself by placing his weight on the trap door. The weight of the condemned then pressed down on a 4x4-inch post which supported the trap door. This post was joined in two places and in turn pressed down a spring. The spring operated a water valve permitting water to run from a can balanced on a cross arm. When the required amount of water ran from the can, a weight slipped off the arm and a weight knocked the 4x4-inch support which automatically let the trap door fall open and the condemned fall to his death. The body drop could be regulated according to the weight and height of the person to be executed. The water valve in the can could be adjusted to regulate the time opening of the trap door. The entire cycle could be completed in a matter of seconds and not exceeding a minute.

have shouted to the Deputy, "What's going on Dick?" And the law officer replied, "Sorry, it's nothing that would interest you, Tom." Whereupon the condemned man said, "Hell, I'm the most interested guy in the world, take this damn curtain down." The request was complied with and Tom Horn watched the construction and perfection of the instrument that would take his life. A barbaric ordeal—but Tom Horn had the nerves for the occasion.

During the day Charles Horn arrived in Cheyenne. He made arrangements to escort his brother's body to Boulder, Colorado, for burial. John C. Coble had pledged to buy the best casket in Cheyenne and to pay all funeral expenses.

Of considerable interest to the public was a letter received by Governor Fenimore Chatterton. The letter threatened the Chief Executive's life unless he immediately commuted the death sentence of Tom Horn to life in prison. The message was written on stationery from the Albany Hotel in Denver. The ultimatum stated that he could not expect to live more than twenty-four hours unless the request was complied with.

At six o'clock, Governor Chatterton ordered Company E and Troop A of the Wyoming National Guard to proceed to Laramie County Courthouse, to surround and to protect it. This move was done to insure that the execution would be carried out. Officials feared there might be an attack against the prison in an attempt to release the doomed man. A guard of ten men was immediately posted around the jail block and in the alley running between Ferguson and Eddy Streets. No person or persons were allowed on the sidewalks or streets near the Courthouse.

The troops were supplemented by deputies stationed at every window inside the Courthouse, as well as at other strategic places in the building.

Shortly after Tom Horn's evening meal, Father Kennedy, a Catholic priest, spoke with the doomed man. Tom was said to have knelt with the priest during the prayers in his behalf.

Following the priest's visit, The Rev. Mr. Watson, of St. Mark's Episcopal Church entered the cell. A Mr. Lovett Rockwell, and Mesdames Robinson and Appel accompanied by Mr. Watson, sang to Tom after the short services were over. Whereupon he bid the clergyman goodbye, and asked him to thank the officers of the jail for this and their many kindnesses to him. Then Reverend Mr. Watson emerged from the Courthouse somewhat elated that Tom Horn had accepted his doctrines.

After the church folk had departed, Tom had a good smoke, and then crawled into his bunk.* A few minutes later Sheriff Smalley came by. He asked, "How do you feel, Tom?" Horn replied, "Feel fine, Ed." "Why?" In a matter of minutes Tom Horn was sound asleep.

In the meantime "Old Cheyenne" was entering into a state bordering on acute indigestion. Hotels and rooming houses were full. Midnight saw the streets crowded and the saloons doing a thriving business. Drinking was heavy—the entire city seemed to be getting riotously drunk. To the condition was added wild rumors to the effect that last ditch effort was to be made just before daylight. Few gave them much thought, if any. One Karl Konotsky, a recent jail-mate of Horn and McCloud added considerable fuel to the fire, by stating he knew that something was sure to pop. He said he had heard McCloud relay a "break" message to the condemned man. Horn was to be liberated by an army of friends—that an armed guard would not be able to stop.

Perhaps in a remote but well-upholstered part of town, men, "big men" were together. Drinking and toasting this, that and everything. Tomorrow it would all be over! Think of it! No more nightmares . . . fears that Horn would tell everything. Once again they could walk the streets of Cheyenne—"free" men. One "loaded" individual might have rationalized, and then come up with something about such work as Horn's being an occupational hazard. While another could have belched and hiccupped simultaneously and espoused on the necessity of the wheels of justice and their grinding out the death verdict. The laughing and drinking could have continued until the wee hours of the morning.

NOVEMBER 20, 1903—THE END OF THE TRAIL

Tom Horn arose early and went about his usual morning toilet procedures. He began thinking about today, then changed his train of thought—he could do it very easily. Tom began humming as he brushed the wrinkles out of his blanket. "Can't let this thing get me down," he mused to himself, "all of us gotta go sometime."

He had more letters to write. About this time Dick Proctor brought in his breakfast. "A nice one," Tom murmured, "bacon,

*There was always a great deal of speculation as to whether Tom Horn actually did accept religion and ask forgiveness. In one of his last statements, he indicated that he had not. At the gallows, a few seconds before his death, Charles Irwin asked him if he had confessed to the preacher or taken on any religion. Horn's reply was "no."

eggs, cakes, bread and black coffee." Just what he liked. The jailer knew Tom's likes and dislikes. Horn "took down" his last meal quickly, as he wanted to get back to his writings. He asked the jailer how many minutes he had left. Proctor told him that it was nine o'clock and that he had a little over an hour of life remaining. Horn said, "I can do a great deal in that time."

At 10 o'clock Sheriff Smalley demonstrated the gallows to those invited to attend the execution. At least those who cared to see the crude device work. The intricate Julian trap-springing mechanism was explained in detail. All transpired within a few feet of the condemned man's cell.

At little later Tom heard John Coble talking to Sheriff Smalley down below in the office. John wanted to bid his friend goodbye for the second time. Permission was granted. The Irwin boys were with him. In the succeeding few minutes a near heart-breaking scene transpired.

"Goodbye Tom," Coble said, "Tom I can't stay... I came to say goodbye. I'm sorry, Tom, but die like the man I know you to be. Tom, fate's against you. You must die. Goodbye, God bless you, goodbye...Tom."

At that point John Coble came near breaking down. His voice was choked with emotion and his eyes filled with tears.

"I want to thank you, John," said Horn. "You did all you could for me. I'll die all right, John. Don't worry about that. I am not afraid, John John... John... I'm not afraid. Say goodbye to all the boys. You know I thank you for all you have done for me. Keep your nerve, John, for I'll keep mine. You know Tom Horn."

Then the jailer opened the cell door. The two men stood there in near embrace with heads bowed... perhaps sobbing a little. With a last goodbye John Coble turned and walked out of the jail. Tom Horn, as near breaking down as he had ever been during the long ordeal, whirled off-balance through his cell door and caught hold of his bed then stood there a few minutes with his face buried in his hands. Suddenly Horn was himself again. The worst was over. He began smoking his last cigar.

"It's tough," said Coble, when he came out of the jail. "I have stood by Tom. His alleged friends have deserted him. I have been abused and called all sorts of names, but I did all I could to save the law from hanging an innocent man. I now give up! I can do no more. Sometime the truth may be known..."

THE EXECUTION

The story was best told by John Charles Thompson to the Denver, Colorado, Posse of Westerners. Mr. Thompson was one of the few witnesses to the hanging. As a young reporter he covered the case in its entirety. This graphic account, used in part here, was published in the 1945 issue of "Brand Book of the Denver Westerners."*

"Word had gone out that the hanging would take place at 7 a.m. At crisp dawn of the 20th crowds began collecting outside the rope barriers. They soon numbered several thousand persons. There was naught to be seen other than the grim walls of the ugly Courthouse, but imagination morbidly pictures what was going on inside. Business virtually was suspended; the 'Roman holiday' spirit was in the air.

"Persons accorded the privilege of observing Horn's last mile were admitted to the Courthouse at 7 o'clock. Guards with rifles ready, herded them into the county clerk's office and entrance to the jail. There were about eight newspaper reporters, and a dozen visiting sheriffs and other peace officers; also the Irwin brothers, big Charlie and little Frank, close friends of Horn who had disdained enmity aroused by their efforts in his behalf. Kels Nickell importantly had sought admittance, but had been denied. There might have been violence had he and the Irwins met there.

"Time marched on at a pace considerably less than that of a victim of locomotor ataxia. 7:30 o'clock came without summons from the Sheriff's office; 8 o'clock, 8:30. Sheriff Smalley came into the corridor, beckoned Charlie Irwin to a corner, spoke to him in tones inaudible to others, handed him an envelope. Charlie, his back in a corner, extracted a paper, scanned it, and nonchalantly pocketed it. Reporters were fired with curiosity; besieged him with questions which elicited no information. Later the county clerk (T. Joe Cahill), at Irwin's request, cleared the rear room of the suite. Irwin invited George H. Evans and me to go there with him. To us he confided that the communication he had received was a letter from Horn reiterating innocence.

"We could copy this, he said and show up the crack reporters covering for the 'metropolitan' press (meaning 150,000 population Denver). Jubilantly, we copied, while Irwin stood guard at the door to prevent intrusion. I took a new sheet of carbon paper, typed a double copy as Evans read the letter to me. I tossed the carbon paper into a wastepaper basket. Then, in turn, we telephoned the message

*Published by permission of the Denver Posse of the Westerners.

to our respective papers, each of which was prepared to issue an extra immediately after the hanging. Smugly, we rejoined the other reporters, unaware that we were about to receive a shocking lesson in journalism resourcefulness and enterprise.*

"Nine o'clock passed, 9:30, 10:00, and still we sweated in the county clerk's offices. Cause of the delay was the sheriff's unwillingness to kill Horn while a last-minute appeal for a reprieve was being made to Governor Chatterton.

"At 10:30 o'clock I received a call from the office. A press bulletin just received from Denver related that the Post had issued an extra there which quoted Horn's letter to Irwin in full. Hot with indignation, Evans and I remonstrated with Irwin, accusing him of bad faith;

---

*The letter read: "To John C. Coble, Esq., Cheyenne, Wyo.

"As you have just requested, I will tell you all my knowledge of everything I knew on regard to the killing of the Nickell boy.

"The day I laid over at Miller's ranch he asked me to do so, and I could meet Billy McDonald. Bill McDonald came up, and Miller and I met him up the creek above Miller's house. Billy opened up the converastion by saying he and Miller were going to kill off the Nickell outfit, and wanted me to go in on it. They said that Underwood and Jordan would pay me. Miller and McDonald said they would do the work. I refused to have anything to do with them, as I was not interested in any way. McDonald said that the sheep were then on Coble's land, and I got on my horse and went up to see, and they were not on Coble's land. I promised to stay all night again at Miller's, as McDonald said he wanted to come up again the next morning.

"He came back next morning and asked me if I still felt the same as I did before, and told him I did. 'Well,' he said, 'we have made up our minds to wipe up the whole Nickell outfit.'

"I got on my horse and left and went on about my business. I went on as John Bray and Otto Plaga said I did, and on the ranch where I got in on Saturday. I heard of the boy being killed there. I felt I was well out of the mix-up.

"I was over in that part of the country six weeks or two months later and saw both, McDonald and Miller, and they were laughing and blowing to me about running and shooting the sheep of Nickell. I told them I did not want to hear of it at all, for I could see that McDonald wanted to tell me the whole scheme. They both gave me the laugh and said I was suspicioned of the whole thing. I knew there was some suspicion against me, but did not pay the attention to it that I should have. That is all there is to it, so far as I know.

"Irwin, who swore I came into Laramie on the run on that Thursday, just simply lied. All of that supposed confession in the United States Marshal's office was prearranged, and everything that was sworn to by those fellows was a lie, made up before I came to Cheyenne. Of course, there was talk of the killing of the boy, but LaFors [LeFors] done all of it. I did not even make an admission, but allowed LaFors [LeFors] to make some insinuations. Ohnhaus, LeFors and Snow and also Irwin of Laramie, all swore to lies to fit the case.

"Your name was not mentioned in the marshal's office. This is the truth, as I am going to die in ten minutes.

"Thanking you for your kindness and continuing goodness to me, I am sincerely yours.

"Tom Horn."

he rejoined as hotly that he had not given us the "double-cross"—that no one other than we two had seen Horn's letter; not even his brother, Frank.

"This colloquy amusedly was observed by a tall, saturnine scribe of the Post's staff named Hamilton. He beckoned me to the rear room. 'Irwin's right,' he said, 'he didn't break down and double cross you. Look here.' He reached into the wastepaper basket beside the typewriter desk, drew out the carbon sheet I had used in double-copying the Horn letter, held it up against the light. There, stenciled as legibly as the copy of the sheets between which it had been imposed, was the letter. 'The next time you wish to keep somcthing a secret,' dryly advised the veteran reporter, 'don't use new carbon paper.'

"This Hamilton, during our long wait, regaled us with stories of executions he had witnessed. They were *passé* for him, he said, no longer aroused more emotion than the killing of a rat. He was directly behind me at the gallows, his body crowded against mine by pressure in the press section. His head drooped, his forehead rested against the back of my head. Later I found the back of my stiff collar sopping, wilted by tears he had shed . . . .

"We newspapermen were crammed into a little space at the edge of the platform adjoining Horn's cell; the visiting sheriffs were marshalled on the first-tier level below. The Irwin brothers, flanked by guards, stood beside them. The executioners and a venerable Episcopal clergyman, Dr. George C. Rafter, an acquaintance of Horn, were on the gangway at the opposite edge of the platform. Beside the Irwins stood two physicians, Dr. George P. Johnston and Dr. John H. Conway. They were gentlemen of the highest integrity whom nothing could have induced to contribute to a criminal conspiracy.

"Horn, his back against the cell grill, was half-reclining on his narrow bed, puffing a cigar. He was perfectly composed. His soft shirt was unbuttoned at the collar, this exposing the scar of the wound he had suffered in a fight at Dixon.

" 'Ready, Tom,' said Proctor.

"Horn arose, carefully placed his cigar on a cross reinforcement of the grill, strode firmly the few steps required to take him to the side of the gallows platform.

"He nodded to the Irwins; sardonically scanned the peace officers below.

" 'Ed,' he commented to Smalley, 'That's the sickest looking lot of damned sheriffs I ever seen.'

" 'Would you like us to sing, Tom?' asked Charlie Irwin.

" 'Yes, I'd like that,' responded Horn.

"So, while Proctor buckled straps that bound Horn's arms and legs, the Irwins, each in a rich tenor, sang a rather lugubrious song popular on the range, *Life Is Like a Mountain Railroad*.

"The clergyman read his church's prayer for the dying Horn, standing relaxed, listened without a tremor.

" 'Would you like to say anything?' asked Smalley.

" 'No,' replied Horn.

" 'Tom,' spoke up Charlie Irwin, 'did you confess to the preacher?'

" 'No,' was the reply.

"Proctor adjusted the noose, formed with the conventional knot of 13 wraps, to Horn's neck; drew a black hood over his head. Smalley on one side and a friend of Horn, T. Joe Cahill, on the other, lifted the doomed man onto the trap.

"Instantly the sibilant sound of running water permeated the breathless stillness; the instrument of death had begun to operate. To the straining ears of the listeners that little sound had the magnitude of that of a rushing torrent.

"Smalley, his face buried in the crook of an arm resting against the gallows tree, was trembling.

" 'What's the matter,' came in a calm tone through the black cap, 'getting nervous I might tip over?'

"Seemingly interminable, the sound of escaping water ran on.

" 'Joe,' said Horn, addressing Cahill, 'they tell me you're married now. I hope you're doing well. Treat her right.'

"Indubitably, he was the best composed man in that chamber of death.

"Still the sinister sound of running water; then mercifully, the leaves of the trap parted with a crash and Horn's body hung through the opening.

"Thirty-one seconds had elapsed since he had been lifted onto the trap!

"He fell only four and one-half feet; his head and shoulders projected above the gallows floor. This drop was not sufficient; his neck was not broken. Proctor had feared to arrange a longer drop, apprehensive that stoppage of the fall of a body so heavy as Horn's might tear the head off. The slam of the massive hangman's knot against the side of Horn's skull knocked him into unconsciousness, however, and he did not suffer. For seventeen minutes the physicians with fingers on his pulse, felt impulses as a mighty heart labored on; then the pulse ceased.

"Tom Horn was dead—unconfessed!

"I did not see him die. Immediately upon his plunge through the trap, the witnesses were required to leave. I hesitated sufficiently to watch the dangling body turn. It made precisely one-half turn—stopped. Proctor's reckoning in this respect had been accurate.

"I was the first man to get out of the courthouse. I emerged at a high lope and was intercepted in the middle of the street by Kels Nickell, who had contrived to get through the police line.

" 'Is the son-of-a-bitch dead?' he demanded.

" 'Yes,' I replied, and loped on—I had an extra to get out.

"An hour later I saw the Horn cadaver on a slab at the Gleason mortuary. There was no mistaking the body—it was that of Horn."

THE END

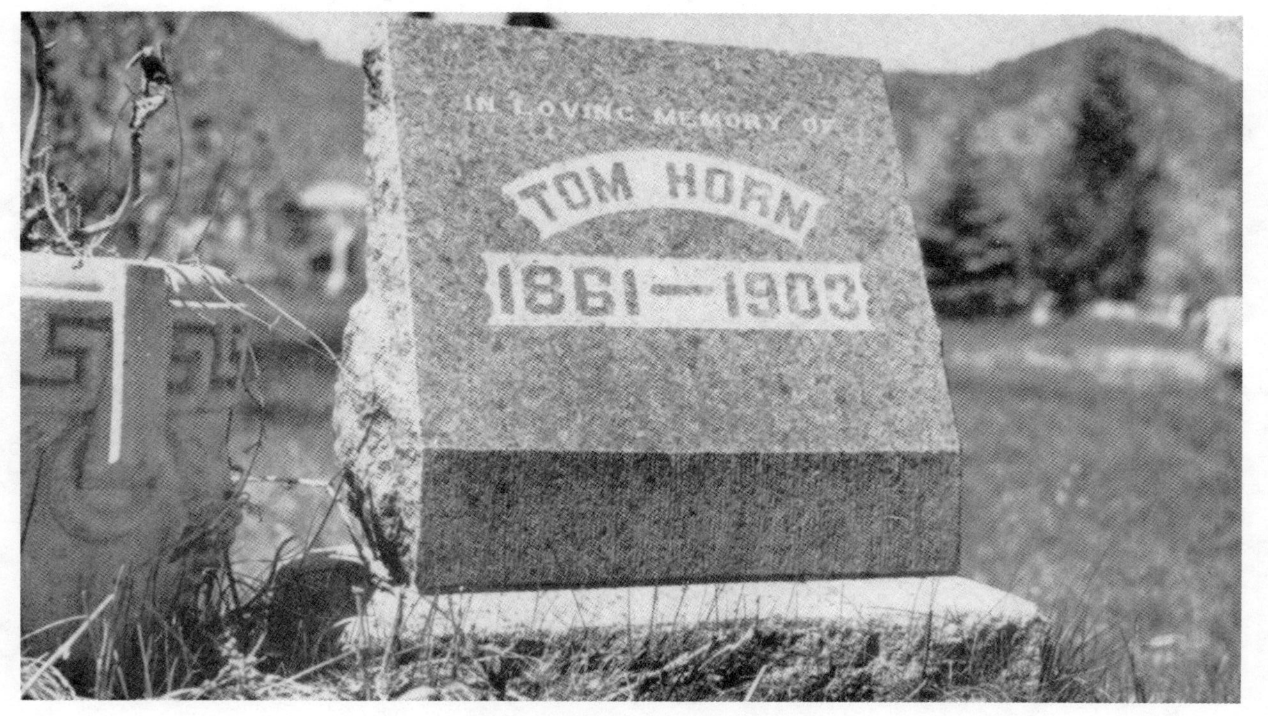

IN LOVING MEMORY...

"You know... in Wyomin' when folks hanker to hang a man, one excuse is as good as another."

—Anonymous

(Courtesy Mr. Fred Mazzula, Denver, Colo.)

BIBLIOGRAPHY

A. NEWSPAPERS:

The complete files (1895-1903) of the following: Denver Post, Denver Times, Rocky Mountain News, Cheyenne Daily Leader, Cheyenne Tribune, Laramie Boomerang, and Laramie Republican.
Boulder Camera, November, 1903.

B. CORONER'S INQUEST REPORTS:

On file in Albany County Courthouse, Laramie, Wyoming, and Laramie County Courthouse, Cheyenne, Wyoming.

C. THE TRIAL PROCEEDINGS:

The State of Wyoming vs. Tom Horn—on file in the Clerk of the Court's Office, Laramie County Courthouse, Cheyenne, Wyoming.

D. PACIFIC REPORTER: Volume 73, Horn vs. State, Supreme Court of the State of Wyoming, St. Paul, West Publishing Company, 1903, pp. 705-729.

E. CORRESPONDENCE:

Tom Horn, Joe LeFors, and W. D. Smith. (Five letters.) December 28, 1901-January 7, 1902. Filed in the First Judicial District of Wyoming, Laramie County Courthouse, Cheyenne, Wyoming.

F. WYOMING STOCK GROWERS ASSOCIATION RECORDS:

On file in the Archives and Western History Library of the University of Wyoming, Laramie, Wyoming.

G. INTERVIEWS:

Dr. Robert H. Burns, Laramie, Wyoming.
Mr. T. Joe Cahill, Cheyenne, Wyoming.*
Mr. Fenimore Chatterton, Arvada, Colorado.*
Mr. Charles Farthing, Iron Mountain, Wyoming.*
Mr. E. E. Fitch, Laramie, Wyoming.
Mr. A. S. Gillespie, Laramie, Wyoming.*
Mr. Harry Hannes, Laramie, Wyoming.
Dr. George P. Johnston, Cheyenne, Wyoming.
Mr. E. S. Lauzer, Cora, Wyoming.
Mrs. Nettie LeFors, Buffalo, Wyoming.
Mr. Ira C. Lesh, Pierce, Colorado.
Mr. M. F. Osterele, Ault, Colorado.
Mr. Axel Palmer, Laramie, Wyoming.*
Mr. Andrew Ross, Pierce, Colorado.*
Mrs. Leslie Snow, Buffalo, Wyoming.
Mr. Mike G. Shonsey, Clarks, Nebraska.
Mr. B. H. Wykert, Ault, Colorado.

*Indicates interview was recorded.

H. SECONDARY WORKS:

Annals of Wyoming, published by the State Historical Department, Cheyenne, Wyoming.

Coe, Charles H., *Juggling a Rope,* Lariat Roping and Spinning Knots and Splices, also the Truth About Tom Horn, "King of Cowboys," Hamley & Company, Pendleton, Oregon, 1927, pp. 86-113.

Colorado Magazine, published by the Colorado State Historical Society, Denver, Colorado.

Cunningham, Eugene, *Triggernometry,* "A Gallery of Gunfighters," Caxton Printers, Ltd., Caldwell, Idaho, 1952, pp. 350-389.

Fowler, Gene, *Timber Line,* "A Story of Bonfils and Tammen," Covici-Frede Publishers, 1934, pp. 169-195.

Hebard, Grace Raymond, "Tom Horn clipping file," Archives and Western History Library, University of Wyoming, Laramie, Wyoming.

Horn, Tom, *The Life of Tom Horn,* "An Autobiography," published privately by John C. Coble, Louthan Book Company, Denver, Colorado, 1904.

Kelly, Charles, *Outlaw Trail,* published by the author, Salt Lake City, Utah, pp. 220-228.

LeFors, Joe, *Wyoming Peace Officer,* "An Autobiography by Joe LeFors," Laramie Printing Company, Laramie, Wyoming, pp. 131-146.

Monaghan, Jay, *Last of the Badmen,* "The Legend of Tom Horn," Bobbs Merrille and Company, Indianapolis and New York, 1946.

Raine, William McLeod, *Famous Sheriffs and Western Outlaws,* Doubleday, Doran & Company, Inc., Garden City, New York, pp. 80-91.

Snow, Leslie, "Tom Horn clipping file," Archives and Western History Library, University of Wyoming, Laramie, Wyoming.

Thompson, John Charles, "The Hanging of Tom Horn," Denver Posse Westerners *Brand Book,* 1945, pp. 111-129.

INDEX